GAMES, STRATEGIES, AND MANAGERS

GAMES
STRATEGIES
AND
MANAGERS

John McMillan

New York   Oxford
OXFORD UNIVERSITY PRESS
1992

Oxford University Press

Oxford   New York   Toronto
Delhi   Bombay   Calcutta   Madras   Karachi
Petaling Jaya   Singapore   Hong Kong   Tokyo
Nairobi   Dar es Salaam   Cape Town
Melbourne   Auckland

and associated companies in
Berlin   Ibadan

Copyright © 1992 by Oxford University Press, Inc.

Published by Oxford University Press, Inc.,
200 Madison Avenue, New York, New York 10016

Oxford is a registered trademark of Oxford University Press

Library of Congress Cataloging-in-Publication Data
McMillan, John, 1951–
Games, strategies, and managers / John McMillan.
p. cm.   Includes bibliographical references and index.
ISBN 0-19-507403-3
1. Management games.   2. Decision-making.
3. Game theory.   4. Management.   I. Title.
HD30.26.M4   1992
658.4'035 — dc20   91-26007

2 4 6 8 9 7 5 3 1

Printed in the United States of America
on acid-free paper

Thanks, Elizabeth

Preface

THIS BOOK is about systematic thinking in making business decisions. It uses powerful tools of analysis borrowed from a deceptively simple-sounding source—game theory. In its technical form, game theory is a highly sophisticated and mathematical subject. But, stripped of its mathematics and jargon, it can be useful to people in managerial situations faced with important decisions of strategy. The aim of this book is to use game theory to codify, as far as possible, the process of decision-making; to seek general principles that illuminate features common to many situations of business negotiating and contracting.

Acknowledgments are due to many. Perceptive comments on the entire manuscript were offered by Herbert J. Addison, Elizabeth Cullen, and Michael Rothschild. For suggestions, advice, and encouragement, I am also indebted to Colin Camerer, Spencer Carr, Vincent Crawford, Christopher Findlay, Herman Gadon, Peter Gourevitch, Theodore Groves, Bengt Holmström, Takeo Hoshi, Hideshi Itoh, Alex Kane, Yoshitsugu Kanemoto, Yong-Gwan Kim, David Kreps, Ping-Sing Kuo, Karen Lai, David Lehr, Gordon MacDonald, George Mailath, Preston McAfee, Paul Milgrom, Frank Milne, Roger Myerson, Eric Rasmusen, John Roberts, Andrew L. Schuller, Joel Sobel, Hal Varian, Birger Wernerfelt, and Robert Wilson. At the University of California, San Diego, useful feedback was provided by students in the Graduate School of International Relations and Pacific Studies and by participants in the Executive Program for Scientists and Engineers. A major debt to the researchers whose ideas I have borrowed is acknowledged in the Reading Guide at the end of the book. Congenial working conditions were provided by the Graduate School of International Relations and Pacific Studies, University of California, San Diego; the Australia-Japan Research Centre, Australian National University; and the Department of Economics, University of Canterbury, New Zealand.

Parts of the book have been published before. Chapter 7 is adapted from "The Economics of Section 301: A Game-Theoretic Guide," *Economics and Politics* 2, March 1990 (also published as "Strategic Bargaining and Section 301," in *Aggressive Unilateralism*, edited by Jagdish Bhagwati and Hugh Patrick, Ann Arbor, University of Michigan Press, 1990). Chapter 12 comes from "Bidding for Olympic Broadcast Rights: The Competition Before the Competition," *Negotiation Journal* 7, July 1991. Chapter 13 is based on "Managing Suppliers: Incentive Systems in Japanese and U.S. Industry," *California Management Review* 32, Summer 1990.

La Jolla, Calif.   J.M.
August 1991

Contents

Contents

PART IV

BIDDING

PART V

THE STRATEGIC MANAGER

I

STRATEGIC
DECISION-MAKING

WHAT IS game theory about, and how can it be used in making decisions? Part I will answer this question by examining several games, which will serve to introduce ideas that are essential for understanding the more sophisticated uses of game theory to be developed later in the book.

Chapter 1 gives a general background to game theory. Chapter 2 gives a more detailed introduction to game theory, introducing some of its basic ideas by working through some simple games. Chapter 3 examines the sources of the gains that result from the players' cooperation, and looks at the tension in games between cooperation and competition. Chapter 4 develops some ideas for decision-making under uncertainty.

1

The Art and Science
of Strategy

MANAGERS ARE continually making strategic decisions. As a manager, you think strategically whenever there are interactions between your decision and other people's decisions: when, in order to decide what you should do, you must reason through how they are going to act or react. What are their aims? What options are open to them? In the light of your answers to these questions, what is the best way for you to act? Game theory provides a tool for thinking about how deals are shaped: a systematic way of thinking about questions of strategy. This book uses ideas from game theory to investigate decision-making in business organizations.

The origin of the word strategy is the Greek *strategos*, meaning leader of an army. Webster's Dictionary defines strategy first in the military sense as the science "of maneuvering forces into the most advantageous position prior to actual engagement with the enemy"; and alternatively as "skill in managing or planning, especially by using strategem." Turning to "strategem," we find listed as synonyms, "artifice, ruse, blind, trick, subterfuge, chicanery, plot, snare." Game theorists, while not excluding these unpleasant connotations, use the word strategy in a broader and less loaded way, simply to mean game plan; a specification of actions covering all possible eventualities. This is the sense in which the word is to be understood throughout this book.

An *aficionado* of strategic situations, Thomas Schelling, characterizes them as "involving two or more participants, each trying to influence, to outguess, or to adapt to the decisions or lines of behavior that others have just adopted or are expected to adopt." The archetypical strategic interaction is the bargaining over price between a buyer and a seller, each trying to guess what the other will accept. Strategic situations are ubiquitous in business and in everyday life. Besides between buyer and seller, they arise between employer and employee, firm and competitor, landlord and tenant, manufacturer and subcontractor, takeover raider and target firm, regulatory agency and public utility; the list is endless. In negotiating, bidding, or contracting, the participants must think through the logic of actions and reactions.

Game theory offers a scientific approach to strategic decision-making. In place of the anecdotes, cases, stories, and examples that are commonly offered as advice to negotiators, game theory gives a systematically structured view.

What Is Game Theory?

The inventor of game theory, John von Neumann, a Hungarian living in the United States, was one of the greatest minds of the twentieth century. The breadth of his activities was extraordinary: from the heights of abstract research—in pure mathematics and theoretical physics—to work that has crucially affected the shape of the world today—helping to develop the atom bomb and the computer. One of his coworkers reported that "if you go in to see him with an idea, inside of five minutes he's five blocks ahead of you and sees exactly where it's going. His mind was just so fast and so accurate that there was no keeping up with him. There was nobody on earth, as far as I'm concerned, who was in this category." When the computer von Neumann helped to build was undergoing its preliminary testing, a race between the computer and von Neumann to solve some complicated arithmetic problem was set up; von Neumann won. The Nobel physicist Hans Bethe said, "I have sometimes wondered whether a brain like John von Neumann's does not indicate a species superior to that of man." A variant of this story had it that he was a demigod come down to Earth, having made a detailed study of humans so as to be able to imitate them perfectly. Von Neumann lived his life with zest. He threw weekly parties, large, loud, and lavish. He was famous among the Princeton academics for his love not only of food and wine but also of jokes, off-color stories and gossip. He had the stereotypical traits of the absent-minded professor. Once he left Princeton to drive to New York for an appointment; halfway there he phoned his wife to ask, "Why am I going to New York?" Contrary to the romantic myth of the effortlessly inspired genius, however, he worked very hard: his wife said, "His capacity for work was practically unlimited." He worked long hours; and often, in the middle of one of his parties, he would go upstairs to his study to work on an idea he had just had.

At the Institute of Advanced Study in Princeton during the Second World War, von Neumann teamed with the economist Oskar Morgenstern, another European expatriate, to produce a long and densely mathematical book, *Theory of Games and Economic Behavior*, which provided a branch of mathematics tailor-made for the study of human interactions. Its importance was immediately recognized: the *Bulletin of the American Mathematical Society* greeted it with the prediction that "posterity may regard this book as one of the major scientific achievements of the first half of the twentieth century."

Von Neumann and Morgenstern named their subject *the theory of games* to draw out the analogy between games in the usual sense of the word, like chess, poker, backgammon, and tic-tac-toe, and other situations in which the participants make decisions that affect each other. As IBM's founder Thomas J. Watson Sr. observed, "Business is a game, the greatest game in the world if you know how to play it." Or as von Neumann and Morgenstern more carefully expressed it, "the typical problems of economic behavior [are] strictly identical with the mathematical notions of suitable games of strategy." In the competition between two firms for market share, say, just as in chess, there are specified rules of play; the players choose their actions from a defined set of available actions; there is a relationship (sometimes perfectly predictable as in chess, sometimes involving chance as in poker) between the players' actions and the final outcome; and no single player has full control over the final outcome, but rather the outcome compounds the separate decisions of two or more people.

"In war the will is directed at an animate object that reacts." When Karl von Clausewitz, the nineteenth-century analyst of military strategy, stated this maxim, he was saying that war is, in our technical sense of the word, a game. Game theory's initial applications, in the early 1950s, were to the study of war. In a duel between a submarine and an antisubmarine aircraft, for instance, the aircraft must anticipate the submarine's evasive actions; in deciding its evasive actions, the submarine must anticipate what the aircraft will do, which means it must anticipate the aircraft's anticipations. Game theory was used, particularly by Rand Corporation analysts such as Daniel Ellsberg (later to gain fame for leaking the Pentagon Papers), to compute best strategies in military situations such as this. From problems of military tactics, the enquiry broadened to address questions of deterrence and cold-war strategy: game theory promised a dispassionate, mathematical analysis of the threat of nuclear catastrophe.

Game theory's most fruitful uses, however, have been in the less destructive, lower-stakes sphere of economics. In business, as in war, the decision-maker must anticipate the reactions of others. Your competitor or employee or supervisor or customer makes decisions that both respond to yours and affect you in some way. The game-theoretic analysis of such actions and reactions is now at the center of economics research. The best and brightest Ph.D. economists graduate from universities like Princeton, M.I.T., Stanford, and Northwestern armed with concepts like *extensive-form games, perfect sequential Nash equilibrium,* the *revelation prin-*

ciple, the *folk theorem,* the *intuitive criterion,* and *incentive-compatibility constraints.* Can such bizarre jargon possibly describe how people actually behave? I will argue not only that it can, but that the insights from game theory can, with some imaginative interpretation, provide useful guidelines on how to behave in actual strategic situations. And, although the theorists need the jargon and the mathematics as conduits of precise thought when they first develop the concepts, their bottom-line conclusions can be expressed in plain English.

What, then, is game theory? In a sentence, *game theory is the study of rational behavior in situations involving interdependence.*

By *interdependence,* we mean that any player in the game is affected by what the others do; and in turn that player's actions affect the others. The outcome depends on everyone's decisions; no one individual has full control over what happens. No man is an island. The players, to the extent that they are aware of these interdependencies, must take them into account when deciding how to act. The interdependencies often generate competition among the participants in a game. Von Neumann's own interest in game theory may have derived from his intensely competitive nature; as he liked to say, "Only a man from Budapest can enter a revolving door behind you and emerge ahead of you." But games are usually not purely competitive exercises; the players also have some common interests. Playing a game can be compared, as we will see, to dividing a pie whose size can increase or decrease as a result of the players' actions. The players have a common interest in increasing the total size of the pie; but conflicting interests as to how the pie is to be divided between them.

By *rational behavior* in our characterization of game theory, no moral judgment is implied. All that rationality means in game theory is that, in their own eyes, the players try to do the best they can. As analysts watching from the outside, game theorists do not presume to judge people's motives; game theorists take the players' objectives as given. You may think the aims are crazy; but if they are being pursued in a purposive, systematic way, then by the definition we are using here that person is being rational. Being rational merely means not consistently making the same mistake. Thus we are attaching to the word rationality a narrow and limited meaning. Whether it is appropriate to think of people as behaving rationally (in our limited sense) is a question of fact, not theory. Are people rational? Clearly not always: psychologists make their living investigating irrational behavior. Although for some types of strategic interactions rationality may seem implausible (think of a conflict between teenage offspring and parent), for other situations it is accurate. Corporations, routinely negotiating deals worth millions of dollars, choose as their managers people who have proven themselves to be effective decision-makers.

Because of the interdependence of the players, a rational decision in a game must be based on a prediction of others' responses. By putting yourself in the other's shoes and predicting what action the other person will choose, you can decide your own best action. This is the essence of the game-theoretic method: "putting yourself in the other person's shoes" will be a recurring theme of this book.

Coping with uncertainty is an inescapable feature of decision-making. Decisions are typically made without full knowledge of their consequences. What is the true quality of the used car you are buying? Will the price of stock you are buying rise or fall? What is the most efficient technology for your firm to adopt? Much of the analysis of this book will be about how to take creative risks. Uncertainty is present in strategic situations because other people's actions are not entirely predictable. Information is typically dispersed; one person has relevant information that the others do not have. Strategists must not only decide what risks are acceptable to them, but also how the other players' uncertainties affect their decision-making. The dispersal of information introduces a role for both offensive and defensive strategies: how to benefit from any informational advantage of your own, and how to curb the other person's informational strengths.

But Does It Work in Theory?

Real-life strategic situations are often extremely complicated. Game theory provides a *model* of this complexity. A model is to the real situation what a road map is to the region it represents. The map is a simplification, a deliberately stylized representation that omits some features of the world and highlights others. If it contained everything in the region it represented it would be so complicated as to be not understandable and therefore useless as a map. Similarly, the models we examine in this book are simplifications. Complexity is dealt with by breaking the situation into its components. The aim is to capture the essence of a negotiation, not to draw a literal picture of it. By exposing the essential features of one situation, we can find a hitherto hidden common core to many apparently diverse strategic situations. Thus it is not an appropriate criticism of the modeling exercises that follow to say "the world is more complicated than your models." This is true by the very nature of a model. The model is inappropriate only if it unduly distorts the actual situation by omitting something crucial.

Since our search is for general principles, no actual strategic situation will be completely encompassed by our models; each individual situation is different. Game theory cannot, by its nature, give all the answers to how any particular strategic situation works. Rather, what game theory does is give partial answers: it takes a piece of a strategic situation, small enough to be feasible for us to understand fully the logic of the situation.

This is a useful exercise provided the chosen piece is commonly found in diverse real-world interactions.

Ronald Reagan once said: "an economist is the only professional who sees something working in practice and then seriously wonders if it works in theory." Although meant as economist-bashing, Reagan's quip neatly encapsulates the economic theorist's method. To say that something works in practice but not in theory is to say it is not properly understood. Seeing if something works in theory will mean, in this book, testing an argument by checking whether it holds up in a fully specified, but simple, model. If an argument does not work in a simplified model, it is unlikely to be valid in more complicated reality. Modeling, then, is a way of testing ideas, by focusing on them one at a time. Modeling means reducing the strategic situation of interest to its essentials.

The aim of the social sciences, according to the philosopher Sir Karl Popper, should be to understand what Popper calls "the logic of the situation." We understand people's actions if we see how those actions are objectively appropriate to the situation; how the observed actions are consistent with rational behavior. Popper's phrase will recur throughout this book, for it neatly encapsulates game theory's method. As game theorists, we will be trying to understand *the logic of the situation*.

Strategic decision-making cannot be completely reduced to a science; there will always be a role for the tricks of the trade. A canny gambler will invariably beat a naive logician at poker. It is valuable, however, to push the scientific approach as far as it will go. Science is organized knowledge, designed to be efficiently communicated: the science of strategic decisions can be learned from a book. By contrast, the art of strategic decisions, like any other art, is best learned through experience. By helping us to think systematically through the issues—to understand the logic of the situation—game theory can give us a short cut to what skilled players have learned intuitively from long and costly experience. Compare playing poker in the usual way, your opponents sitting across the table from you, with playing it in separate rooms via computer terminals. Game theory can analyze the computer-terminal version of poker (at least in principle; in practice a complete analysis would be mathematically very complex, involving billions of multiplications and additions). But game theory is of little help in understanding the extra features present in the across-the-table version—the information conveyed by body language and tone of voice. Analogously, some of the general aspects of business negotiations can be captured by game theory, but other aspects—the personal and the idiosyncratic—cannot. Game theory, then, is a limited but (as this book aims to show) powerful aid to understanding strategic interactions. John von Neumann wrote a game-theoretic analysis of poker; and he was an enthusiastic—but not always successful—poker player.

The Payoff

This book is about making good decisions. Is it a good decision to spend valuable time reading this book? What is the payoff?

Game theory cannot—and does not claim to—provide cut-and-dried answers to questions of how to behave in any actual strategic situation. Game theory does not purport to tell managers how to run their businesses. Decision-making cannot be reduced to a computer program. There is more to most negotiations than can be encompassed in a mathematical formula. Negotiation is, as noted, art as well as science. Game theory does not eliminate the need for the knowledge and intuition acquired through long experience. What, then, does game theory offer?

Game theory offers a short cut to understanding the principles of strategic decision-making. Skilled and experienced managers understand these principles intuitively, but not necessarily in such a way that they can communicate their understanding to others. Game theory provides a language for expressing these principles. The stylized games that we will work through in this book serve as finger exercises in strategic decision-making. Game theory is, therefore, a way of economizing on experience: game theory makes it possible to grasp the principles of strategic thinking.

Game theory, like any general theory, provides links; it shows that many apparently diverse situations have the same essential structure. Knowledge that comes from experience, by contrast, is specific to its origins: it may not be apparent that the same ideas apply elsewhere, and so the knowledge may not be utilized to its full potential. Experience teaches you to see the trees; game theory helps you to see the forest.

We will see in the chapters that follow that many situations that look quite different from each other have a common strategic core. A procurement manager trying to induce a subcontractor to search for cost-reducing innovations faces, in essence, the same problem as an entrepreneur negotiating a royalty arrangement with a manufacturing firm to licence the use of a new technology, or a sales manager devising a commission-payments scheme to motivate salespeople, or a production manager deciding between piece-rate and wage payments to workers, or a firm's compensation committee designing a managerial incentive system. (Ideas relevant to these topics will be developed in Part III.) A manager's decision on how low to bid for a government contract has much in common with an antiques collector's decision on how high to bid in an auction, which has much in common with a takeover raider's decision on what price to offer for a firm. (See Part IV.) A negotiation between a corporation and a foreign government over the setting up of a manufacturing plant proceeds, in some respects, in the same way as the haggling between the buyer and the seller of a used car, which proceeds in much the same way as the bargaining between a labor union and an employer. (See Part II.) Understanding the common core of strategic situations can lead to improved decision-making.

Summary

Most business situations are *interactive,* in the sense that the outcome emerges from the separate decisions of different people. Good decisions, therefore, require that each decision-maker *anticipate* the decisions of the others. Such decisions, being anticipatory, must be made under *uncertainty.* Game theory is designed to help us understand interactive decision-making.

The next three chapters introduce some of the basic ideas used in game theory: how to understand the logic of situations in which, in order to decide what you should do, you must anticipate what others will do. Tools for interactive decision-making will be developed. We begin our exploration of game theory, in Chapter 2, by looking at games as pure games.

2

Playing Games as Games

GAMES IN the technical sense of situations involving interdependent decisions can also be games in the everyday sense of the word. In this chapter we will see some games that work both as brainteasers and as introductions to some of the main ideas of game theory. The most effective way to learn game theory is to do it: for this reason, you should try to reason each of these games through before reading the solution that follows.

THE PRISONERS' DILEMMA

A pair of transients, Al Fresco and Des Jardins, have been arrested for vagrancy. They are suspected of complicity in a robbery, but the evidence is inadequate to convict them. The district attorney interrogates them in separate cells and offers each the following deal. "If you confess and your friend does not, you will be released and your friend will have the book thrown at him; and the other way around if he confesses and you do not. If both confess, both will receive moderately long sentences. If neither confesses, both will be convicted of a minor vagrancy charge." Specifically, the promised jail sentences, in months, are as in the following table, with the first number in each pair representing Al's sentence and the second Des's. (A minus sign is put in front of each of the numbers to remind us that, in the reverse of the usual interpretation, here more is worse.)

Des: **Al:**	Confess	Don't Confess
Confess	(-8, -8)	(0, -15)
Don't Confess	(-15, 0)	(-1, -1)

What does rationality dictate that our players do? (Or, is there honor among thieves?)

What is the logic of the situation represented in this table? Imagine Al's reasoning process; should he confess or not? If Al believes, for whatever reason, that Des is going to confess, then (reading down the first column) Al sees he has a choice between 8 months in jail (if he confesses) and 15 months in jail (if he does not confess). Confessing is clearly his best strategy in this case. If, on the other hand, Al believes Des will not confess, then (reading down the second column) Al sees his choice is between going free (if he confesses) and 1 month in jail (if he does not confess); again, confessing is best for him. Although, to work through the logic of the situation, Al had to make conjectures about what Des would do, in the end these conjectures were irrelevant. Regardless of what Des does, Al's best action is to confess. Now notice that Des is in exactly the same situation as Al, so Des reaches the same conclusion; Des also rationally confesses. Thus the *equilibrium* of this game, the outcome of simultaneously rational decisions by both of the players, has both confessing.

This looks paradoxical. Compare the confess/confess equilibrium (which results in 8 months' jail for each) with the alternative of neither confessing (which results in 1 month's jail for both). Both would be better off if neither confessed. There is a contradiction between what is individually rational and what is collectively rational. The pursuit of individual gain results in both being worse off than they need be. Each would be better off if they could succeed in cooperating. But they cannot: if one decided to act in their mutual interest by not confessing, then, by the logic already given, it is in the interest of his rival to confess.

Let us introduce some economics jargon to describe this situation. Call an outcome *efficient* if there is no alternative outcome that would leave some players better off and none worse off. To reverse this definition, an outcome is not efficient if there is another outcome that the players unanimously prefer. In the prisoners' dilemma, the $(-1, -1)$ outcome is efficient (as, for that matter, are the $(-15, 0)$ and $(0, -15)$ outcomes). We have found that the equilibrium of the prisoners' dilemma game is not efficient.

What the prisoner's dilemma shows, in the words of the mathematician Robert Aumann, is that "People who fail to cooperate for their own mutual benefit are not necessarily foolish or irrational; they may be acting perfectly rationally." The prisoners' dilemma is a paradigm for many diverse business and economic interactions. For example: Two firms are competing to sell the same product; the logic of profit maximization forces each to set a low price when both would earn more profits if each set a higher price. Two nations trading with each other are driven by rational, national-interest calculations to erect trade barriers when both would be better off if they were eliminated. Fishermen overfish their common fishing ground and destroy their industry, to everyone's loss.

A potential buyer and a potential seller bargain so hard that they fail to reach agreement on a price, despite the fact that there exist prices such that both would have been better off had the sale occurred.

THE RATIONAL PIGS

Two pigs, one dominant and the other subordinate, are put in a box. There is a lever at one end of the box which, when pressed, dispenses food at the other end. Thus the pig that presses the lever must run to the other end; by the time it gets there, the other pig has eaten most, but not all, of the food. The dominant pig is able to prevent the subordinate pig from getting any of the food when both are at the food. Assuming the pigs can reason like game theorists, which pig will press the lever?

For the sake of definiteness, let us attach some hypothetical numbers to this game. Suppose 6 units of grain are delivered whenever the lever is pushed. If the subordinate pig presses the lever, the dominant pig eats all 6 units; but if the dominant pig pushes the lever, the subordinate pig eats 5 of the 6 units before the dominant pig pushes it away. To fill in all the possibilities, we must make some assumption about what happens in the unlikely event that both press the lever simultaneously. Suppose the subordinate pig can run faster so, if both press, it gets 2 units of the food before the dominant pig arrives. Finally, suppose pressing the lever and running to the other end requires some effort, the equivalent of one-half a unit of food. Our game then is represented by the following matrix (with the first number in each pair being the subordinate pig's amount of food and the second the dominant pig's):

Dominant Pig:	Press	Don't Press
Subordinate Pig:		
Press	(1.5, 3.5)	(−0.5, 6)
Don't Press	(5, 0.5)	(0, 0)

To solve this game, let us anthropomorphically endow the pigs with deductive capabilities. Consider first the subordinate pig's reasoning. "Suppose I predict that the big pig will press the lever. Then I get 1.5 if I press and 5 if I don't. If, on the other hand, I predict it will not press, I get −0.5 if I press and 0 if I don't. Thus regardless of what it does, I am better off not pressing than pressing." Now imagine the dominant pig's thought process. "If I predict the small pig will press the lever, I get 3.5 if I press and 6 if I don't. If I predict it will not press, I get 0.5 if I press and 0 if I don't." Our dominant pig now does seem to face a dilemma. Its *best response* is different depending on what it conjectures its rival will do: it should not press if it conjectures the subordinate pig will press; but it should press if it conjectures the subordinate pig will not. How can it decide what its best action is? To resolve this quandary, the dominant pig must put itself in the shoes of the subordinate pig. Doing so, it sees, as we saw, that the subordinate pig's best action is unambiguous: don't press. Thus if it presumes that the subordinate pig is rational, it knows it should use its best response to its rival's not pressing: thus it is in its interest to press the lever. (Notice that the dominant pig's chain of reasoning is more complex than the logic we encountered in the prisoners' dilemma, in that its choice of action depends on its prediction of what its rival will do.) Rational behavior, therefore, indicates a surprising conclusion: the dominant pig presses the lever, and the subordinate pig gets most of the food. Weakness, in this case, is strength.

Animal behaviorists have actually conducted experiments of this sort. In most experimental trials, the dominant pig did actually push the lever. The pigs behaved like game theorists. Of course, few would argue that the pigs actually went through this intricate chain of reasoning. But the outcome was *as if* they had. There is an important general lesson here. Over a sequence of plays, it is possible to converge on the rational outcome by trial and error, ending up with a situation that looks identical to what rational play would generate. In the pig experiments, what probably happened was that the small pig tried pressing the lever. Eventually it learned that it got nothing for its trouble and ceased pressing. Then the large pig, after seeing that it was getting no food, found that the only way for it to get some was to press the lever itself. The pigs thus "discovered" the rational solution to the game. Game-players do not have to be mathematicians in order to succeed in playing rationally.

In contrast to the prisoners' dilemma, the pigs game generates no conflict between individual rationality and collective rationality. The outcome could not be changed without making one of the players (the subordinate pig) worse off. The dominant pig or an outside observer might question the fairness of the outcome (the pig that does the work gets the smaller return); but there is no alternative that the players unanimously prefer.

Similar games arise in less trivial circumstances. Consider, for example, how OPEC worked when it was an effective cartel. OPEC's success was probably due to the willingness of its largest member, Saudi Arabia, to act unilaterally to keep oil prices high. When one of the smaller members increased its output of oil, the Saudis reduced their own in compensation. This was not altruism on the Saudis' part; rather, it arose from the logic of the situation. The Saudis were in an analogous position to the big pig. Both the Saudis and the smaller producers knew that OPEC would collapse unless the Saudis limited their own production; and the smaller producers took advantage of this, getting a free ride on the Saudis' efforts. Saudi Arabia captured for itself a large enough share of the benefits of the high prices that it was rationally willing to bear a disproportionate share of the cost of maintaining the cartel.

Consider also incentives within an international alliance, the North Atlantic Treaty Organization. As a measure of burden-sharing, let us compute for each member country the ratio of military expenditures to national income. Then, for the sake of comparison across countries, let us divide this number by the alliance-wide average. The resulting number will exceed one if the country's share of the costs of collective defense exceeds to its income share; it will be less than one if the country's defense expenditures are a smaller fraction of its income than the average. For the period 1950 to 1984, the United States's relative defense burden so defined was 1.27. All other countries in the alliance had relative defense burdens of less than one (Britain had 0.96, Greece 0.96, France 0.89, Portugal 0.88, Turkey 0.87, Netherlands 0.66, Germany 0.65, Norway 0.59, Belgium 0.58, Italy 0.50, Canada 0.49, Denmark 0.45, Luxembourg 0.20, Iceland 0.00). Only the largest member of NATO, the United States, contributed more than the average share to collective defense. The logic of this might be analogous to the pigs, with the United States playing the dominant pig's role. (Of course, both NATO and OPEC involve much more complex interactions than the pigs game, so this can only be part of the story.)

THE LOCATION GAME

Two beer vendors, Ms Bud and Ms Weiser, operate on a beach. They are required to charge the same price, but they can choose where to locate themselves on the beach. Their customers, sunbathers, do not like to be near each other, so they are spread evenly along the beach. Sunbathers also are averse to walking, so they purchase one can of beer from the vendor closest to them. Where on the beach will the vendors, seeking large sales, locate themselves?

The answer is that the two vendors locate themselves right next to each other, in the middle of the beach. This is established as follows. If one vendor, say Bud, had already chosen her location, where should her rival, Weiser, place herself? Suppose the locations on the beach were as follows:

          B   *   W

With this configuration, Bud sells to all customers to the left of her; Weiser sells to all to the right of her; and they share equally those between them, Bud getting those to the left of the mid-point (denoted * above), and Weiser getting those to the right of the mid-point. Given Bud's location, Weiser can easily calculate that she could increase her sales by relocating leftwards: by doing so, she shifts the mid-point and so takes some of Bud's customers. Thus the situation depicted above could not be an equilibrium of the game. It follows that the best response of Weiser to any given location of Bud is to locate right next to Bud, on whichever side of the beach is the longest. Where will Bud locate herself? What we have found so far is Weiser's best response to an arbitrary decision of Bud. But Bud is in an identical situation to Weiser. By repeating the foregoing logic, interchanging the names of the players, we find that Bud's best response to an arbitrary decision of Weiser is to locate just next to her.

To complete our solution of this game, let us define the *equilibrium* of the game (strictly, the *Nash* equilibrium, after the mathematician John Nash) to be a situation such that each of the players is doing the best he or she can, given the other's actions. Thus, at an equilibrium (of this or any other game), all players are simultaneously acting rationally; each is using his or her best response to the others' actions, which are in turn best responses. At an equilibrium, no individual could have done better by acting differently. Conversely, the players' actions do *not* form an equilibrium if one of them has an alternative action that would have made him or her better off. The logic of best responses and equilibrium will be invoked repeatedly through this book. In the location game, for Bud's location to be a best response to Weiser's at the same time as Weiser's location is a best response to Bud's, it must be that each is located right next to each other, exactly in the middle of the beach.

The logic of this game is more subtle than that of the earlier games. In the prisoner's dilemma and the pigs' game, at least one of the players had a uniquely defined action that was best regardless of the other player's action. The location game is different: both players, in calculating their best actions, must simultaneously conjecture what their rival is going to decide to do.

Puzzles that the location game might resolve include: Why do gas stations often cluster together? Why do different airlines flying a given route schedule simultaneous departures? Why do New York City's street peddlers of watches and radios cluster on the same blocks? Why do competing television networks target their programs at bland, middle-of-the-road tastes? We can stretch this game still further if, instead of customers on a beach, we think of voters as being evenly distributed along a left-right spectrum, and political parties competing for votes by choosing where to locate themselves ideologically. The game-theoretic prediction is that the parties place themselves in the center of the political spectrum, contesting the vote of the least ideological voters. (The very name of one of Canada's two main parties, the Progressive Conservative Party, seems to be an attempt to straddle this political middle ground.)

NEGOTIATING WITH A DEADLINE

Mortimer and Hotspur are to divide $100 between themselves. Each of the bargainers knows that the game has the following structure:

Stage 1: Mortimer proposes how much of the $100 he gets. Then either Hotspur accepts it, in which case the game ends and Hotspur *receives the remainder of the $100; or Hotspur rejects it, in which case the game continues.*

Stage 2: The sum to be divided has now shrunk to $90. Hotspur makes a proposal for his share of the $90. Then Mortimer either accepts it and gets the remainder; or rejects it, in which case each receives nothing and the game ends.

What will Mortimer demand at the first stage?

Mortimer knows that Hotspur will squeeze as much out of the negotiation as he can—"in the way of a bargain, mark you me, I'll cavil on the ninth part of a hair," Shakespeare has Hotspur say in *Henry IV*. What is the least Mortimer can induce Hotspur to accept? To answer this Mortimer must put himself in Hotspur's shoes, and imagine the game has reached the second period. Hotspur is now in a strong position: he knows that Mortimer gets nothing if he rejects Hotspur's offer, so Mortimer is better off accepting any division that gives him more than zero. Thus Hotspur can demand for himself almost all of the $90, leaving Mortimer just enough so that he does not say no out of spite—one cent, perhaps, or one dollar. Hotspur therefore gets $90 less a small amount if the game goes to the second round. Thus, from the perspective of the first stage, Mortimer can predict what Hotspur will do. Mortimer knows that Hotspur knows that he, Hotspur, can assure himself of (close to) $90 if he rejects Mortimer's first-stage offer. Hence Mortimer knows that the least Hotspur will accept in the first round is $90; the best Mortimer can do is demand $10 for himself. With both players having gone through this chain of reasoning, the actual play of the game is straightforward: Mortimer immediately offers Hotspur slightly less than $90, and Hotspur immediately accepts.

This game shows the power of a deadline: the last person to make the offer can capture most of the remaining gains from trade. In reality, the rules of the game rarely specify the sequencing of offers. Thus there is likely to be scrambling to be the last to make an offer; to get your own offer in just before the deadline so that your bargaining partner has no choice but to accept. This is a risky strategy; it runs the risk that the deadline will pass before agreement is reached. Often actual negotiations end just before the deadline; this deadline effect perhaps is an explanation for this.

Good bargainers, like good chess players, look several moves ahead. The essence of the foregoing argument was "putting yourself in the other's shoes." Although the agreement occurs in the first period, it is shaped by the possibility of a second period. Each bargainer thinks through the other's rational responses to all possible contingencies. The forward-looking logic that we used in solving this game is (as we will see in Chapters 5 and 6) a general tool for thinking about bargaining.

THE INHERITANCE GAME

An aged mother wishes to give an heirloom to one of her several sons. She wants to ensure that it goes to the son who most values it. But the mother has failed to inculcate honesty in her sons; since each wants the heirloom, they have an incentive to exaggerate its worth to them. The mother therefore devises the following scheme to reveal the most deserving recipient. She asks the sons to tell her confidentially how much they value the heirloom, and promises to give it to the one who reports the highest valuation. (The yuppie offspring measure the value of everything in dollar equivalents.) To finance one last holiday for herself, she will extract a payment from the recipient, equal not to what the recipient reports, but to the second-highest reported valuation. Will the mother's scheme make honesty the best policy?

The mother, by requiring the son who reports the highest valuation to pay the second-highest reported valuation, will indeed induce honest reporting. Consider what your reasoning would be if you were one of the sons. One option is to report exactly what the heirloom is worth to you. Another is to exaggerate its worth. The amount you pay if you receive the heirloom is independent of what you say it is worth (because, by the rules specified, the amount you pay is equal to someone else's reported valuation.) The only effect of your report is to determine whether or not you are awarded the item. Hence exaggerating its worth can only change the likelihood of getting it. In particular, exaggeration results in the possibility that you make the highest report when you would not have, had you been honest; that is, the second-highest report, the one you now beat, is more than your true valuation. But this means that what you must pay, the amount of the second-highest report, is more than what you believe the heirloom is worth; exaggerating cannot be in your interest. Conversely, would you want to understate the item's value? Understating changes the outcome only when you would have won with an honest report, but now you report a valuation lower than one of your sibling's, so you do not get the item. Again, this cannot be in your interest. The mother's scheme works.

The truth is obtained at a price, however. The money received by the mother is less than the successful son's actual valuation of the heirloom. That son in effect earns a profit, equal to the difference between his own valuation and the second-highest valuation. This sum of money can be thought of as what the mother loses as a result of her informational disadvantage.

The idea that you can induce self-interested people to tell the truth by cunningly designing the way payments depend on reports is powerful, and has more significant applications than the contrived game analyzed here. Some examples of these applications will be developed in

Chapters 6, 9, and 11; others include the following. A state regulatory agency must decide what price a telephone company may charge. The price should reflect the company's production cost; but the regulatory agency knows less about costs than the company itself, so it must rely on the company's reports. Can the regulator induce the telephone company not to overstate its costs? Some neighbors propose building a neighborhood park. They want each household's contribution to the construction cost to reflect the household's valuation of the park. How can they overcome each householder's temptation to free-ride on the others' efforts by claiming not to care about the park? A communications satellite is shared by several users. The cost of operating the satellite is to be divided according to the profit each user earns from it. How can the users be induced to reveal their profits?

Summary

The games analyzed in this chapter, simple as they are, have served to introduce some of the most important ideas of game theory, ideas that will underlie the analysis in the rest of this book. Several basic concepts were introduced. *Best response* means a player's best action when faced with a particular action of his or her rival. *Equilibrium* is the outcome that results when all players simultaneously are using their best responses to the others' actions; thus at an equilibrium all players are doing the best they can given the other players' decisions; that is, all are playing their best responses. If, conversely, the game is not at an equilibrium, then at least one of the players could have done better by acting differently. An outcome is *efficient* if there exists no alternative feasible outcome that would leave some players better off and none worse off.

The prisoner's dilemma exhibited a feature that more complicated games often have: although everyone acts rationally, the outcome looks irrational. The equilibrium, in other words, is not efficient. The players, in rationally pursuing their own interests, produce a situation that is in no one's interest.

The pigs game, the location game, and the negotiation game illustrated, in successively more subtle settings, the use of best-response reasoning. Rational behavior in games requires putting yourself in your rival's shoes. In order to compute your own best action, you must make some conjecture about what action your rival will choose; to anticipate others' responses and counter-responses. If you believe your rival is at least as clever as you (believing the contrary may be just fooling yourself), then this conjecture should be based on the presumption that your rival will likewise act rationally.

Often in games information is dispersed: some players know things that other players do not. The inheritance game showed that it is possible for a player who lacks some needed information to design a strategy that reduces—but does not completely eliminate—his or her informational disadvantage. The player can learn the information; but must pay for it.

In the next chapter, we examine the potential gains from cooperation among game-players, and how these gains can be achieved.

3

Understanding Conflict and Cooperation

THE TWO essential aspects of any strategic situation are conflict and cooperation. Rarely are different people's aims identical; interactions typically involve some (polite or impolite) conflict. Equally rare are situations of pure conflict, in which one person's gains equal the other's losses. Even the fiercest conflict has some commonality of interest, some scope for cooperation. (In war, the combatants usually respect conventions of how prisoners should be treated.)

Playing a game is like dividing a pie. Players are often faced with contradictory motives. Their actions affect the size of the pie, and all participants agree in wanting the pie to be as large as possible. But their interests are at odds when it comes to dividing the pie; all want their own shares to be as large as possible. The players' attempts to increase their own shares may have the side-effect of decreasing the size of the pie. A tension exists between seeking a large total pie and seeking a large share of the pie. Expressed in simple terms, this is one of the central ideas of game theory.

Where do the gains from cooperation come from? Can these gains be realized? This chapter investigates the sources of the mutual gains accruing to game-players.

The Gains from Trade

Why do people buy and sell? Because they gain something. This may seem so elementary as not to need saying. It is, however, worth examining the sources of these gains. Imagine a trading situation. This can be of any kind: a simple transaction between a buyer and a seller in which the only decision is the price; an agreement by one party to work for another in exchange for payment; or a complicated contract between firms that specifies in detail what will be done in a long list of contingencies.

If trade takes place it must be a good thing. More precisely, voluntary trade must be mutually beneficial. The argument is straightforward: given our assumption that people are rational, if the transaction were not beneficial to one of the parties, it would not have taken place. The ability to veto the transaction prevents consenting adults from being exploited.

The idea of gains from trade is more subtle than it seems at first. The legal system often in effect denies it. For example, a voluntary transaction between a buyer and seller of cocaine is illegal; the law in this case does not accept that people can judge for themselves what is best for them. But this takes us beyond the restricted notion of rationality that we are using throughout this book, which takes as given people's aims and asks how these aims are pursued most effectively.

Even if we do not question the rationality of the buyer and the seller, we must be careful how we interpret the proposition that voluntary trade is a good thing for the parties involved. Rarely do both buyer and seller know everything they would like to know. In an ordinary transaction like the sale of a car, the buyer is necessarily less knowledgeable than the seller about the car's quality. After buying the car and driving it for some weeks, the buyer may discover that it is defective and the price was more than it was worth. Because someone lacks information, mistakes can be made. After the fact, one of the parties might regret the transaction that was freely made. But this possibility does not contradict our proposition about the gains from trade, provided we state it a little more carefully, recognizing that information is rarely perfect.

We must also be sure when we apply the proposition that the transaction is indeed voluntary. "Give me your money or I'll shoot you" has an aspect of voluntariness: you have a choice. But you did not choose to participate in the transaction; this is the key. We want "voluntary" to mean that there is choice from the outset.

Our amended version of the proposition is: *voluntary trade is mutually beneficial, evaluated according to the parties' own tastes and with the information they have at the time of the transaction.*

It follows that there are *gains from trade*. Any sort of transaction—between buyer and seller, employer and employee, landlord and tenant—results in gains for both parties. The distribution of these gains is often uneven. It might be argued that it is sometimes unfair, in that one person gets much more of the gains than the other. Here we are on shakier grounds, however, because reasonable people can disagree on what constitutes fairness. But regardless of notions of fairness, we can certainly conclude that both are better off than if the transaction had not taken place.

From this elementary argument we have derived a conclusion of great importance. Trade is a form of creation. The social act of trading produces value just as surely as the physical act of manufacturing something. Exchange is a game without a loser; both sides win.

Sources of Gains from Trade

How can there be gains from trade? An obvious answer is that buyer and seller differ in some way. Among the reasons for such differences are the following.

Differences in preferences. The buyer may simply value the item more highly than the seller, so there is a price that leaves both feeling they are better off as a result of the transaction. Remember that these may be entirely subjective evaluations; game theorists are not so presumptuous as to judge what people should want. How much an individual enjoys eating ice cream or owning a Rembrandt depends only on the individual's tastes. It is possible, however, to measure this subjective worth of an item: simply ask the individual what its dollar-equivalent value is. What is the lowest price the seller would accept? What is the most the buyer would offer? Assuming honest answers can be induced—and the inheritance game of Chapter 2 illustrated that it is sometimes possible to structure incentives so as to achieve honest answers to questions such as these—this gives us a measure of subjective evaluations.

Comparative advantage. The most common source of gains from trade is differences in the productive capacities of buyer and seller. The seller may be able to produce the item more cheaply than the buyer; the seller, in other words, has a comparative advantage in producing the item. It is in your interest to specialize in doing that at which you are relatively efficient. This is why, 1960s hippie ideology notwithstanding, modern households do not try to be self-sufficient. Imagine trying to produce by yourself all the food, clothing, and everything else you use. Your standard of living would be much lower. There are gains from trade in specializing in selling your labor services and using the proceeds to buy your consumption needs. In exactly the same way, comparative advantage is the basis of trade between nations: a low-wage country produces goods that use labor intensively, exporting them to a high-wage country in exchange for goods whose manufacture requires more capital, and both countries benefit.

One important source of comparative advantage, in turn, is *economies of scale*. Sometimes there is synergy from having people work as a team: there are gains from having people work together rather than separately, dividing the labor and having each specialize in a part of the production process. An employer, the owner of capital equipment, and a group of workers can gainfully trade their services, benefiting from the economies of mass production.

Differences in beliefs. If the value of the item is uncertain at the time of the transaction, and the buyer believes it is worth more than the seller, then mutually gainful trade is possible. The buyer of a used car might believe it is worth more than the owner, who knows its faults. Or the owner of some corporate stock might believe the price is about to fall, while a buyer, having access to different stock-market information, believes it is going to rise. In such cases, at the time of the transaction—though not necessarily later—both buyer and seller perceive themselves to have gained.

Differences in beliefs as a basis for trade should be treated with caution: are the different beliefs consistent with both parties behaving rationally? The potential buyer of a used car should be aware of the fact that one possible reason for the owner's willingness to sell is that the car has hidden defects. Of course, it may be a perfectly good car, and the seller may simply want to trade up. But the seller's willingness to sell provides information to the buyer about the likelihood that the car is defective. The rational buyer will factor this into the decision about how much to offer for the car. The precariousness of differences in beliefs as a source of gains from trade is most clearly seen in the case of stock-market trading. People do not buy shares for the pleasure of owning part of a particular company; they are trading solely for their earning potential. Suppose the owner of certain shares believes, on the basis of his or her own information about the general state of the economy and the health of this firm in particular, that the shares are overpriced. Nevertheless, there is someone willing to buy at the current price. Should the owner sell? Apparently the potential buyer's information indicates the opposite of the owner's information. If the owner is not only rational but believes the buyer is behaving rationally, then the owner should infer, from the buyer's willingness to buy, that the buyer has some additional information. Similarly the buyer should infer from the owner's readiness to sell something of the owner's information. Rational individuals will use the information conveyed by the offers to buy and sell to revise their own assessments of the stock's value. As a result, the differences in beliefs should be reduced, perhaps by enough to discourage either the buyer or the seller from going ahead with the transaction. Groucho Marx warns against trades based solely on differences in beliefs: "I wouldn't want to belong to a club that would accept me as a member" can be rephrased into "I wouldn't want to buy from anyone who'd want to sell to me." Differences in beliefs provide a shaky source of gains from trade. Relying on your own superior intelligence or on the gullibility of your negotiating partner is hardly a safe way to make money: when the dust clears you might find that you have been the gullible one.

Achieving Efficient Outcomes

A major part of any negotiation consists of identifying potential gains from trade. This involves looking for win-win situations, moves that would make not only you but also your negotiating partner better off. It may not be obvious at the outset just what the sources of mutual gains are. Experienced negotiators are skilled at creating unexpected gains from trade, based, as we have seen, on differences between the bargainers in preferences, in productive capacities, in beliefs. Thinking creatively about the possibilities for mutual gain—ways of expanding the pie to be divided—is an essential part of negotiating. In the negotiations between a computer manufacturer and a supplier of semiconductors, for example, the buyer might be more concerned than the seller about delivery time, because the computer manufacturer's entire production schedule depends on the availability of the semiconductors, while the supplier can relatively easily speed up the production of semiconductors. The supplier, on the other hand, might be concerned about the stability of its sales, because the revenue earned from its other customers is subject to wide fluctuations. Thus a mutually beneficial deal could be crafted under which the supplier promises speedier delivery in exchange for the buyer's offering a longer-term contract.

If the realized gains from trade are as large as is feasible, we call the transaction *efficient*. More precisely, as we saw in the last chapter, efficiency means that it would have been impossible to have restructured the transaction so as to make some participants better off and none worse off. An efficient outcome is reached when all mutually beneficial changes that are feasible have been used up.

It is tempting to suggest that all transactions must be efficient. Remembering our underlying hypothesis that individuals behave rationally, would sensible people not just agree to do what is in their joint interest? Unfortunately not. If the world were efficient, labor negotiations would never end in a strike; pollution and congestion would not be matters of public concern, for those affected could negotiate acceptable compensation for their grievances; and government intervention to control monopolies would be unnecessary.

As we saw with the prisoners' dilemma in Chapter 2, the individually rational pursuit of a large share of the pie often sabotages efficiency. There is a unanimously preferred alternative, but the logic of the situation prevents its being reached. A tension between cooperation and conflict is present in most games. Rational actions by each of the individuals can result in an outcome that no one likes. In a piece of game theory

jargon that has become a trendy buzzword, most games are *nonzero-sum:*
the total gains vary depending on the players' actions. In a *zero-sum*
game, by contrast, the total gains are constant; what one wins, the other
loses. A zero-sum game is a game of pure conflict, like an athletic contest. The players' actions affect only the distribution, and not the size, of
the pie. Few if any economic games are zero-sum; in most business
games the size of the pie is determined by the players' actions, so that
seeking a large share of the pie might result in reducing the total size of
the pie.

The tension between conflict and cooperation is illustrated by the decisions of two firms competing to sell the same product. Consider the
following stylized representation of competition between two firms.
Cournot Ltd and Bertrand Ltd, purveyors of mineral water, compete by
choosing one of two possible prices, high and low. Each firm's profit
depends not only on its own price, but also on the price of its rival. A
firm earns the highest possible profit when it charges the low price while
its rival charges the high price; moderately high profit when both firms
charge the high price; moderately low profit when both charge the low
price; and the lowest possible profit when it charges the high price and
its rival charges the low price, as represented in the following table (with
Cournot's profit being the first number in each pair and Bertrand's the
second):

Bertrand: **Cournot:**	High Price	Low Price
High Price	(10, 10)	(1, 15)
Low Price	(15, 1)	(4, 4)

What price will each charge?

A little thought shows that, although the numbers are different, this
game is exactly equivalent to the prisoners' dilemma analyzed in the last
chapter. If Cournot believes that Bertrand is going to charge the high
price, then Cournot earns higher profit from the low price than from
the high price ($15 profit rather than $10 profit). If, on the other hand,
Cournot believes Bertrand will charge the low price, Cournot is still better off charging the low price ($4 profit versus $1 profit). Regardless of
what its rival does, Cournot's best decision is to charge the low price.
Similarly, Bertrand rationally charges the low price. Thus the equilibrium of this game, the outcome of simultaneously rational decisions by
both players, has both charging the low price, even though both would
would earn higher profits if both charged the high price. The equilibrium is not efficient; the pursuit of individual gain results in both players
being worse off than they need be. To repeat the argument in reverse:
an efficient outcome would have both firms charging the high price and
earning high profits. But, if such an outcome were ever attained, each
firm would have an incentive to undercut the rival firm's price, thereby

capturing most of the market and earning still higher profits. Since both firms reason in this way, mutual undercutting takes place, resulting in a low-price, low-profits equilibrium. The logic of the game induces an outcome that is, from the viewpoint of the firms, inefficient.

The game of competition between firms, with its inefficient outcome, is typical of games in general. In most games there is a tension between making the total pie as large as possible and getting a large share of the pie. By the very nature of a game, players' actions affect not only themselves but also the other players. But players have no incentive to take account of their effects on others when they choose their actions. In the firms' competition just analyzed, an increase in price by one would increase the other's profit; but this is not taken account of by the firm contemplating the price change. As a result, games often have inefficient outcomes. Gains from trade exist; but the logic of the situation can mean that the maximum gains from trade are not realized. Can the players somehow achieve cooperation and overcome the prisoners' dilemma?

Suppose the players can get together before the game is played, and they can credibly promise each other that they will charge the high price. If each is confident the other will not undercut the agreed price, each can go ahead and set the high price, and total profits will be maximized. But it is essential that these promises are irrevocable for, as we saw, the prisoners' dilemma logic means that, if each believes the other is going to charge the high price, each has an incentive to respond by charging the low price. In the face of the players' temptations to break their promises, how can the promises be made credible?

One way of achieving irrevocable promises is to write contracts, with severe legal punishment for breach. The British Parliament in 1834 conferred on companies the "privilege" of suing and being sued. The wording is significant. It is indeed a privilege to be able to be sued, for this means it is possible to make enforceable agreements, thus escaping inefficiencies of the prisoners' dilemma type.

Contracts can, however, only sometimes solve a prisoners' dilemma. It depends on the environment of the specific game whether contracting is feasible. First, the legal system will enforce only certain kinds of contracts. If our firms were operating in nineteenth-century Germany, where cartels were legal, they could write contracts to set high prices. But such contracts are not only unenforceable but illegal in most countries today. Second, informational issues constrain what can be contracted. In practice most contracts are incomplete. It is often infeasible to specify in the contract what should happen in every possible event: the world is too complex to allow planning for all contingencies. Unspecified contingencies leave open the possibility of prisoners'-dilemma behavior. Also, for a contingency to be enforceably contracted, it must be observable not only to the contracting parties but also to an independent third party, for it must be possible to prove in court that a breach of contract has taken place. Players cannot credibly promise to act in a certain way if it is impossible to verify those actions. For these reasons, in many situations, game inefficiencies cannot be corrected contractually.

An alternative way of escaping the prisoners' dilemma arises in ongoing interactions: in games played repeatedly. Suppose Cournot Ltd and Bertrand Ltd meet each other not just once (as our argument implicitly assumed), but every week over an indefinitely long future. Then the possibility of future retaliation, as we will see, provides a sanction for enforcing cooperative agreements. In repeated games, agreements can be self-enforcing.

What changes if the game is played repeatedly? The game now has a history and a future. Thus the players can make their actions contingent on what their rivals did in the past; they can reward or punish rivals' past behavior. A firm gets an immediate payoff, as we saw, from price cutting. But, as we will see, the repetition of the game provides a sanction to induce each firm not to charge the low price. To see one kind of outcome to this repeated game, suppose the firms adopt the following strategy: on the first play of the game, each charges the price consistent with maximizing joint profit, that is, the high price. On subsequent plays, each continues to do this unless, at some play in the past, its rival has charged the low price. In this event, it responds by charging the low price. In other words, each firm threatens the other with a price war: if it deviates at any stage, it will be punished by being faced with low profits over the indefinite future. Is this an equilibrium of the repeated version of the game between Cournot Ltd. and Bertrand Ltd.? Suppose Cournot knows that Bertrand has adopted this strategy: is Cournot deterred from charging the low price? Cournot faces a trade-off. If it charges the low price, it receives in this period the highest possible profit, given Bertrand's high price, or $15. But then it suffers from the lowered profits when Bertrand retaliates in the subsequent periods, earning $4 in each future period. If, on the other hand, Cournot plays cooperatively and continues to charge the high price, it earns $10 in each period. Is the sequence of $15 followed by a stream of $4 profits better than the stream of $10 profits? If Cournot evaluates future profits as being worth as much as current profits, then, since the stream of future profits extends indefinitely, the future loss that results from price cutting ($4 instead of $10) outweighs the current gain ($15 instead of $10). The same logic applies to Bertrand, faced with Cournot's threat to retaliate against any price cutting. Thus it is not in either firm's interest to cut its price. The repeated game is in equilibrium if each firm adopts the strategy of retaliating against any price cutting by the other firm by itself charging the low price in future plays of the game. This makes the efficient outcome (10, 10) an equilibrium of the repeated game. The paradoxical feature of the prisoners' dilemma—that rational actions lead to an outcome that neither player wants—is thus eliminated.

Retaliation, then, need not be a destructive force but can have positive effects. (Anyone who has played a contact sport like rugby knows that the possibility of retaliation actually makes the game safer.) Agreements—tacit or explicit—are worthless without some way of enforcing them; and retaliation provides an enforcement mechanism. Paradoxically, you can be better off when your rivals have the ability to harm you than when they do not.

That concern for the future can generate cooperation is a straightforward enough conclusion: we did not really need game theory to teach us that. The payoff that we get from the precision that game theory brings to our thinking is that, surprisingly enough, this conclusion is quite fragile, and must be carefully qualified. The players might not succeed in cooperating, even though the future is hanging over them. Three caveats must be appended to the idea that cooperation can occur in ongoing relationships.

First, the foregoing argument omitted part of the logic of repeated games. Our arithmetic weighed the firm's current gain from price-cutting against its future losses after its rival retaliates. A dollar received now is worth more than a dollar received a year from now (because if you had it now it could have accumulated interest by next year), so the comparison of the alternative profit streams depends on the interest rate. For the threat of retaliation to work, the threatened player must care enough about future returns. For this to be the case, the future returns must not be too long delayed, and the interest rate must not be too high; otherwise the player will succumb to the temptation of immediate profits and charge the low price, producing the prisoners'-dilemma outcome. Cooperation, therefore, depends on the costs of delay. For cooperation to be equilibrium behavior, the players must be sufficiently patient; they must value future returns highly enough.

A second caveat is that, to be able to retaliate, it must be possible to see any deviations. Suppose that our firms cannot directly observe their rival's price, so they must infer the rivals' behavior from their own sales. Suppose, in addition, that total demand for their product fluctuates unpredictably. Then if they see that their sales are abnormally low, they cannot distinguish the cause: was it because total demand was low, or was it because the other firm defected by underpricing? The firm risks retaliating when the rival did not in fact defect; and not retaliating when it did. Both types of error weaken the retaliatory sanction. If the uncertainty is large enough it can destroy the possibility of cooperation.

A third caveat is that cooperation is not the only equilibrium of the repeated game. Suppose one of the firms doggedly charges the low price, regardless of what its rival does. Then the best the rival can do is also to charge the low price. This is self-reinforcing; that is, it is an equilibrium. Hence game theory does not *predict* that cooperation occurs in a repeated game; game theory says only that the repetition makes cooperation *possible*. Many outcomes are consistent with all of the players behaving rationally, and it is possible to be trapped in a low-level equilibrium. Cooperation is just one of the outcomes of the repeated game.

The conclusion is therefore regrettably indeterminate. Many different outcomes can emerge from the interactions in an ongoing game. Efficient, cooperative outcomes are possible; but so are outcomes like the prisoners' dilemma. Concern for the future only sometimes generates cooperative behavior.

How do real game-players play in repeated games? A huge number of laboratory experiments have been done, putting subjects, usually undergraduate students, in a repeated prisoners'-dilemma situation and letting them play for real money. In the experiments, as in the theory just outlined, no clear-cut pattern emerges; the subjects play cooperatively some of the time and noncooperatively some of the time. Typically, they cooperate in the early plays of the game, and then revert to noncooperative play toward the end of the experiment. Surprisingly, males have been found to cooperate more than females. More consistent with stereotype, sociology students cooperate more than economics students. A study of plea-bargaining in trials with more than one defendant—literal prisoners' dilemmas—found that the prisoners did not behave as in the simple prisoners' dilemma game: they usually cooperated with each other.

Does It Pay to Be Trustworthy?

A cautionary note: we tend piously to think that cooperation is always a good thing, but games like the prisoners' dilemma and the firms' competition show that this is not necessarily so. If the two firms succeed in cooperating and achieving what is, from their point of view, an efficient outcome, the result is that they charge a high price, and the public is exploited. The prisoners, if they can cooperate so as to avoid the prisoners' dilemma, thwart justice. What we are describing as the efficient outcome is efficient in only a limited sense: it is efficient from the point of view of the players in the game. It is not necessarily efficient in a wider game in which effects on other people are incorporated. Successful cooperation need not promote the social interest.

Cooperative behavior does, nevertheless, often correspond to ethical behavior. Let us change our game and suppose Cournot Ltd and Bertrand Ltd are not competing to sell the same product; rather, Cournot is selling some component to Bertrand that Bertrand uses in its production process. Opportunistic behavior, analogous to charging the low price in the previous game, is possible on both sides. Cournot could deliver items that it knows are defective. Bertrand, pleading changed circumstances, could insist the price be renegotiated downwards after Cournot has sunk the costs of retooling needed to produce this particular item. Everyone knows that such opportunistic behavior occurs on occasions. The remarkable thing is not that it occurs, but that it does not occur more often.

Sam Goldwyn got it wrong. Contrary to his maxim, "An oral contract isn't worth the paper it's written on," oral contracts can often be relied on. The insight captured by the repeated game is that reputation is an asset. Relationships among firms—either competitive, as between firms selling similar products, or complementary, as between a manufacturing firm and a parts supplier—usually persist over time. In an ongoing relationship, the people you are dealing with might be deterred from taking immediate advantage of the situation by the long-term damage to their reputations. Concern for the future may prevent a firm from squeezing the last cent of profit from its trading partner. There is, literally, no future in it. People often cooperate because, in an ongoing situation, it is in their interest to do so. The business world relies heavily on the logic of repeated games. Businesspeople often eschew written contracts, relying instead on exchange relationships, even when considerable risks are involved. When a written contract is used, it is often left deliberately vague, with much left to be resolved later by mutual consent; for such a transaction to work, trust is needed.

Can you trust the person you are dealing with? People often behave honorably simply because they are honorable. Most people value honesty for its own sake: to put it in crass terms, they are prepared to forsake some monetary gains in order to do the right thing. But, as we have seen, sometimes there is an additional force at work, reinforcing native virtue. In an ongoing relationship it may pay to act honorably. The retaliation possibilities inherent in the ongoing game mean that cooperation can be sustained. Selfish individuals can cooperate: egotists can play as if they were altruists. Some people refuse to sell shoddy goods because they want to do what is right, others because they know it would cost them future sales. The bottom line is the same regardless of the vendor's motivation: the buyer can count on the quality of the offered merchandise. It is important to remember, however, that if the players are purely self-interested, outcomes other than cooperation are possible in repeated games; the players' concern for the future cannot always be relied on to produce cooperative behavior. The answer to the question: "does it pay to be trustworthy?" is "maybe."

Summary

An exchange creates gains for both parties. The gains from trade arise from differences between buyer and seller: in their preferences, productive capacities, or expectations. An important part of negotiating consists of exploring the possibilities for mutual gain.

Game interactions—the effect of one player's actions on the other player—mean that the outcome of a game is often not efficient; there is some alternative outcome that each of the players would prefer but which, because of the logic of the game, is not attained. To realize the gains from trade, the players must somehow overcome this game logic.

Contracting, if it is feasible, is one way of avoiding the prisoners' dilemma; each player promises to eschew mutually harmful acts. Alternatively, the repetition of the game can generate cooperation; the possibilities for retaliation that repetition introduces can make it in the players' interests to cooperate. In an ongoing relationship, a player might refrain from squeezing out all possible current profits out of concern for the long-term effects of such behavior. But concern for the future only makes cooperation possible; it does not guarantee it. For the future to weigh heavily enough to provide an effective sanction it must be that (a) the players are sufficiently patient and (b) any player's deviations from agreed behavior can be sufficiently accurately observed by the other players. Even if these conditions are met so that cooperation is potentially worthwhile, many outcomes are consistent with rational behavior and there is no guarantee that cooperation will be achieved: the players might be trapped in a low-level equilibrium with no cooperation occurring.

Most games are more complicated than the prisoners' dilemma, in that they have a wider range of possible outcomes. Even if the players succeed in cooperating, there is usually still a role for bargaining: over which of the many possible cooperative outcomes is achieved. What shapes the agreement in this bargaining game? This question will be addressed in Part II. Before turning to bargaining, however, we must develop some tools for thinking about decision-making under uncertainty; this we will do in the next chapter.

4

Weighing Risks

ALMOST every decision in business—for that matter, almost every decision in life—involves some uncertainty. There are not many sure things. Not everything that affects the ultimate outcome of the decision can be known at the time the decision must be made; risk-taking is inescapable. Reflecting this, the games to be analyzed later in this book will contain uncertainty as an essential ingredient. A seller does not know how highly a potential buyer values what is being negotiated over, so does not know how high the price can be driven without losing the sale. An employer does not know the ability of a new employee at the time of hiring. The owner of a firm cannot observe how assiduously the manager promotes the firm's efficiency. A firm contracting to do some work cannot predict at the time of agreeing to a price exactly what its costs will be.

How does uncertainty affect the structure of transactions? How is it possible to make a rational decision without knowing exactly what consequences will follow? In this chapter, we develop an analytical framework for thinking systematically about risky decisions. In what follows we discuss risk-taking in terms of gambles. The ideas are, however, intended to be applicable to decisions usually given more dignified names, such as choosing a firm's line of business or investing in the stock market.

Probability

Imagine having to make a decision when confronted with uncertainty. Let us suppose you have done your homework and have discovered the range of possible consequences of your decision. (Eventualities that are completely unforeseeable raise additional difficulties which, since they are the subject of ongoing and uncompleted research in economic theory, we will ignore here.) Only one of the possible eventualities will actually occur. How should you weigh the alternatives?

The first essential component of a rational decision in the face of uncertainty is knowledge of the relative likelihood of the alternative possible outcomes. In order to think precisely about decisions involving uncertainty, we borrow from statistical theory the concept of *probability*. Probability, which measures the relative likelihood of a particular thing happening, is represented by a number between zero and one. A probability of zero means that the event in question is impossible; a probability of one means it will definitely happen. If you add up the probabilities attached to all possible outcomes, you get a total equal to one (since, by definition, one of these outcomes is sure to happen). When you toss a coin, the probability of heads is one-half, the probability of tails is one-half. When you throw a die, there is a one-sixth probability of any particular number coming up. Odds at horse races reflect probabilities: if a horse has odds of five to two, its probability of winning is 5/7 (that is, 5/[5 + 2]).

In your rational decision process, then, you begin by listing all the possible outcomes that could follow your decision. You then estimate the probabilities of the different possible outcomes: that is, assign a number between zero and one to each of the possible outcomes, in such a way that these probabilities sum to one. In some situations these probabilities can be deduced easily: using simple arithmetic you can compute the probability that a roll of a pair of dice will show a total of seven; using less simple arithmetic but the same principles you can calculate the probability of getting a royal flush in a poker hand. In other situations probabilities are harder to impute: you need to use some guesswork to assign probabilities to the possible future prices of the stock you are contemplating buying. Experience you and others have accumulated in similar situations in the past can provide useful information to help you assign these probabilities.

The Expected Return

How can you, as decision-maker, assign a valuation to a risky choice, when, by definition, you do not know what the outcome is going to be? To give this question some more definite content, imagine a single toss of a coin. If it comes up heads, you win $100; if tails, nothing. The probability of each outcome is one-half. What is the value to you of this gamble? To answer this question, we borrow another concept from statistics.

Although the coin is actually to be tossed only once, imagine it is to be tossed many times. Then the average payoff per toss would be approximately $50, because the toss would come up heads about half the time.

Define the *expected return* from the single coin toss to be the average return of the (hypothetical) many coin tosses. (Technically, the expected return is computed by multiplying the payoff from any particular outcome by the probability that that outcome arises, and then summing over all possible outcomes. In the foregoing case, this is just $(100 \times 0.5) + (0 \times 0.5)$, or 50, as we said already.) We will take expected return as our basic way of evaluating uncertain events. To repeat, this involves treating unique events *as if* they were played over many times so that the uncertainty is virtually removed.

How much would you be prepared to pay to participate in a gamble like this single coin toss? Presumably the most you would be prepared to pay is the expected return: that is, $50 for the equal chance of $100 and nothing. The reasoning is the same kind of "as if" logic as before. If this were not a single gamble but a long series of gambles, you would just break even by paying $50 per coin toss; by paying anything more you would be certain to lose money in the long run.

But would you pay as much as $50 to participate in the gamble? Few people would. Our calculation of the expected return ignores the fact that people dislike risk. How is the distaste for risk-bearing incorporated in rational decision-making?

The Risk Premium

If you were offered the choice between receiving $50 for sure and receiving a 50% chance of $100 and a 50% chance of nothing, which would you pick? Most people would take the $50. People tend to prefer a certain outcome to a gamble with the same expected return: in economics jargon, they are *risk averse*.

Consider now the experiment of gradually reducing the amount of money offered for sure as the alternative to the 0/100 gamble. How low would this sum have to go before you preferred the gamble to the certain outcome? The more risk averse you are, the further this amount will have to be lowered. The difference between $50 and the amount at which you will take the gamble is called the *risk premium*. If, for example, you would switch from taking the sure thing to taking the gamble at $40, you have a $10 risk premium. Your risk premium is a measure of how cautious you are toward this particular gamble. In any situation, not just in the stylized situation just described, the risk premium is defined to be the difference between the expected return of the gamble and the amount of money that, if received for sure, the individual regards as equivalent to the gamble. In other words, the risk premium is the answer to the question: *how much money would you be prepared to give up to rid yourself of this risk?*

The size of the risk premium depends on three different things. The first is the psychology of the individual; how cautious or adventurous the person is. Your risk premium toward the chance that your house will fall down in an earthquake is higher the more circumspect your nature. The second is the size of the risk itself: the odds of the alternative outcomes. Your risk premium toward earthquake damage to your house would be greater if you lived in California than if you lived in Iowa. Finally, the risk premium depends on the objective size of the potential loss. Your risk premium on earthquake damage will be higher if your house is worth $1 million than if it is worth $200,000. A given individual has different risk premiums toward different risks; and different individuals facing the same risk can have different risk premiums.

Buying insurance is an expression of risk aversion. By purchasing insurance the individual obtains, for the price of the insurance premium, a certain outcome in place of an uncertain one. The risk premium measures the most the individual would willingly pay to be completely insured against this particular risk.

Avoidance of all risk is not the aim of rational people, even if they are risk averse. Rather the aim is to find the right amount of risk. Risk is inherent in any decision that commits resources for the prospect of future returns; avoiding risk means avoiding most opportunities for gain. Rational decisions involve finding the ideal amount of risk to accept, given the individual's degree of risk aversion and the costs of reducing risk. When, for example, should you purchase insurance? If the insurance company asks a price higher than your risk premium for the particular risk in question, you would rationally refuse to buy the insurance, preferring to face the risk despite being risk averse.

Measuring Risk Attitudes

Science, as Lord Kelvin said, is measurement. Risk aversion is not merely an theorist's toy; it is possible to measure it. One way is to observe market data: economists have inferred risk-aversion measures from studying farmers' decisions on what crops to plant, or individuals' purchases of property and liability insurance. And psychologists have developed ways of measuring risk aversion in the laboratory, by using questionnaires designed to elicit the subjects' risk aversion.

Psychologists find that women, older people, the married, and the first-born tend more than others to avoid risks. Risk aversion affects the choice of occupation: not surprisingly, commission salespeople have been found to be less risk averse than average, while public-sector employees and bankers are more risk averse than average.

A study of the risk attitudes of U.S. and Canadian managers finds that chief executive officers are more willing to take risks than lower-level managers; that managers in small firms are more willing to take risks than managers in large firms; and that managers with a graduate degree are more willing to take risks than managers with a bachelor's degree or high-school training. Contrary to national stereotypes (the risk-taking American, the cautious Canadian), this study finds no evidence that risk aversion is systematically related to nationality.

The rich and successful are consistently found in such studies to be less risk averse than average. The causality could go in either direction; probably it goes both ways. The rich might be more willing to take risks because the prospect of losing, say, $1000 is less worrying if your annual income is $1 million than if it is $20,000. On the other hand, the rich might have acquired their wealth through their willingness to accept risks.

The Risk Attitudes of Firms

Firms are less averse to risk than people. Large firms, in particular, often have a risk premium that is close to zero; in terms of our simple example, they are just as happy with the gamble offering $50 expected return as with the $50 for sure, and definitely prefer the gamble to receiving, say, $49.95 for sure. This is because their owners are stockholders with diversified investment portfolios.

The idea of diversification is summarized by the adage "Don't put all your eggs in one basket." Common-sense as this saying is, it is worth thinking through its logic. Imagine you have 100 eggs. When you carry a basket, there is a probability of, say, 10% that you will drop it. If you put all your eggs in one basket, you will end up with either 100 eggs or none; the expected loss is 10% of 100, or 10 eggs. Suppose instead you put each egg in a separate basket, and the probability of dropping any one basket is still 10%. If we assume this probability is the same regardless of how many other baskets are dropped, then the expected number of baskets dropped is 10. Thus the expected number of eggs lost is 10, the same as if you had put all your eggs in one basket. If you are risk neutral, you are indifferent between using one basket and 100. If you are risk averse, however, using 100 baskets is crucially different from using one. With one basket, you actually get either 100 eggs or none. With 100 baskets, you might end up with any number of eggs between zero and 100. You are more likely to get some intermediate number of eggs than either extreme of zero and 100. Being risk averse means you prefer this situation; you prefer not to put all your eggs in one basket.

The eggs-in-baskets story is translated into less trivial terms by considering an investor who is choosing between owning 100% of one firm and owning a 1% share of 100 firms. A risk-averse investor prefers the diversified portfolio. The stock market makes it possible for investors not to put all their eggs in one basket.

The foregoing argument assumed that the probability of dropping any one basket is the same no matter how many other baskets are dropped. This need not be the case. It may be that dropping one makes it less likely you will drop another; in this case the gains from diversification are still greater. Or it may be that dropping one indicates you are clumsy and increases the likelihood you will drop others. In this case the gains from diversification are reduced; but the diversified portfolio remains preferable for a risk-averse individual (except in the extreme case in which dropping one basket means that for sure you will drop all the others). For risk-averse investors, this means that a well-designed investment portfolio—a portfolio that minimizes the likelihood of bad outcomes—contains stocks whose prices tend to move in opposite directions and (to the extent possible) avoids grouping stocks whose prices tend to move together.

A corporation traded on the stockmarket is usually owned by many individuals. If the corporation's stock makes up only a small fraction of each of its owners' portfolios, then the owners will care little about the risks the corporation faces. If your eggs are spread over many baskets, you worry little about the risks to any one basket. The corporation, unlike its individual owners, can afford to undertake activities that have high expected return even though they have a high risk. A widely held firm, in other words, is much less averse to risk than any of the people who own it.

Profits come from seeking slight edges. Just as a sportsperson who refuses to take risks does not often win matches, a firm that is unadventurous does not earn high profits. A firm that accepts any gambles with a positive expected profit will have both larger gains and larger losses than a firm that is more cautious; but over the long run the firm that is less risk averse will tend to have larger profits. Making risk-averse decisions means, by definition, turning down some opportunities with uncertain but—on average—positive net returns. A risk-neutral firm (that is, one with zero risk aversion) therefore has a competitive edge over a risk-averse firm. An eighteenth-century proverb said: "Boldness in business is the first, second, and third thing."

When we are subject to risks that we find unacceptable—of our house burning down or our car being stolen—we purchase insurance. If owners of corporations could buy insurance against their business risks, diversified ownership would not be necessary. Why are such insurance policies not available? As the Nobel laureate Kenneth Arrow pointed out, insurance against business risks would be subject to what is aptly called *moral hazard*. The very fact of being insured would change the insured person's incentives in a perverse way. Just as insuring your car against theft dulls your incentive to take care to prevent theft, with insurance against business risks the businessperson would have less of a stake in the firm and so would do less to prevent losses, increasing the likelihood of losses occurring. For this reason, many types of business losses are uninsurable. As we have seen, however, diversification of ownership serves as a substitute for insurance.

Diversification comes at a cost. The more baskets your eggs are spread over, the less time you can put into guarding any one basket. Mark Twain put the case against diversification in *Pudd'nhead Wilson*. "Behold, the fool saith, 'Put not all thine eggs in one basket'—which is but a manner of saying 'Scatter your money and your attention', but the wise man saith 'Put all your eggs in one basket and—WATCH THAT BASKET'." Stockholders with diversified portfolios are not able to do much monitoring of their firms. Managers may be left free to pursue their own interests at the expense of the owners' interests. Thus the gain from diversification—the reduction in risk—must be weighed against the loss from diversification—the reduction in monitoring.

We have seen that firms are usually less risk averse than people, and that, over the long run a firm tends to make higher profits the less risk averse it is. It does not follow, however, that firms are completely indifferent to risk. Decisions are made by people, not firms. The people running the firm must be made in some way personally accountable for their decisions, in order to encourage them to make good decisions. But, to the extent that managers are held accountable for their decisions, they bear the risk that things might turn out badly through no fault of their own. Thus the managers' decisions will reflect their own risk aversion. The firm will take risk-averse actions even if its stockholders would prefer it to be less cautious (more on this in Chapters 9 and 10).

The Gains from Trade Again

Recognizing that people or firms can differ in their degree of risk aversion gives us another source of gains from trade, additional to those listed in the last chapter. The fact that one individual worries more about risks than another means that there may exist an opportunity for mutually gainful trade. If the buyer, say, fears risk more than the seller, and there is some way of shifting some of the buyer's risk onto the seller, then a mutually gainful bargain would have the seller bearing some of the risk in exchange for getting a higher price. This is how insurance works; there is a mutually gainful trade in which the insurance company absorbs the risk of, say, a house burning down in exchange for a fee paid by the owner. Less obviously, many contracts have insurance as one of their implicit functions. Thus an employee who is paid a fixed salary is sheltered from the risk of fluctuations in the firm's profits. A military contractor doing research for the government with a cost-plus contract, under which all costs are reimbursed no matter how high they become, is sheltered from the risk of any unforeseeable cost fluctuations.

Imagine General Motors negotiating with a firm with 50 employees molding plastic into steering wheels. For General Motors, the contract is tiny relative to its overall operations, and it has other sources of supply of steering wheels, so any risks associated with this particular contract are negligible; toward this contract it is risk neutral. For the small, closely held steering-wheel manufacturer, in contrast, the contract is vital; the firm is risk averse to any fluctuations in earnings from this contract. The difference in risk attitudes means that buyer and seller can create a mutual gain by means of a deal that shifts some of the risk associated with the deal from the seller to the buyer. Consider first a contract that specifies a fixed price to be paid for each steering wheel delivered. If there are unpredictable fluctuations in the price of the plastic used as raw material, then with this fixed-price contract all of the risk of these cost fluctuations is borne by the steering-wheel manufacturer. Now consider an alternative contract, under which General Motors permits the supplier to pass on, in the form of a higher price for the steering wheels, some specified fraction of any raw-material cost increases. Suppose further that this alternative contract is designed at the outset so that the average price it will yield (averaged over the possible fluctuations in the price of plastic) is the same as the price in the fixed-price contract initially considered. General Motors, not caring about the risk per se, perceives itself to be equally well off with either contract; but the risk-averse steering-wheel manufacturer definitely prefers the latter contract because it offers some protection against risk. It follows that a similar contract, allowing some passing on of cost increases but yielding a somewhat lower average price to the steering-wheel manufacturer, would leave both firms better off than under the fixed-price contract. The shifting of risk in exchange for the price concession is mutually beneficial. General Motors in effect acts like an insurance agent, taking on some of the risk of unforeseeable increases in the small firm's production costs in exchange for what amounts to an insurance premium, the lowered average price it must pay to the small firm. Thus there is a gain from trade in risk. (This is not the end of the story: the contracts differ also in their effects on the two firms' actions. Chapters 8, 9, and 13 will investigate in more detail the creation of mutual gains in situations such as this.)

Summary

The prescription for rational decision-making under uncertainty that emerges from this chapter is as follows. First, list all the possible eventualities. Second, assign probabilities to them. Third, compute the expected return from each action available to you. Fourth, if you are risk averse, subtract from each expected return the appropriate risk premium. Finally, choose the decision that yields the highest risk-adjusted expected return.

The size of the risk premium depends on how risk averse the decision-maker is, as well as how much variability in there is in the potential returns. Firms are usually less risk averse than people.

   This chapter has developed tools for thinking about how to take decisions under uncertainty. Since most strategic decisions involve uncertainty, these tools will be used in the following chapters to analyze a variety of strategic managerial decisions. From a theorist's point of view, the risk-neutral case is easier to think about than the risk-averse case (simply because only expected returns have to be calculated; it is not necessary to go on to compute the risk premium). Since our aim in the following chapters will be to understand the logic of the situation in as simple a way as possible, we will usually think of our game-players as being risk neutral. The exception to this will be in Chapters 9, 10, and 13, where the consequences of risk aversion are the focus of interest.

II

NEGOTIATING

W HAT DOES it mean to say that someone is in a strong bargaining position? What determines who gets the better of the deal? How can you structure a deal so as to take advantage of superior information you have, or to mitigate the other person's informational advantage? Chapters 5 and 6 offer ways of thinking about negotiation strategies. Then Chapter 7 illustrates the application of bargaining theory by looking at how international trade negotiations are structured.

5

Gaining Bargaining Power

WHAT CAN game theory teach us about negotiating? Negotiation has an irreducible component that is pure art. The tricks of the trade are essential. But to some extent what goes on in negotiations can be analyzed scientifically: this is the purpose of game theory.

Does it matter how you go about negotiating? Should you arrive at the negotiating table punctually or deliberately late? Should you call your opponent by given name or surname? Do national characteristics matter: should you negotiate differently with a Japanese than with an American? Does it matter what you wear? In what follows, we ignore the etiquette and the psychological aspects of negotiation; instead we focus on the fundamentals. The personality of the negotiators can affect the outcome, but in idiosyncratic ways that cannot be encapsulated by theory. In fact, testimony from experienced negotiators often discounts personality and emphasizes substance. A U.S. State Department report on foreign-affairs negotiators' experiences, for instance, emphasizes substantive matters, such as the need for adequate expertise and information gathering, and downplays the role of the personality or culture of the negotiator. What is being negotiated is more important than who is doing the negotiating.

Bargaining power is a slippery concept: to say that you did well in a negotiation because you were in a strong bargaining position is not to say anything very informative. The question to be addressed is: what are the sources of bargaining strength?

The Archetypical Bargaining Game

The prisoners'-dilemma game is in one sense typical of most games, in that it contains elements of both conflict and cooperation. But there is another sense in which it is too simple to be a model for actual games.

If cooperation is somehow achieved, then the story is at an end; there is only one outcome that cooperation can lead to in the prisoners' dilemma. Real-world games have an additional layer of conflicting interests. Many efficient outcomes usually exist, resulting in the possibility of conflict over how the gains from cooperation are to be shared. Bargaining occurs over which one of the many efficient outcomes is to be reached.

The simplest kind of business deal involves a buyer and a seller bargaining over the price of some object, a car, say. (When third-person singular pronouns are used in what follows, the seller will be referred to as "she" and the buyer as "he.") Imagine that the seller knows exactly how much the buyer would value owning the car; that is, the most the buyer would be willing to pay: $1100, say. And the buyer knows the value to the seller of keeping the car; that is, the very lowest price the seller will accept: $1000, say. By changing the labels of the characters, this could be converted into a story about other negotiations such as between labor and management. (It is unrealistic that each bargainer knows precisely how much the item is worth to the other: this leaves no role for such common bargaining tactics as bluffing. But we will start with this simple model and add the complications of private information in Chapter 6.) For any negotiation to be potentially fruitful, there must be some overlap of interests—there must be some potential gains from trade. With the numbers we have chosen this is indeed the case. If any price between $1000 and $1100 is agreed upon, both buyer and seller perceive themselves to be better off than without the deal. There are gains from trade of $100; and essentially the bargaining is over how to divide the $100. For simplicity, in what follows we will therefore think of the bargaining as being over the $100.

This simple game is similar to the prisoners' dilemma in that there is a possibility of an inefficient outcome: failure to reach agreement in this model is analogous to the confess/confess outcome in the prisoners' dilemma. But it is more complicated than the prisoners' dilemma in that there are many efficient outcomes. In this simple game, efficiency means merely that the $100 is successfully divided between the two players. Any agreement to divide the $100 serves to maximize the size of the pie; any such transaction results in an increase in total value of $100. The inefficient outcome, breakdown, yields a zero increase in total value.

Does our simple model predict a particular negotiation outcome? The seller, in deciding how much to ask for, must conjecture how much she can get away with; that is, the highest price the buyer is likely to accept. Similarly, the buyer, in choosing whether he should reject the seller's offer, must estimate what price the seller would agree to. Imagine the seller asks for, say, $73.21. Is it rational for the buyer to accept? It is, if the buyer believes that, in the future rounds of the bargaining, the seller will never yield, but go on demanding $73.21. With this belief, the best the buyer can do is accept immediately: the most he will get is the remainder of the gains from trade, $26.79. Is it rational for the seller to start with the offer of $73.21? It is, if the seller believes that the buyer believes that the seller will not settle for less than $73.21. Thus, if both buyer and seller have particular beliefs about the other's intentions, it is rational for the seller to ask for $72.31 and for the buyer to accept immediately. But of course there is nothing magical about the number $72.31. Any division of the gains from trade, with anything from zero to $100 going to the seller, can result from particular sets of beliefs. We cannot yet predict the outcome of the negotiation process. The outcome depends crucially on each negotiator's belief about what price his or her opponent will find acceptable.

How much bargaining power do either of the bargainers have in this situation? Bargaining power is a notoriously vague and slippery concept, so much so that some analysts argue the term is so misleading that it is better to avoid using it. Our game of dividing $100, however, suggests a precise way of formulating the idea of bargaining power. The seller is in a strong bargaining position if, first, the buyer believes the seller will refuse to settle for anything less than a large share of the gains from trade; and, second, the seller knows the buyer believes this. Suppose, for example, the buyer—for whatever reason—believes that the seller will settle for nothing less than $95, and that there will be an impasse if he holds out for an outcome that gives him more than $5 and the seller less than $95. Then the agreement is likely to give the seller $95, for the buyer prefers receiving the $5 from this agreement to receiving nothing if he forces an impasse. The buyer's belief about what the seller will settle for is such that the agreement gives the seller most of the gains from trade; the seller is in a strong bargaining position.

Thus the question: "how much bargaining power does each of the bargainers have?" has been turned into the question: "what does each bargainer believe about the other's willingness to settle, and about the other's beliefs?" This reformulation clarifies our thinking but is, in itself, not much of an advance, for we have not yet said anything about what determines the bargainers' beliefs about their rivals' thinking. Where do these beliefs come from? How sensible is it for the buyer to believe that the seller will never reduce his demand below $72.31, or $95, or any other sum between zero and $100? We must look next at how such beliefs are formed.

Forming Beliefs

As noted, there are many possible mutually acceptable divisions of the $100 in our archetypical bargaining game. Which outcome is reached is determined by each of the bargainers' beliefs about what the other will

settle for. In order to say which of the many possible outcomes will be
reached we must find what shapes these beliefs.

Like a good chess player, as noted in Chapter 2, a good negotiator
looks several moves ahead, and asks: what is likely to happen if I reject
the current offer? The answer will depend upon the objective facts of
the situation. Let us add some more structure to our simple bargaining
game by supposing that each of the bargainers has some alternative to
fall back on should the negotiations fail. Suppose, for example, that the
seller of the car has a firm offer from someone else of $1040, and the
buyer knows of another equally good car that is obtainable for $1090.
Suppose, moreover, that each bargainer knows the other's alternative.
The effective gains from trade are now the difference between $1090
and $1040, or $50, rather than the $100 initially. The alternative oppor-
tunities shrink the range of prices to be bargained over. And the range
is shrunk asymmetrically: the range of possible agreements has moved,
relatively, in the seller's favor, reflecting the fact that the seller's fallback
is more attractive than the buyer's (in the sense that the seller, in invoking her alternative opportunity, would get a net gain of $1040 minus
$1000, or $40; while the buyer in, invoking his alternative opportunity,
would get a net gain of $1100 minus $1090, or only $10). If the seller
had a still better alternative opportunity—say, an offer of $1070 for the
car—then the range of possible agreements would shift still further in
the seller's favor.

The more attractive a bargainer's alternative opportunities are, the
better the negotiated outcome will be for that bargainer. The alternative
opportunities overhang the negotiations, affecting each bargainer's expectations of what the other will settle for, and shaping the terms of the
agreement. The credibility of bargaining positions is the key here. It is
credible to the seller that the buyer will hold out for a favorable settlement when either the seller knows that the buyer has a tempting alternative opportunity; or the seller knows that the buyer knows that the
seller has a tempting alternative opportunity. Alternative opportunities,
therefore, are a source of bargaining power. (Before we accept this argument, we must test it by seeing whether it stands up in a fully specified
model; this is done in the Appendix.)

"Necessity never made a good bargain," said Benjamin Franklin. If
you are negotiating for a raise in pay, your boss will tend to find your
case persuasive if you have a job offer from another employer for more
than your current salary; that is, if you have an attractive fallback. On
the other hand, your bargaining position is shaky if you are easily re-
placeable; that is, if your boss has a good fallback. It is often possible,
with effort and some luck, to improve your fallback options, by searching for better alternatives either before beginning the negotiations or
during the negotiations. This search might consist of seeking alternative
potential negotiating partners; or it might be simply thinking of what
you could do if the negotiations fail. Such search is productive, because

it improves your bargaining power. If you want a raise in your salary, it may be worth seeking outside offers even if you do not intend to leave your current job. A corporation that is the target of a hostile takeover attempt often seeks a friendly firm with which to merge. Also under the heading of improving your fallback position comes the classic military tactic of attacking the enemy just before the opening of scheduled peace talks. In July 1988, for instance, Iraq launched an offensive on a broad front against Iran one week before a United Nations–sponsored meeting to negotiate an end to the Iran-Iraq war. Since a bargainer receives a bigger share of the pie the more attractive is his or her fallback, the investment in time, money, and effort in developing alternatives will generate a return for you even if the negotiation results in agreement and none of the alternatives you find are activated, because the terms of the agreement will have been moved in your favor.

One potent way of improving your fallback position is to generate competition on the other side of the bargaining table. The use of competition as a bargaining strategy will be examined in some detail in Chapter 11. Also, your bargaining power is inversely related to how good your opponent's alternatives are. Thus, knowing what the other's alternatives are is crucial to a realistic assessment of what you can expect to achieve in the bargaining. An aggressive bargainer might even try to worsen the other's alternatives.

A second determinant of the strength of bargaining positions, additional to the bargainers' alternative opportunities, is the relative cost incurred by the two bargainers if the agreement is delayed. Time is money. During negotiations over the price of a car, for example, the seller loses the interest she could be earning if she had the money from the sale; the buyer must pay taxi fares while he does not own the car. In the case of union-management negotiations, the cost of a delayed agreement includes wages foregone by the workers during a strike and profits and market share lost by the firm. Such variables as the size of the union's strike fund, the level of the firm's inventories, and the firm's alternative production facilities determine the costs of delay.

The costs of delay shape the terms of the negotiated agreement, for they shape each bargainer's expectations of what the other will agree to. The more impatient your opponent is to settle, the better (from your point of view) is the agreement you can hold out for. The seller's share of the gain from trade is higher the less her own cost of waiting is; and it is higher the greater the buyer's cost of delay is. The converse holds for the buyer. Thus the possibility of delay shapes the outcome, in that the higher one party's cost of delay, the smaller that person's share of the rationally negotiated gains from trade. (Again, the details of the logic are given in the Appendix.) Patience is not only a virtue, rewarded in heaven; patient bargainers—those with low costs of delay—get their rewards now.

The members of a Los Angeles neighborhood association discovered that the return extractable from an opponent's cost of delay can be huge. Objecting to a newly built luxury hotel, the homeowners forced the project through months of hearings, while the hotel, sitting empty, lost $800,000 a month. Finally the developer, desperate for a settlement, agreed to pay more than a million dollars into a neighborhood preservation fund.

Baseball players have already discovered that bargaining power increases as the opponent's cost of delay increases. In 1980 the Major League Players Association, after three months of fruitless bargaining with the owners, voted for an unconventional strike. They would strike when the preseason exhibition games were scheduled, then go back to work for the first six weeks of the regular season, but then go on strike again if no agreement had been reached with the owners. What explains this on-again-off-again strike? The players earn a steady salary through the season, but no salary during the exhibition games. The owners, by contrast, receive revenue at a varying rate during the season: it is abnormally low in the first six weeks of the regular season. The players' income foregone from striking during the preseason was zero. The owners' revenue foregone later in the season, that is, their waiting cost, was high. Both times the players chose to strike, they were in a strong bargaining position: first when their own waiting cost was small, and later when the owners' waiting cost was high.

Sometimes, imaginative ways can be found to increase the opponent's cost of delay in agreement. A union negotiating with a restaurant owner, instead of simply striking as the restaurateur expected, arranged for hundreds of its sympathizers to enter the restaurant, order a cup of coffee, and occupy all of the tables for the duration of the lunch hour. Similarly, actions that lower a bargainer's own cost of delay strengthen that bargainer's position. A union, for example, can do this by accumulating a strike fund; and management can do it by holding inventories of finished goods to prevent lost sales in the event of a strike.

Thus, as a negotiator, you should try to find out your own and your opponent's cost of delay. If yours is lower, you have an advantage: you may be able to get a better deal by explicitly or implicitly threatening to delay the agreement. The terms of the agreement will move in your favor if you can reduce your own time costs or raise those of your opponent.

Focal Points

Bargaining games usually have not one, but many possible agreements that leave both bargainers better off than at the status quo. In our game of dividing $100, any payoff to the seller between $1 and $99, with the buyer getting the remainder, makes both seller and buyer better off than they would be with no agreement. This multiplicity is likely to be still greater when we leave our simple models and look at actual negotiations, with many bargainers and many issues on the table. The complexity of some negotiations is impressive. For example, when the Empire State Building was sold in the early 1960s, over 100 lawyers, working for 34 parties, produced a contract 400 pages long. Theory cannot be expected to produce a clear-cut prediction of the outcome in such cases. There is an inherent indeterminacy in bargaining: often there are many possible points of agreement.

In some stylized bargaining games (like the two solved in the Appendix) there is only one outcome that is consistent with both bargainers doing the best they can; thus there is a unique prediction about where the bargaining would end. Such clean results are, however, artifacts of these models' contrived simplicity. A multiplicity of outcomes is more typical in bargaining games. What can we predict about which outcome will be reached when many outcomes are consistent with rational behavior?

We consider once again the game of dividing $100, but now we omit the special structure of the earlier games: there are no alternative opportunities and no costs of delay. Instead, any of the two bargainers can make a proposal for the division of the $100 at any time. There is no disadvantage to either bargainer from delaying agreement, except that there is a fixed deadline imposed from outside: if agreement is not reached before the deadline, neither bargainer gets anything. Game theory now offers no clue to how the $100 will be divided, as we saw at the start of this chapter. Depending on each bargainer's beliefs about the other's expectations, any division at all is a possible outcome of this game. There is not enough structure in this game to pin down what beliefs are rational and therefore produce a unique outcome. We must therefore look not to mathematical theorems but to less formally developed ideas to further our understanding of negotiations.

As we have seen, a bargaining agreement is reached when the bargainers' expectations converge: when they share mutually consistent beliefs about what the other will agree to. That the outcome is theoretically indeterminate means that there are many possible outcomes that can be generated by mutually consistent expectations. Suppose, however, that there is something about the bargaining situation that serves to highlight a particular outcome. Such an outcome can be a *focal point* upon which an agreement can coalesce. Thomas Schelling, who conceived the idea of the focal point, talks of "the intrinsic magnetism of particular outcomes."

Unlike our earlier concepts, the focal point is not precisely defined. For this reason it must be used with care, lest it degenerate into a question-begging concept: a particular outcome occurs because it occurs. This trap can be avoided by listing at the outset the possible determinants of focal points. There are several: for example, a particular outcome might be highlighted by precedent ("we do it this way because it's always been done this way"); or by some mathematical symmetry (equal shares); or because an impartial mediator suggests a solution.

Focal points have been studied (by the economist Alvin Roth and various coauthors) by putting undergraduate students in simulated negotiation situations and observing their actions. The students bargained for tokens, which were essentially lottery tickets, and were paid real money at the end of the experiment. The experimenters could make the tokens worth more to one bargainer than his opponent by offering them different-sized prizes. The bargainers were given a fixed time to reach agreement; in the event of no agreement, they earned nothing. They bargained via linked computer terminals, so they did not know who they were bargaining with and could not make deals on the side.

The simplest game examined in the Roth experiments had each player valuing the tokens equally, and each being informed of this. This corresponds exactly to the game of dividing $100 mentioned above; as we saw, game theory predicts no particular outcome. In strong contrast to the theory's agnosticism, the experimental results were unambiguous. The students almost always agreed to a 50–50 split. Evidently, mathematical symmetry, or perhaps fairness, is attractive to bargainers.

The experiments were then complicated by introducing a difference between the bargainers: each token was now worth four times more to one of the bargainers than to the other. The bargainers were informed about this difference. Now agreements tended to cluster around two points: either genuine equal division (that is, each getting equal value out of the agreement, so that the tokens were split 80–20, with the player who valued the tokens less getting more of them), or nominal equal division (that is, a 50–50 split of the unequally valued tokens). Thus there were two focal points, with the choice between them being apparently arbitrary. During the negotiation, both players argued for the focal point that most favored them; but one of them eventually had to give in for agreement to be reached.

A further set of experiments then examined the choice between the two focal points. The players played the same bargaining game several times, but their bargaining partner was now a computer (although they were led to believe they were bargaining against people). The computer was programmed relentlessly to demand one particular 50–50 split: in some cases the nominal 50–50 split, in others the genuine 50–50 split. Eventually the bargainers went along with whichever division the computer had led them to expect. This provides experimental verification for the notion that the bargaining outcome is determined by each bargainer's expectations of what his rival will agree to; and that these expectations can be established through experience.

Then the experiment was changed once more. Neither bargainer was told how highly his opponent valued the tokens. As in the first and simplest experiments, most of the agreements now divided the tokens equally. But this equal-division focal point was equal in name, not necessarily equal in substance. The genuine equal-value focal point, however, was destroyed because none of the players knew where it was, since none knew how highly his rival valued the tokens.

The interesting finding of these experiments is the marked tendency for the bargainers to settle for a 50–50 split, despite the fact that the units by which the 50–50 split was defined were arbitrary. The tokens were often not equally divided by their value to the bargainers, but by the number of tokens; the 50–50 split was nominal rather than genuine. In the absence of a unique bargaining equilibrium, there seems to be a powerful tendency to settle for equal shares. But how is equality to be defined? It does not seem to matter much. Given the many possible ways of dividing the pie, what seems to be needed to get agreement is a commonly agreed way of keeping score: and it does not seem to matter that the units in which the score is kept have no real meaning.

The bargainers failed to reach agreement in about one-fifth of the negotiations. This is surprisingly frequent given the contrived simplicity of the experimental bargaining situation. We can conclude that the exact, true division of the pie is less important to the negotiators than the fact that the negotiations do not break down. Any division of the spoils is better than ending with no agreement. Hence the *appearance* of equal division may be enough to generate agreement. There is an advantage to what we might call "phony precision" in negotiations. Phony precision helps produce agreement: the appearance of a 50–50 split is all that is needed.

Hence, during complicated negotiations, a good strategy seems to be to look for some way of defining a focal point upon which agreement can coalesce, thus avoiding breakdown. Find a method for measuring your own and your opponent's concessions, even if the measure does not really capture their objective value.

Commitment as a Bargaining Technique

We now consider yet another way in which bargainers' expectations of each other are formed: one of the bargainers manipulates his or her rival's expectations. Suppose that the seller, making the first offer, announces that the buyer must take or leave her offer, saying that if the buyer rejects the offer she will refuse to bargain further and neither of them will get any of the $100. Moreover, the seller is able to convince the buyer that she will indeed carry out this threat if the buyer rejects her offer. What does the seller demand?

This game is easily solved. The seller demands all of the $100 minus a few pennies. The buyer is faced with a choice between getting nothing and getting the small amount the seller is offering; he rationally accedes to the seller's demand. The seller's commitment serves to shape the buyer's expectations of what the seller will settle for. (Here we are working to the full our assumption that each bargainer always prefers more money to less. Realistically, most of us would, in the buyer's position, reject the seller's offer as an insult. But the argument is easily patched up to allow for spite and hurt feelings. The buyer's pride has a price. If the buyer prefers getting, say, $5 and feeling aggrieved to getting nothing at all, then the seller rationally demands $95 and the buyer rationally accepts.)

The best bargaining strategy, therefore, is to refuse to bargain. Being able to make commitments while your opponent cannot means that you have much of the bargaining power. This is, in Thomas Schelling's words, "the paradox that the power to constrain an adversary depends upon the power to bind oneself." Of course, nothing is a paradox once understood. The gains from commitment seem paradoxical because it would seem to be better to have more flexibility of action rather than less. But the point is that when using commitment as a bargaining technique, you choose for yourself the position to which you are committed. Flexibility is in fact useful at one stage of the process: it is good to have a wide range of choice over what position you are going to commit to. It is good to have flexibility *before* the negotiations begin, but to be inflexible *during* the negotiations.

Commitment must be all or nothing. Being partially committed is like being partially a virgin. The seller must make the buyer believe that her commitment is irrevocable. If the buyer thinks that the seller might, despite her protestations, actually be willing to bargain, then it is not rational for the buyer to accept the pittance he is offered. If the buyer does come back with a counteroffer, then the situation has changed for the seller. She is now faced with getting zero if she persists with her threat, or some share of the $100 if she bargains. After the fact, it is in the seller's interest to renege on her commitment if she can. But the ability to renege eliminates the gains from commitment. For the commitment strategy to work the other party must believe the commitment will be maintained even if, with the benefit of hindsight, the committed party regrets the commitment.

Thus a commitment strategy must be believable if it is to work. How can commitment be achieved? One way is for the seller to put her reputation at stake. If the seller plans to be in business for a long time, then she can convincingly argue to the buyer that she cannot afford to renege on the promise she made. The cost of reneging on her current commitment would be the inability to make credible commitments to others and therefore the loss of bargaining power in other negotiations. This is why precedent matters to negotiators: granting a concession in the current negotiation makes less plausible to your future negotiating partners your claim that you are committed to what you are asking for.

Another way of achieving commitment is to hire an agent to do the negotiating, and require the agent to follow a set of procedures that are publicly known. Trying to bargain with a department-store clerk is usually futile: the store can make its price quotes firm by requiring its salespeople to follow its price list. The government achieves commitment in its contracting with firms by binding its negotiators to procedures that are explicitly and precisely set out in a publicly available book of rules. A bureaucrat's ploy suffered by everyone at some time is an appeal, sincere or not, to this kind of commitment: bureaucrats say "no" without pain to themselves by saying "the rules won't allow me to do what you ask."

A more dramatic way of achieving commitment is to burn bridges; to arrange things so that, should you renege, you will suffer some severe punishment. For instance, a corporate raider attempting to take over a company wrote a clause into the loan agreement financing the takeover that said that, if he raised the price he was offering for the company, his loan interest rate would rise by 1.5%. This credibly committed him to his initial offer, and persuaded the target's owners that there was no point in haggling over the price. Another example of achieving commitment comes from semiconductor firms in Silicon Valley. It is common practice for a semiconductor firm that has developed a new, proprietary chip to license another firm to produce the chip in competition with itself. Why does the innovating firm give up what seems to be a potentially lucrative monopoly on the new chip? User firms must make a large investment in retooling in order to be able to use the new chip. They will be reluctant to do the necessary retooling if they are worried about how reliable the supply of the new chips will be. Licensing allows the innovating firm credibly to promise a reliable supply of the chips, for if delivery is late the firm will lose sales to its licensed competitor.

Why should governments refuse to deal with hostage-takers when it seems to be the humane thing to do? Because from a longer-term perspective, with a view to discouraging future hostage-takers, it is better for the government to maintain its reputation for not dealing with terrorists. Although governments often claim they are committed not to deal with hostage-takers, the facts tend to belie the claim. The U.S. government tried to negotiate an arms-for-hostages swap with Iran. The Israeli government once traded 1150 prisoners for 3 Israelis. The French government routinely deals with terrorists. The reason is obvious: the temptation to save the hostages' lives is overwhelming. Within the context of the single situation, it is rational to negotiate. But from a longer-term perspective, it weakens the government's position. How can governments credibly commit themselves not to succumb to this humane impulse? A *New York Times* op-ed writer once suggested that a way for the U.S. government to achieve commitment would be to make use of its constitutional separation of responsibilities. This would involve the Congress, at the request of the President, passing a law that bars the President from negotiating for hostages (except, perhaps, in some unusual, precisely specified circumstances). Future presidents would be visibly committed, and thus they would be in a strong bargaining position.

Since the ability to make commitments yields bargaining power, a good defensive tactic is to pre-empt your opponent's commitments. In *The Art of War,* Sun Tzu advises a general attacking a city or fortress always to leave an escape route open to the enemy. It is not a good idea to pick a battleground where the enemy have their backs to the wall. Another defensive tactic is to check whether your rival's commitment is indeed firm. As we have noted, if you call your opponent's bluff and reject her initial offer, it may not be in her interest to carry out her threat to refuse to negotiate. Everyone tries to bargain when buying a car or a house. But questioning commitments can be effective in other, surprising circumstances. Supermarkets and hotels sometimes, if asked, will submit to haggling over prices. Most people do not question doctors about their prices. But the Carpenters' Union Benefit Fund of New York has found that five minutes' worth of negotiation over the telephone saves their members an average of over $1000 each in out-of-pocket expenses for surgery.

Our discussion has presumed that only one of the two negotiators has instruments with which it is possible to make commitments. If, however, both have this capacity, they may commit themselves to incompatible demands. Hence commitment is a risky strategy. If you use it and it works, its payoff is high: you earn most of the profit from the transaction. But if your opponent simultaneously tries to use it, the negotiations can be destroyed. For a time, General Electric in its labor negotiations used a strategy known as Boulwarism (named after Lemuel R. Boulware, the G. E. vice-president of employee and public relations who introduced it in the 1950s), under which its initial offer, chosen after careful research into wages and working conditions in G.E. and its competitors, was its final offer. Although this take-it-or-leave-it offer was intended to be fair and acceptable to the workers, the union strongly opposed this technique—understandably, given, as we have seen, the amount of bargaining power to be gained from commitment. One union response was likewise to present a set of demands and announce they were inflexible. Another was to behave disruptively during negotiations. Another was to strike. Yet another was to complain to the National Labor Relations Board, which found that G.E. was guilty of an unfair labor practice; the adjudicator considered the lack of real concessions by G.E. during negotiations as evidence that G.E. was not bargaining in good faith. By 1970, the union's opposition had induced G.E. to cease using the commitment strategy.

The lesson from this is therefore: examine whether either you or your opponent has the ability to make binding commitments. If you can while your opponent cannot, you should commit yourself before the negotiations begin in such a way that you receive most of the gains from trade. This is the most powerful negotiating technique.

Summary

The process of bargaining consists of coordinating the bargainers' expectations about which of the many possible agreements is to be reached. We have seen several alternative determinants of the bargainers' expectations of what the other is willing to settle for. The internal logic of the situation can shape the bargainers' expectations. Thus the relative attractiveness of the bargainers' fall-back options and the relative impatience of the bargainers help decide their relative bargaining strength. Forces from outside can also shape the bargainers' expectations. The mathematical symmetry of the 50–50 split can establish a focal point upon which expectations coalesce. The ability of one of the bargainers to make commitments lends credibility to the position the bargainer has staked out.

What advice for negotiators does game theory generate? The most important idea we have learned in this chapter is the value of putting yourself in the other person's shoes and looking several moves ahead, to try to predict the other person's responses to your offers. "If I do this, how will my opponent respond; what is it rational for me to expect my opponent to do?" Thinking in terms of this forward-looking reasoning, we have identified several components of bargaining success.

First, if the structure of the game gives one of the bargainers the ability to make commitments, that bargainer is in a strong position. It is therefore a good idea to maneuver yourself into making an all-or-nothing offer if it is feasible to do so.

Second, you will get a better outcome the more attractive your alternatives to agreement and the less attractive your opponent's alternatives. Thus it is worth investing time, effort, and money in developing your alternatives. You will earn a return on this investment even if agreement is reached and none of the alternatives is actually called into use, because the terms of the agreement will have been moved in your favor.

Third, you should estimate both your own and your rival's cost of waiting (including opportunities foregone during the bargaining); if his cost of delay is larger than yours, you have an edge in the bargaining. Patience is a virtue not only in its own right but also as an aid to squeezing more for yourself out of the agreement.

Fourth, in complex negotiations, it pays to look for some way of defining a focal point upon which an agreement can coalesce. There are usually many possible agreements that would leave all better off than at the status quo. Find a method for measuring concessions, even if the measure is, by objective criteria, arbitrary or even meaningless. Phony precision is useful in producing the appearance of equal division and thereby reducing the likelihood of breakdown.

Uncertainty is present in all negotiations, as mentioned earlier, but our analysis of bargaining has so far had little to say about it. In the next chapter we examine how bargaining strategies reflect the strategic use of information.

6

Using Information
Strategically

A VITAL ASPECT of actual negotiations has been omitted from most of
our analysis so far, in that knowledge has been assumed to be perfect.
We have represented each bargainer as knowing the other's valuation,
alternative opportunities, costs of delay, and commitment possibilities.
But, in fact, uncertainty is an essential ingredient of most negotiations.

Negotiators go to great lengths to learn their opponents' aims and to
conceal their own. Good labor-union negotiators, for example, prepare
themselves by researching the firm's production costs and profitability.
At the same time, the firm's negotiators ascertain what wage the workers
could earn elsewhere; and, more subjectively, they try to assess the mood
of the workers, to see how determined they are to achieve their demands. During the negotiations, various tactics are used to elicit information. At the extreme, there are recorded instances of a company
trying to learn the union's limits by bugging the union committee's de-
liberations. More routinely, information and misinformation are released in a calculated way during the negotiations. Tricks like exaggerated impatience, feigned anger, excessive friendliness, and personal
abuse are used to try to make opponents inadvertently reveal their true
aims. Defensive responses to such ploys include pretending ignorance
of details and submitting many demands so as to mask the important
ones.

A game theorist cannot hope to model the full complexities of information transmission and concealment via the negotiation process. This
is one of the reasons why negotiation is not completely reducible to a
science and is necessarily to some extent an art. But game theory can
help us understand the strategic uses of information in negotiations,
showing why some tactics work and the limits of what negotiators can
achieve. In this chapter we look at the problems the uneven distribution
of information can cause: mutually beneficial deals might fail to be

made. And we examine strategies that can serve to mitigate an informational disadvantage as well as strategies for communicating information in ways that will be believed.

Bargaining under an Informational Handicap

We add private information to the simple buyer-seller bargaining analyzed in the last chapter by supposing that the seller does not know exactly how highly the buyer would value owning the car that is for sale.
We illustrate the issues with the following contrived game (which, simple
though it is, serves to highlight some effects of information on bargaining strategies and bargaining outcomes). The seller has many cars for
sale, each of which cost the seller $1000. The seller knows that there are
two kinds of potential buyers: one kind of buyer values this car at $1040
(that is, such a buyer would pay up to $1040 for the car); the other kind
of buyer values it at $1100. The population of potential buyers contains
the same number of each type. The seller has no way of distinguishing
one type of buyer from the other.

The seller makes a take-it-or-leave-it offer to any potential buyer who
appears. We have seen that the ability to make commitments is a source
of bargaining power. Another source of bargaining power, as we will see,
is knowledge. If the seller knew exactly how much any buyer was willing
to pay for the item, the seller could extract all of the gains from trade.
But when the seller operates under an informational handicap, not
knowing any buyer's willingness to pay, the seller cannot get all of the
gains. In making the take-it-or-leave-it offer the seller risks either demanding too high a price and losing the sale (when the buyer has the
lower valuation), or setting too low a price and foregoing some profits
(when the buyer has the higher valuation). The best price balances the
risks of these two kinds of loss.

What price should the seller charge to make profits as high as possible? Since the different types of buyer look the same to the seller, the
seller must offer the same price to all. If the seller charges any price up
to and including $1040, every potential buyer makes a purchase (since
both types of buyers are willing to pay at least this much). If the price is
set anywhere between $1040 and $1100, only the high-valuation buyers
(who make up 50% of the potential buyers) make a purchase. Clearly
the only two prices that are candidates for the best price are $1040
(which yields more profit than any lower price) and $1100 (which yields
more profit than any price between $1040 and $1100). Charging $1040
means earning a profit of $40 from every potential customer. Charging
$1100 means earning a profit of $100 from each successful sale, but only
selling to half the potential buyers, and averaging $50 profit per poten-

tial buyer. Setting the higher price yields the higher profit; but at the cost of missing out on some potentially profitable sales.

Even with the low-valuation customers, there is a potential gain from trade: they value the car at $40 more than it costs the seller to supply it. But the seller, ignorant of how highly any individual customer values the car and therefore forced to set the same price for all customers, rationally sets a price that excludes the lower-valuation customers. The privacy of information means that some potential gains from trade fail to be realized. In bargaining under private information, therefore, as in the prisoners' dilemma, the pursuit of individual gains can lead to an outcome that, if it were possible, both participants would like to change. The negotiation might break down (as it did in this example in the case of the lower-valuation customers) even though a mutually advantageous agreement exists. The result from this simple model is striking: the seller rationally asks for such a high price that there is a 50% chance that no agreement is reached, even though both parties know some price exists that would be profitable for each of them. The exact number 50% is an artifact of the contrived model. But the simple model illustrates a point that holds true in more realistic settings: each bargainer's attempt to grab a large share of the gains from trade when he or she does not know the other's limit results in a significant probability of breakdown.

Gains from trade need not be lost. If the different buyer's valuations were close enough together, there would always be a sale. Suppose that the lower-valuation customers value the car at $1060 instead of $1040. Then the seller can earn a profit of $60 per customer by charging $1060. The seller now does better by selling to all than by focusing on the upper end of the market. No gains from trade are lost in this case; but the high-valuation customers get a windfall, paying $40 less than what they would be willing to pay. These are profits lost to the seller, in the sense that, if it were possible to distinguish the customers and price differentially, the seller could extract another $40 from each high-valuation customer. The customers' private information about their valuations, therefore, results in some of them (the high-valuation ones) getting a better deal than they would if the seller had full information.

Two general lessons emerge from these very simple models of exchange with differential information. Private information can result in no exchange being made, even though potential gains from trade exist; and in other cases it can be a source of bargaining power, resulting in extra gains going to the holder of the information.

Francis Bacon said knowledge is power. Game theory corroborates Bacon's aphorism. The seller is in a powerful bargaining position by virtue of being able to make commitments. The buyers, however, get some countervailing power from the seller's lack of knowledge. Whereas, with full information, the seller could extract all of the gains from trade, the seller's lack of knowledge can result in gains going to some of the buyers.

Screening: Overcoming an Informational Disadvantage

The seller misses out on potential profits, in the second case above, by charging less than the high-valuation customers would be willing to pay. Is there anything the seller can do to mitigate the informational handicap and reduce the amount of unexploited gains from trade? So far, we have depicted the uninformed parties as being relatively passive in the face of their uncertainty, despite their ability to dictate the terms of the transaction. Often, an uninformed party to a negotiation can be more sophisticated than simply demanding a fixed price. The uninformed party can sometimes structure the negotiations so as, in effect, to induce the other party to reveal the information. We call such activities *screening*.

We saw in the last chapter that costs of delay are a source of bargaining power. Let us augment our simple story of the car-seller faced with two kinds of buyers by supposing that the buyers incur costs if agreement is delayed. Specifically, suppose that agreement can be reached either when a buyer enters the seller's store, or one week later. A buyer evaluates costs and benefits one week hence at only 80% of their current value; the seller, by contrast, faces no costs of delay. The seller chooses, and commits herself to, not simply a single price, but a price schedule: a price to apply immediately, and a price to apply if the sale is delayed to next week. What is the buyer's best price schedule?

One possible strategy for the seller is to ask for a relatively high price in the first period, in the hope that the buyer has the high valuation; and to drop the price in the second period, on the assumption that the buyer must have the low valuation if he rejects the first-period offer. Will this strategy work? Consider the second case above; the high valuation is $1100 and the low valuation $1060. If the seller demands too high a price in the first period, then a buyer with the high valuation has the option of rejecting the first-period offer and waiting for the lower price in the second period. Suppose the seller offers a first-period price that ensures acceptance by a high-valuation buyer. What price will be charged in the second period, if it is reached? Since the seller is sure that reaching the second period without agreement means that the buyer must have the low valuation, the seller can charge $1060 in the second period. Given that the second-period price is going to be $1060, what is the seller's best first-period offer? The seller wants to set the price at the highest level that a high-valuation buyer would accept. Call the first-period price p. If the buyer with the high valuation accepts this price, his net gain is $1100-p$. The buyer's alternative is to wait until the second period and pay $1060. The key from the seller's point of view is that delay is costly to the buyer: second-period gains are worth only 80% of first-period gains. Thus purchasing in the second period yields a net return to the high-valuation buyer of $0.8 \times (1100 - 1060)$, or $32. It follows that the first-period price p is low enough to induce the high-valuation buyer to purchase immediately if $1100-p$ exceeds 32, or p is no higher than \$1068. The best first-period price for the seller to set is therefore \$1068. By adopting the policy of pricing the item at \$1068 at the first stage and \$1060 at the second, the seller induces the buyer to purchase at the first stage if he has the higher valuation, and at the second if he has the lower valuation.

From this strategy, the seller earns a profit of \$68 half of the time (when the buyer has the high valuation) and \$60 half of the time (when the buyer has the low valuation), for an average profit of \$64 (compared with the profit of \$60 with the nonscreening strategy considered above). The strategy of starting with a high offer and then reducing it succeeds in screening the buyers: by their choice between purchasing immediately or waiting, the buyers reveal whether they have the high or low valuation. A buyer who buys at \$68 is seen to have the high valuation; one who is prepared to endure the cost of waiting is revealed to have the low valuation., Delay causes a loss for the buyer; this loss is larger the more the buyer values the car, so high-valuation buyers are more impatient to settle than low-valuation buyers. The seller succeeds in screening the buyers by taking advantage of the buyers' impatience.

Bargaining typically consists of a series of offers and counteroffers, with the seller starting high and the buyer starting low, and eventually, perhaps, reaching agreement somewhere in the middle. The foregoing model shows, in a simplified way, a rationale for haggling. The seller, uncertain of any buyer's evaluation, starts with a high price and then lowers it. The seller can thereby induce the buyers to reveal their valuations. Buyers with the high valuation are relatively impatient to settle, for they lose more by waiting than buyers with the low valuation would. Thus buyers with the higher value will be prepared to settle relatively early for a high price; while buyers with the lower valuation will wait until the price falls. By enduring the costs of holding out, low-valuation buyers credibly prove their low valuation. Thus the purpose of haggling, with the seller starting at a high price and coming down, is to reveal information about the other party's limit.

Haggling does not always work, however. Similar reasoning to that just given shows that, in the first case considered above (with buyers' valuations being \$1040 and \$1100), the seller could succeed in screening by setting a first-period price of \$1052 and a second-period price of \$1040 (earning a profit of \$52 from the high-valuation buyers and \$40 from the low-valuation buyers, for an average profit of \$46). The seller would not want to do this, however, for more profits would be earned by, as before, fixing the price at \$1100 in each period and selling only to the high end of the market (thereby earning a profit of \$100 from 50% of the buyers, for an average profit per potential buyer of \$50). The seller is better off demanding the fixed price than trying to screen the buyers. The buyers' valuations are too widely spread for screening to be a profitable strategy for the seller. Once again, we have found a prisoners'-

dilemma outcome: some gains from trade are left unexploited. No sale is made to low-valuation customers even though they are willing to pay more than the seller's cost.

Even when screening works, as in the former case, there are still some losses caused by the uneven distribution of information. It is sometimes, as we saw, in the seller's interest to screen the buyers, so as to be able to charge a higher price to the high-valuation buyers. But screening means that the low-valuation buyers must wait until the second week to receive the car; and waiting, by hypothesis, is costly to the buyers. Thus not all of the potential gains from trade are realized: the pie to be divided between buyer and seller is not as large as it could be.

Haggling used to be the normal way goods were bought and sold, and is still the norm in developing countries. In most retail selling in advanced economies, however, haggling was replaced a century or more ago by simple fixed-price policies, although it still occurs in the selling of large consumer goods like cars. In dealings between suppliers and processors or manufacturers and distributors, prices are usually established by negotiation. How does the seller choose between haggling and fixing prices? We have seen that the gain from using haggling is that it enables the seller to discriminate among buyers with different demands, and thus to earn extra profit. For high price-tag items, the gains from discriminating among customers are probably large. In the sale of small consumer goods, however, these gains presumably are outweighed by other considerations, such as the fact that the selling is often done by an employee who might not be depended upon to bargain in the employer's interest.

Delay is not the only device a negotiator can use to reduce an informational handicap. It is often possible, by imaginatively exploiting the structure of the game, to induce the other party to reveal what he or she knows. A seller, for example, can use quantity discounts to do this. Suppose some buyers' demands are larger than others': more precisely, some buyers would be willing to pay a higher price for a given quantity of the item than other buyers. Typically, however, the seller cannot distinguish between a high-demand buyer and a low-demand buyer. One strategy for the seller is simply to charge a flat price, calculated on the basis of the average buyer's demand. A more profitable strategy, however, is to offer a lower price to those who buy a relatively large quantity. The seller can induce the high-demand buyers to purchase large quantities and the low-demand buyers small quantities, thus screening the buyers by the size of their purchases. By a judicious choice of the size of the quantity discount, the seller may earn more than by setting a single, nonscreening price. Another decision that is structurally similar is that of an employer whose employees' productivities differ in a way the employer cannot observe. The employer can induce the employees to reveal their productivities by designing a payment scheme that makes remuneration depend in a particular way on the employees' outputs; thus salespeople are paid commissions depending on their sales (more on this in Chapter 9).

Information and Bargaining Breakdown

Some general lessons emerge from these simple models. How negotiations proceed is determined by the information each of the bargainers has. Knowledge can be a source of bargaining power, in the sense that bargainers can get a better deal if their information is private than if it is public. But information that is unevenly distributed can also generate bad outcomes, of the prisoners'-dilemma type: it can result in failure to reach agreement, even though it would be in principle possible to craft a mutually beneficial deal. Screening by delay in some cases can be an effective defensive strategy for a bargainer in the face of an opponent's informational advantage. But delay—in effect, a temporary breakdown in the negotiations—also has a prisoner's dilemma aspect: to the extent that delay is costly for either party, the total gains from trade would be higher if delay could be avoided.

The breakdown of negotiations does not necessarily mean, therefore, that someone has acted against his or her own best interests: breakdown can be a perfectly rational phenomenon when information is private. When you do not know what your opponent's limit is, it is a good strategy to push hard enough that some of the time you will overreach. With the benefit of hindsight, overreaching in this way will in some cases be seen to have been a mistake. But with the information available at the time of negotiating, this can be a sensible bargaining technique. It is rational, in other words, for the seller to give the impression that her limit price is higher than it really is: to claim a "rock-bottom price" that is higher than the lowest she could profitably accept. For the seller, there is both a cost and a benefit from setting her resistance point higher than the lowest profitable price. The cost is obvious: if the buyer's resistance point (which the seller does not know) is lower than this, the negotiations break down, even though a price could have been found that would have left both buyer and seller satisfied. The benefit to the seller of setting a resistance point higher than his or her true limit is that, in the event that the buyer's resistance point exceeds the seller's and agreement is reached, he has ensured that the price is higher than it might otherwise have been. The buyer reasons similarly. Observers of labor-management negotiations have noted this phenomenon. The union tries to exploit the fact that its target is not known to management by setting a resistance point at a higher wage than its true minimum. The management similarly sets its resistance point at a lower wage than its true maximum. Contrary to the interpretation often given by labor-relations experts, our model shows that this is not necessarily the result of anyone's behaving irrationally. Rather, it can be caused by both parties trying to squeeze as much advantage as possible from the secrecy of their own limits, under the handicap of not knowing the other party's limit. What is seen with the benefit of hindsight to be inefficient may well be, during the nego-

tiations, perfectly rational behavior. Labor negotiators do, in fact, usually avoid the inefficient outcome, a strike, despite both sides' striving
for bargaining advantage: 85% of contract renewals in U.S. manufacturing industry are settled without strikes.

The efficiency losses from bargaining breakdown can be spectacular,
as is illustrated by a contracting failure in the U.S. oil industry. Oil forms
in pools beneath the ground. Usually several firms control tracts above
any pool and the oil can migrate beneath the tracts; thus several firms
compete to extract from the pool. A prisoner's-dilemma incentive results
in excessive extraction rates: each extracting firm tries to extract as
quickly as possible because it knows that any oil it leaves in the ground
can be extracted by its neighbor. Geology defines an optimal extraction
rate: extracting the oil too fast reduces the amount that it is feasible to
extract (because the gas that facilitates pumping the oil out is dissipated).
Thus the outcome of the separate extractors' decisions is inefficient, as
in the prisoners' dilemma. The solution to this inefficiency is easy to see.
If the entire oil pool were the property of a single firm, it would clearly
be motivated to extract at the efficient rate. This single-extractor solution can in principle be mimicked when there are multiple firms if they
delegate to a single individual the right to make all extraction decisions:
in oil-industry jargon, this is known as unitization. Since more oil will
then be extracted, a scheme for paying the firms could in principle be
devised that left all better off than they would be with unrestricted extraction. In practice, few U.S. oil fields are successfully unitized in the
absence of government regulation. Huge amounts of oil are wasted because of this bargaining failure: unitization would result in between two
and five times as much oil being recovered as in the absence of unitization. This is a dramatic instance of a game in which the players' attempts
to seize a large share result in a shrinking of the total to be divided. Why
is an efficient outcome so rarely negotiated in the oil-field game? The
foregoing game suggests an answer. Oil pools are not homogeneous: the
amount of oil varies from lease to lease. By drilling, a firm learns only
about the productive potential near its well. Each therefore forms private estimates of the values of the leases. In a unitization agreement,
each firm is assigned a revenue share based on its lease's value; each
therefore has an incentive to exaggerate the value of its own lease. As
our simple theory shows, this can be enough to cause the negotiations to
break down. In fact, unitization agreements are sometimes reached early
in the life of the field, before any wells are drilled and the firms have
acquired their private information; or late, after much of the oil has
been extracted and the information has become public. Consistent with
our theory, it is at the intermediate stage when information is private
that agreement is so difficult to reach.

The lesson from this simple game is, therefore, that bargainers should
try to learn the valuation their rivals attach to the item being negotiated.
For an identical reason, it is in bargainers' interest to conceal their own

valuations from their rivals, to try to bluff their opponents into overestimating the minimum they are willing to settle for. But doing so risks breaking up the negotiations.

Some sensitive ethical issues must be pondered by bargainers who are making use of their private information: bluffing involves deception. Buyers who reveal exactly how high a price they are willing to pay are not often going to end up with good deals. Playing your cards close to your chest sounds an innocent enough strategy; but a delicate boundary separates withholding information from lying. Even ethical game-players should, however, understand the strategic uses of information, if only to be aware of how information-based strategies can be used against them by bargainers less honorable than themselves.

Considerations of longer-run self-interest also arise, almost inseparable from the ethical issues: if you plan to continue in the business, it may not pay to get a reputation for deceptiveness. ("Would you buy a used car from this man?") A reputation for honesty can be a powerful advantage in bargaining. Reputational issues are amenable to game-theoretic analysis, along the lines of the repeated-game model of Chapter 3. Extending that analysis, we can deduce that ongoing interactions can generate incentives against using mutually harmful strategies. In an ongoing situation, people may refrain from cheating because it is in their interest to do so. Concern for the future may prevent a firm from squeezing the last cent of profit from its trading partner. Because of the many possible outcomes in repeated games (as we saw in Chapter 3), however, there is no guarantee that this enlightened behavior will actually emerge. (The "used car" jibe has, after all, some point to it.)

Signaling: Using an Informational Advantage

We now reverse the question: instead of asking how to induce others to reveal to you their private information, we ask how you can communicate any private information of your own.

Imagine you have some information relevant to the negotiation that reflects well on yourself. If you simply announce what you know, the other party has no reason to believe you, knowing that, unless you are unusually self-effacing, you have an incentive to exaggerate your own worth. How can you credibly convey this information?

One way is to ask an independent third party who is also privy to the information to confirm your assertion. But this option is often not available since the information is truly private. Another way is to rely on your reputation for honesty. If you have operated in this market for a long time and intend to continue to do so, then the other party, knowing that your reputation for honesty is one of your assets, will trust your statements since it is not in your interest to devalue this asset. But with many kinds of transactions you do not have the visibility or longevity in the marketplace that is necessary for such a reputation to develop. How else can you credibly communicate?

Suppose there is some action that is costly for you to take, and the other party can see you taking it. Moreover, and this is the key, this action is more costly if you are lying than if you are telling the truth. Then the other party might infer, from your taking the action, that you are indeed telling the truth. We call such actions *signals*.

Signals are a form of credible communication. The other party is willing to believe you because you have put your money where your mouth is. Your action speaks louder than your words. That signaling can be described in clichés shows how pervasive it is.

Imagine you are negotiating for a job. You know that you could do the work well if you were hired. You could try telling the employer of your great qualities; but why should the employer believe you? The other applicants are unlikely to admit they are unable to do the work. Credentials can serve as a signal of your quality, provided those credentials are harder to get for an inefficient worker than for an efficient worker. Or suppose you want to borrow a large sum of money from a bank. You intend to repay the loan, but of course every prospective borrower says that. Your claim that you intend to repay looks more plausible if you have taken the trouble in the past to establish a good credit record; your credit record serves as a signal.

We first look at what happens when signaling cannot occur; when there exists no action that can serve as a signal. As we will see, when information cannot be credibly communicated, markets do not function well: some potentially gainful trades cannot be consummated. Then we introduce the possibility of signaling. We will see that signals can indeed successfully communicate information. But the signaling does not necessarily take a cost-effective form. Worse still, the mere existence of a method of signaling does not ensure that any signaling actually takes place: the market may get stuck in an equilibrium in which no one succeeds in signaling.

The Market for Lemons

Let us now change our illustrative game. Instead of the thinking of the uncertainty as being in the buyer's valuation, suppose there can be variations in the quality of the item for sale; and quality cannot be observed by the buyer. How does uncertainty about quality affect the bargaining between buyer and seller? Again, for the sake of concreteness, let us think of this as a market for used cars. Cars come in two types: high quality and lemons. Sellers know the quality of the cars they are selling, but buyers cannot observe quality before buying. We assume that buyers do, however, know the proportion of cars that are lemons. Potential buyers may be reluctant to purchase, because of the risk of getting a lemon. But, to make matters worse, the proportion of lemons offered for sale may be higher than the overall proportion in existence. This is because owners of good cars may be deterred from offering them for sale because the good cars must sell for the same price as lemons, since they look the same to buyers. But a good car is, of course, worth more to its owner than a lemon. The price for which it can be sold may be less than the value of retaining the car.

For the used-car market to exist, the price of cars must be low enough for buyers to accept the risk of getting a lemon. But the price must also be high enough for owners of good cars to find it in their interest to sell their cars rather than to continue using them. These two requirements may be inconsistent. If the proportion of lemons in existence is high enough, the market will cease to operate. Potentially gainful trades exist, but cannot be made. The bad cars drive out the good. The following stylized example makes this point more precisely.

It is known that 60% of the cars of a particular model were faultily built. To a buyer, a car in good order is worth $2000, and a lemon is worth $1000; to a seller, they are worth $1500 and $500, respectively. A seller knows the quality of the particular car. Any buyer knows that the proportion of lemons in existence is 60%, but the buyer cannot recognize a particular car's quality until after purchasing it. At what price will this model of car sell?

The first point to notice is that, since a buyer cannot recognize a lemon, only one price will rule in this market. A seller may claim that the offered car is of high quality and so it should fetch a high price, but (given what we have put into the game) the buyer has no way of verifying such a claim and should ignore it. For a buyer, ignorant of the true quality, the car is worth $1000 with 60% probability and $2000 with 40% probability. Its expected value is therefore $1000 \times 0.60 + 2000 \times 0.40$, or $1400. This, then, is the most a buyer is willing to pay for the car. If we assume that there are more potential buyers than cars for sale, the price is driven up to this limit—provided the market operates at all.

The caveat "provided the market operates" is significant. Will sellers be willing to sell at $1400? The owners of lemons, valuing them at $500, are better off selling their cars at this price than keeping them. But what about the owners of the good-quality cars? They will not want to sell at this price, for the value to them of owning the car is $1500. The owners of good cars will withhold them from the market. But then the basis of our calculations is wrong; the foregoing arithmetic assumed that the proportion of lemons on the market was the same as the proportion in existence. We have found yet another kind of bargaining breakdown attributable to the privacy of information, distinct from those discussed earlier in this chapter. Potential gains from trade exist between owners of good-quality cars and buyers (owners value them at $1500 and buyers at $2000, for a gain from trade of $500). But since the buyers cannot distinguish good cars from lemons, no trade in good cars take place. A form of Gresham's Law applies: the bad items drive out the good.

Similar difficulties due to the dispersal of information arise in insurance markets. A premium computed on the basis of the life expectancy of the typical member of an age group will look like a bargain to those who expect to die soon, and a bad deal to those who know they will probably live a long time. Thus insurance companies offering life insurance must expect that a disproportionate number of unhealthy people will be attracted. This explains why a healthy 65-year-old may find it hard to purchase insurance at any price.

The privacy of information does not, however, always cause breakdowns in situations such as this: provided the proportion of lemons in existence is small, all of the gains from trade are realized. If we change our used-car story so that lemons make up 40% of the cars in existence (rather than 60%), then a buyer would perceive the value of a car to be, on average, $1000 \times 0.40 + 2000 \times 0.60$, or $1600. This, then, is the most buyers, unable to distinguish good cars from lemons, would be willing to pay. Sellers of both types of car are willing to put their cars on the market at any price above $1500. The market is, in this case, able to function (with the price somewhere between $1500 and $1600) despite the uneven distribution of information.

Even if, as in this latter case, the gains from trade are fully realized, the uneven distribution of information causes some to gain and some to lose relative to what would be the case if the buyers were as well informed as the sellers. Owners of good cars receive a lower price than they would with full information. These losses caused by the informational asymmetry are in effect transferred to the lucky buyers of the good cars, who get them at a bargain price.

Is there anything the owners of good cars can do to distinguish themselves from the owners of lemons? Sometimes market participants succeed in overcoming the difficulties caused by the quality uncertainty. If the sellers are in business over the long term and therefore value their reputations for honesty, then their claims about the quality of particular cars might be credible. Reputation is, in fact, one way in which markets often overcome informational asymmetries. But reputational effects cannot be relied on to remove all of these difficulties, as the stereotype about used-car salesmen's probity attests. Of course, actual markets are more subtle than the lemons game: there are many sources of information about product quality. The buyer of a used car can have it checked by an expert before buying. An insurance company can insist on medical checks of its customers. But such sources of information often cannot completely eliminate the informational disparities between buyer and seller: some scope typically remains for the problems just discussed. We next examine actions the informed party to a negotiation can take to communicate credibly his or her information.

Signaling in Markets

The owners of good cars in the foregoing story have an incentive to signal their cars' quality to potential buyers. Simply claiming the car is good will not work: as we already discussed, such a claim is not credible. The seller must find a signal. Guarantees are sometimes offered by used-car dealers. It is more costly for the seller of a low-quality item to offer a guarantee than for the seller of a high-quality item. Thus a guarantee can work as a signal.

Signals such as guarantees can overcome informational frictions, so that mutually gainful trades are made despite the dispersal of information. But signals do not always work; and when they work, they often do not work efficiently. To make these points, let us for the sake of variety change our story from a fable about used cars to a tale of hiring.

An employer wants to hire a worker. Two kinds of worker exist: highly productive and less productive. If of the high-productivity type, the worker will generate $200 worth of output; if of the low-productivity type, $100 worth of output. Productivity is an innate characteristic of a worker: workers know their own productivity, but the employer cannot observe it before hiring. Competition from other employers forces this employer to offer to pay the worker the full amount of his productivity as perceived at the time of hiring. Before entering the job market, the worker can choose to receive education, completion of which gives the worker a diploma. This education has no direct effect on productivity, but is observable by the employer. We assume that earning the diploma costs a low-productivity individual more than a high-productivity individual (both in monetary terms—extra fees must be paid because getting to a passing level takes longer—and in extra effort and worry). Specifically, to earn the diploma costs a high-productivity individual $60 and a low-productivity individual $120. Will the worker's educational level serve to signal his innate productivity?

Notice that this game is constructed so that education does satisfy the requirements of a signal: the signal is observable by its intended recipient; and it costs a low-productivity worker more to signal than a high-productivity individual.

An equilibrium of this game consists of a set of self-confirming beliefs. The worker and the employer begin with beliefs about how signals are to be interpreted. For the system to be in equilibrium means that, after each acts on these beliefs, neither sees anything to indicate the beliefs are mistaken. Suppose the employer believes that anyone who has the diploma must be of high productivity, and anyone without the diploma must be of low productivity. The employer therefore offers to pay a wage of $200 if the worker has the diploma and $100 if he does not. A high-productivity worker who has the diploma therefore earns a net return (wage minus education cost) equal to $(200 − 60), or $140. If the same individual chooses not to earn the diploma, he is hired (given the employer's beliefs) as an unproductive worker and paid $100. That the former number is the larger means that education is profitable for a productive worker. Similarly, a low-productivity worker earns a net return of $100 if he has no diploma. But if he chooses to earn the diploma, he is mistakenly hired as a high-productivity worker, is paid $200, and earns a net return of $(200 − 120), or $80. Thus it pays the low-productivity worker not to get the diploma. The employer's beliefs about the relationship between education and productivity are confirmed in the marketplace: the worker chooses to earn the diploma if he is productive and chooses not to if he is unproductive. Signaling succeeds in this example: anyone with the diploma is in fact a productive worker. The market does succeed in overcoming its informational difficulties, in separating low-productivity from high-productivity workers.

There is an essential arbitrariness to the level of credentials required in this example. All that is required for the diploma to serve as a signal is that it be hard enough to earn in order to deter low-productivity individuals from getting it; but not so hard to earn so as to deter high-productivity individuals from getting it. How is the credential set? The model is silent on this, but presumably it is determined by history or custom. The diploma is the qualification everyone believes is necessary for this job, because that is the way things are customarily done: it is the social convention about how much signaling is needed to achieve credibility. Comparisons across different countries of the credentials required of job applicants suggest that signaling equilibria are indeed arbitrary. For example, corporations hiring management trainees in Germany often require a Ph.D.; in the United States, an M.B.A. is typically required; but in Japan, all that is needed is an undergraduate degree from a prestigious university. An applicant for a faculty position in British and Australian universities, at least until recently, required only an undergraduate or a Masters degree; U.S. universities ask for a Ph.D.; and German universities require the *Habilitation*, which is an extra degree beyond the Ph.D.

Another layer of arbitrariness exists in signaling games. It is also possible that, despite the fact that signaling is possible, the system gets stuck in an equilibrium in which no signaling takes place. Signaling need not work. Suppose that the employer believes that the diploma is meaningless: that, although an individual with the diploma must be of high-productivity, an individual without the diploma could be either a high or a low-productivity worker. This can be a self-confirming belief. Suppose 40% of the hiring pool are low-productivity workers and 60% are high-productivity workers, and the employer knows this. Acting on the belief that an individual without the diploma could be of high or low productivity, with probabilities of respectively 0.60 and 0.40, the employer computes the expected productivity of such a worker to be (0.60×200) + (0.40×100), or $160; this is the wage the employer offers. Individuals who have the diploma, on the other hand, are assumed by the employer to be high-productivity and accordingly are paid $200. In these circumstances, does it pay a high-productivity individual to incur the costs of earning the diploma? The net return to a high-productivity individual who earns the diploma is wage minus education costs; that is, $200 − $60, or $140. This is less that what this individual would earn without the diploma (which we saw to be $160), so education does not pay. (And if it does not pay a high-productivity worker to become educated, it must not pay an low-productivity worker to incur the still higher education costs.) Thus no worker receives education. The employer's initial beliefs are confirmed, for the proportion of uneducated workers who turn out to be less productive is indeed 40%. Thus this is an equilibrium in which no signaling takes place. Given the employer's history-determined beliefs about how to interpret educational signals, no one finds it profitable to become educated, and no communication takes place. Even though a device exists with which to signal—the diploma—no signaling takes place. The high-productivity workers have no cost-effective way to signal their high productivity. This caveat must be borne in mind when thinking about signaling: it cannot always be guaranteed to work.

"Wasteful" Expenditures as Signals

The general lesson from our stylized education stories is that expenditures that yield no direct benefit in themselves can serve as communication devices. Any expenditure that is oservable by the intended recipient of the signal, and that the recipient knows to be less costly to make for "good" senders than for "bad" senders, might work as a signaling device. Examples of signaling abound.

Imagine your firm produces brake linings, and you want to persuade the procurement executive of an automobile manufacturer to purchase your product rather than your competitors' brake linings. You expect that, after the auto firm has used your product once, it will be convinced of its quality and will then buy it repeatedly. You say, "try it, you'll like it." But how can you induce the auto firm to try it, given that it knows that you would be making the same claims for your product even if it were of low quality? How can you credibly communicate its value when the potential buyer knows you are not disinterested?

The signaling idea suggests that expenditures that are in themselves wasteful can serve a useful communication purpose. In the case of trying to sell the brake linings, any obviously extravagant expenditures can serve as signals. Such apparently nonutilitarian devices as wining and dining the potential customer, or providing lavish promotional brochures, or locating your office at a high-rent address, or even burning money in front of the customer do not in themselves say anything about the quality of your product, and they may appear to be wasteful. But they work as communication devices because the potential buyer, the recipient of the signal, knows that you are relying on continuing sales to cover the apparently frivolous costs you are incurring. The buyer knows that you know that, if your product were of low quality, the buyer would not continue to buy it after one initial purchase, and so you would not be able to cover your promotional expenses.

The game of love works similarly: the gift of a diamond ring signals that the suitor has in mind a long-term relationship and not just a one-night stand.

The basic requirement for a signal is met by such "wasteful" expenditures: they are more costly in net terms (that is, taking into account any future profits from repeat sales to satisfied customers) for a low-quality producer than for a high-quality producer. As in the job-market game that we solved in detail, however, wasteful expenditures do not necessarily work as signals. The mere existence of a means of signaling does not ensure that communication actually occurs in the market. But it is possible that the outcome to which this market evolves does involve signaling.

Signaling is pervasive. For a further example, imagine you have invented a new manufacturing process. Since your wealth is limited, you must persuade a venture capitalist to fund your fledgling company. You know your process will work; but the venture capitalist hears dozens of similar proposals every day. To separate yourself from the pack, you can signal your own information by offering to make your own stake in the project relatively large. By putting, say, your house and car at risk should the project fail, you credibly communicate your belief that it will not. The venture capitalist will still want to check the reliability of your judgment; but the signaling means that the venture capitalist need not question your sincerity.

A final, more trivial example of signaling: restaurants in Japan are famous for representing their menu by plastic models. A good rule for a tourist in Tokyo is never to enter a restaurant whose models look unrealistic or unappetizing. Good models are quite expensive; the quality of the model is a signal, in our precise sense, for the quality of the food.

Summary

Negotiation strategies depend on what information is available to all and what information is private. We have seen strategies to defend yourself against another's informational advantage, and strategies to exploit your own informational advantage.

Signaling is a way of communicating information about yourself in a way that the other party will believe. For an action potentially to work as a signal, it must not only cost you something to undertake it, but also the other party must know that it would cost you more to do it if you are misrepresenting your information than if you are being truthful.

In the face of another's superior information it is sensible in some cases to push your own position far enough to risk a bargaining breakdown. Thus bargaining under incomplete information has some prisoners'-dilemma character. The attempt by you as bargainer to use the privacy of your information to capture a large share of the gains might cause the negotiation to break down even though the possibility for a mutually advantageous agreement exists. When information is unequally distributed, breakdown does not necessarily mean that either party has acted irrationally.

An informational disadvantage can be partially overcome by inducing the other party to reveal private information by his or her actions. If you do not know the limits of what your opponent is willing to accept, and if your opponent incurs costs of delay, you should haggle. Use the delay inherent in the process of offer and counteroffer to deduce what you can about the smallest share of the gains from trade your opponent is willing to accept. If the value of agreement to your opponent is large, he or she will be impatient to settle, because of the value of the time spent in negotiation. Thus starting with a demand for a large share of the gains from trade and gradually reducing it serves, in effect, to induce your opponent to reveal the valuation.

Another way of reducing your informational handicap is available if you have more than one potential trading partner. Playing one bidder off against another—using competition—can induce them to reveal at least part of what they know. This we delay taking up until Chapter 11.

Next, in Chapter 7, we illustrate the uses of the bargaining theory so far developed by looking at how some international negotiations have proceeded.

7

Negotiating International Trade Agreements

WHILE THE players in the games so far considered have been people or firms, games are also played among nations. This chapter will discuss international trade negotiations. Business negotiations are usually conducted behind closed doors; it is difficult for outside analysts to get detailed information about how they proceeded. When governments negotiate, by contrast, the news media pay close attention. Trade negotiations among nations therefore provide a useful case study illustrating the bargaining theory of Chapters 5 and 6.

Nations regularly negotiate agreements on the rules governing their trade with each other. Since the Second World War, the main forum for such negotiations among non-Communist nations has been the General Agreement on Tariffs and Trade (GATT). GATT has had remarkable success in reducing tariffs on trade among developed nations. When GATT began in 1947, tariffs were typically around 50% or more—a significant barrier to world trade. After successive negotiations over three decades, these tariffs were virtually eliminated, permitting a vast increase in the volume of international trade, and a resulting increase in the wealth of the Western nations.

GATT has not, however, succeeded in removing other kinds of trade barriers. Government regulations that discriminate against foreign producers, and hidden subsidies that aid domestic producers (especially in agriculture), have been discussed at great length in GATT with little real progress in freeing trade in the affected areas. Why has GATT succeeded so well over tariffs, and failed over the nontariff barriers?

GATT's inability to reduce nontariff barriers has prompted the U.S. Congress to legislate unilateral action against nations that it perceives to have "unfairly" closed their borders to U.S. firms, threatening to restrict entry into the U.S. market in retaliation if the offending barriers are not removed. What are the determinants of the success or failure of aggressive bargaining tactics?

The Players' Aims

Nations are much more complex entities than people or firms. In order to model nations as players in a game, we are forced to confront the issue of what aims each nation pursues. (We will avoid the more fundamental question of whether it makes any sense to represent a nation as having a coherent and consistent set of objectives.)

What aims do a nation's representatives pursue during trade negotiations? They do not pursue free trade as an end in itself, as economic theory would in most cases recommend. Underlying the positions usually taken by the negotiating nations is the idea that exports are a good thing and imports are a bad thing. Economic theory, in contrast, views the purpose of the economic system as to provide people with consumption goods: imports achieve this, and exports are merely a means to this end, paying for the imports. As we saw in Chapter 3, there are gains from trade among individuals; for exactly the same reasons, there are gains from trade among nations. National income is highest when a country specializes in producing those goods that it is relatively efficient at producing, and importing other goods. With some exceptions, trade restrictions prevent the attainment of efficient production and pre-empt the gains from international trade. Thus a lowering of tariffs and other trade barriers would increase overall national well-being. Why then do trade barriers persist?

Any change in trade policy, even one that in net terms benefits the nation, inevitably has redistributive effects; it helps some groups in the nation and harms others. For this reason the process of trade-policy formation is highly politicized. The aims actually pursued by the trade negotiators reflect the workings of the domestic political system and the competing claims of import-industry groups, export-industry groups, and consumers. The resulting agenda takes more account of some groups' interests than others', because political power is spread unevenly over the different interest groups; hence some industries are favored with protection from foreign competition. The protection of agriculture by Japan and the European Community, for example, results from the political influence of farmers.

Trade barriers also exist for reasons other than the political power of certain interest groups. First, if a country is large enough to be able to affect world prices by changing the amount it imports, it may be in its interest to use tariffs to manipulate world prices to its own advantage. A country whose imports and exports make up a significant proportion of world trade can, by judiciously setting tariffs, raise the world price of its exports and lower the world price of its imports. Second, especially in the case of newly developing nations such as South Korea, import restrictions are used as a way of promoting the development of selected industries. Picking winners is, however, hard to do: most governments have not been notably successful at it. Third, a nation may erect trade barriers out of considerations of risk sharing: it might be judged inappropriate to force one sector of the economy to bear the full brunt of adjustment to any unforeseen changes in the international economy. Over time, an industry might lose its competitiveness *vis-à-vis* foreign producers. To shelter this industry's workers and owners from loss of income, it might be given trade protection. A study of the results of one round of GATT negotiations for the United States, for example, found that smaller-than-average tariff reductions occurred in declining industries and industries with a high proportion of unskilled or old workers. Evidently the U.S. negotiators, reflecting either political-power or risk-sharing considerations, sought to protect those industries that would be hardest hit by trade liberalization.

For reasons that are complex (and sometimes, but often not, justified by economic analysis), therefore, international trade negotiators place a positive value on their nation's trade restrictions. This is implied by the very language used in GATT: tariff reductions are called "concessions." A trade negotiator usually prefers lower foreign trade restrictions and higher domestic trade restrictions.

Repeated Games and the Enforcement of International Agreements

The international game of setting up trade restrictions has some prisoners'-dilemma character. A country may wish to impose import restrictions, for any of the reasons just given. But if two countries simultaneously impose trade restrictions against each other, they produce an outcome that is worse for both of them than free trade would have been. To those who decide tariff policy, the best outcome is to have high tariffs while the other country has low tariffs; the next-best situation is both having low tariffs; the next-best is both having high tariffs; and the worst outcome is having low tariffs while the other country has high tariffs. This is a prisoners' dilemma, exactly as in Chapter 2. The equilibrium— if the countries both pursue their short-run interests—has both countries imposing high tariffs. The logic of the situation traps both countries into imposing trade restrictions that end up being against their own interests.

Nations sometimes regard their existing trade restrictions as bargaining chips, only to be given up in exchange for foreign nations' opening access to their markets. The suggestions by proponents of free trade that trade restrictions are self-defeating and should be unilaterally revoked are sometimes resisted on these grounds, which essentially restate the prisoners' dilemma logic. Even though freer trade would benefit both, neither country would benefit from a unilateral move toward free trade.

Because of the prisoners'-dilemma nature of trade restrictions, there is a role for international negotiations to try to find mutually beneficial reductions in trade restrictions. Negotiations among nations are always subject to an impediment that is only sometimes present in negotiations among firms or individuals. No international authority with the coercive power to enforce contracts exists. Hence international agreements must be self-enforcing.

The international enforcement mechanism fits the repeated-game model of Chapter 3: if one country pursues its immediate interests, departing from a pre-existing agreement to maintain low tariffs, then the other country retaliates by increasing its own tariffs. The law of international trade relies on *lex talionis*—the law of retaliation in which the punishment resembles the offense committed. The rules of GATT specify that the sanction against a country's breaching an agreement by raising its tariffs is that its affected trading partners retaliate by raising their own tariffs on the offending nation's exports. The GATT rules state that the retaliatory increase in tariff must be "substantially equivalent," which in practice means that the value of imports affected by the retaliatory tariff increase equals the value of exports affected by the initial, offending tariff. For instance, in 1984 the European Community retaliated against the United States' imposition of tariffs on European specialty steels by imposing tariffs on a long list of U.S. exports, including plastics and steel.

Retaliation is sometimes criticized as a destructive force in international relations. The repeated-game argument, to the contrary, reveals that retaliation is a positive force: it is the very basis upon which the ability to make cooperative agreements rests. Meaningful agreements can be reached only if there exists some sanction that can be invoked in the event of nonperformance. It is in each nations' own interest that its trading partners be able and willing to retaliate against it. The ability to retaliate does not, however, by itself ensure a cooperative outcome; as we saw in Chapter 3, many outcomes are consistent with rational behavior in repeated games, including the prisoners'-dilemma outcome.

GATT tries to ensure that its member states' trade regulations are what it calls "transparent": that is, easily observed and understood by outsiders. This can be explained in repeated-game terms. Retaliatory strategies work as an enforcement mechanism in a repeated game only if one player's deviations from agreed behavior are observable to the other players; the more disguisable are deviations, the less cooperative are the outcomes that can be supported as equilibria. Transparency, then, is essential to GATT's ability to maintain agreements.

Finding Focal Points in International Negotiations

In most negotiations, as we saw in Chapter 5, there are many potential agreements that would leave all participants better off than the status quo. An inherent indeterminacy exists in negotiations. Achieving cooperation to avoid the prisoners' dilemma is only part of the negotiators' problem: there are many different cooperative outcomes, with different divisions of the gains from cooperation and so with the possibility of disagreement over which of them should be chosen.

The concept of the focal points was developed in Chapter 5 as one way of modeling how the bargainers select one particular outcome from the many mutually acceptable possible outcomes. Agreement requires that there be some coordination of each bargainer's expectations of what the other will settle for. A focal point emerges if there is some feature of the bargaining situation that serves to focus each bargainer's attention on a particular outcome, and thereby to coordinate the bargainers' expectations. A particular outcome can be highlighted as a focal point by historical precedent and/or some mathematical symmetry; in particular, equal division—somehow defined—can often serve as a focal point.

GATT can be interpreted as providing a forum for communication to establish focal points. GATT provides an established set of procedures for negotiation. It generates precedents, and embodies a set of norms and rules. Having existed since the end of the Second World War, GATT's rules and customs, though often breached, are widely recognized as the appropriate way to conduct trade policy.

One of the main features of the GATT negotiating procedure is the so-called principle of reciprocity, under which one nation rewards another nation for liberalizing its trade by liberalizing its own trade to an equal extent. Reciprocity is not defined in GATT's rules; but custom has given it a precise definition. Countries in effect trade tariff reductions in such a way as to achieve a perceived balance of concessions. The size of a tariff reduction is measured for these purposes as being the percentage tariff cut multiplied by the volume of existing imports affected. Thus, out of the many possible directions of mutual tariff reduction, reciprocity selects for consideration a few possible directions. The reciprocity custom serves to focus the negotiators' attention on a small subset of the possible tariff-reduction combinations; it establishes a focal point.

Reciprocity therefore has the useful effect of reducing the extent of arbitrariness in the negotiating process. But the norm of reciprocity is itself arbitrary: one expert in international law has described it as an "absurd" and "naive" way of measuring the value of a tariff reduction. The percentage tariff cut multiplied by the volume of imports affected in no way measures the economic consequences of the tariff reduction. A more meaningful measure of the economic consequences of a tariff cut would be based on some prediction, albeit necessarily inexact, of the change in imports that will be generated.

If reciprocity is viewed in focal-point terms, however, its arbitrariness is not a drawback. Because of the multiplicity of possible outcomes that would leave all bargainers better off than at the status quo, the negotiation process is itself arbitrary. Reciprocity serves to establish a focal point because it is a simple rule cemented by longstanding custom. Its exactness is its virtue. A more meaningful but less exact rule, requiring estimates of how imports and exports will respond to the proposed tariff cuts, would leave more scope for disagreement among the bargainers and therefore result in a greater likelihood of bargaining breakdown.

In the bargaining experiments by Alvin Roth and his coauthors, summarized in Chapter 5, the bargainers showed a marked tendency to settle for a 50–50 split, despite the fact that the units of measurement by which the 50–50 split was defined were arbitrary: the 50–50 split was nominal rather than genuine. Given the multiplicity of mutually acceptable agreements, these experiments suggest that what is needed for settlement to be reached is a commonly agreed way of keeping score in the process of mutual concession-giving; and it does not seem to matter that the units in which the score is kept have no real meaning. The exact, true division of the gains from agreement is less important to the negotiators than the fact that the negotiations do not break down. Hence the appearance of equal division may be enough to produce agreement. There is an advantage to what, in Chapter 5, we called "phony precision" in negotiation.

International trade negotiators, then, engage in quid-pro-quo bargaining, looking for simple and exact ways of measuring each others' concessions, almost without regard to whether they measure the true value of the concessions. According to an experienced participant, trade negotiations often end up as "long battles fought with hand calculators."

Reciprocity is also applied in negotiations about the removal of trade barriers other than tariffs, with trade negotiators expecting "payment" for any liberalization in their nation's trade that they offer. In the Tokyo Round of negotiations (1973 to 1979), for instance, in exchange for a change in its method of assessing taxes on distilled spirits, the United States extracted tariff reductions from the European Community and Canada. The United States negotiators carefully calculated in dollar terms what they were giving and receiving over this tax issue; although, once again, the measures of the gains and losses made no economic sense.

Most nontariff barriers—such as government regulations that discriminate against foreign producers or hidden subsidies to domestic producers—cannot be measured as unambiguously as tariffs. The focal-point model of the bargaining process suggests that, if the parties could agree on a common definition of how to measure the trade barrier, then they would have moved a long way toward an agreement to reduce them. However—for this very reason—agreeing on a common definition may itself present difficult, sometimes insuperable, problems. This is illustrated by the struggles among the GATT members over the definitions of subsidies, quantitative restrictions, and so on. The absence of simple quantitative measures that would permit focal points to emerge might explain GATT's lack of success in eliminating nontariff barriers to trade.

The Bargaining Power of Nations

As noted, international trade negotiations ordinarily proceed according to the norm of reciprocity, under which one country offers increased access to its own market in exchange for similarly increased access to a foreign market. While this system has succeeded in removing tariff barriers, it has worked less well in lowering other kinds of restrictions to trade, such as discriminatory government regulations, because of the difficulty in establishing focal points.

The U.S. Congress, in response to what it perceived as the continuing use of unfair trading practices by some of its trading partners, unilaterally changed this negotiating procedure, by having the United States threaten to limit a targeted foreign country's access to the U.S. market unless that country increased its purchases of U.S. goods. Section 301 of the 1974 Trade Act enables the President to retaliate against foreign countries' trade-restricting policies that reduce U.S. exports. The so-called Super 301 provision of the 1988 Omnibus Trade and Competitiveness Act strengthened these retaliatory provisions by focusing on countries rather than sectors within countries; by specifying a process of investigation and negotiation, to be followed by retaliation should the United States' demands not be met. Whereas under reciprocity the deal is "If you help me, I'll help you"; under Section 301 it is "Unless you help me, I'll hurt you."

The U.S. Congress, incidentally, did not invent this aggressive technique of trade bargaining. As long ago as the seventeenth century it was used by the government of Flanders, which retaliated against England's prohibition of imports of its lace by prohibiting the importation of English woolens. Flanders's action was successful: England removed the offending trade barrier. Adam Smith, the original free-trader, approved of Flanders's action. "There may be good policy in retaliations of this kind, when there is a probability that they will procure the repeal of the high duties or prohibitions complained of."

Nor are threats to withhold market access unique to the United States in the present day; they are successfully used elsewhere. China once threatened to cease its grain purchases from the United States if proposed new textile import restrictions were imposed. Malaysia induced Sweden to remove import restrictions on rubber boots by threatening to stop its imports of Swedish trucks. Chile secured access for some of its agricultural products into Japan by threatening to cease its importation of Japanese cars. Nevertheless, for the sake of definiteness, in what follows we shall talk of the United States as being the initiator of the aggressive bargaining.

The use of aggressive tactics is predicated on the user country's belief that it is in a strong bargaining position *vis-à-vis* its trading partners. Is this belief well founded? What are the sources of international negotiating strength? Bargaining power, according to our analysis in Chapter 5, depends upon each bargainer's expectations about what the other is willing to agree to. Agreement is reached by a process of coordination of these expectations. Being in a strong bargaining position means that your rival expects you not to settle unless you receive a large share of the gains from agreement; and, moreover, you know that this is what your rival expects.

We argued in Chapter 5 (and in more detail in the Appendix) that one of the determinants of the bargainers' expectations about what the other will accept is the relative attractiveness of their alternatives to agreement. Each bargainer's payoff is higher the better his own alternative and the worse his opponent's. Alternative opportunities are a source of bargaining power: they overhang the negotiations, affecting each bargainer's expectations of what the other will settle for and shaping the terms of the agreement. Extrapolating from this simple game, we can conclude that one can improve one's bargaining position by taking actions that would result in a higher return for oneself in the event that the negotiations break down. And a more aggressive way of improving one's bargaining position is to worsen one's opponent's alternatives. This is the intent of aggressive bargaining strategies like Section 301, in requiring that the foreign country's access to the U.S. market be limited should the negotiations fail. Our model suggests that implementing Section 301 increases the United States' bargaining power, in the sense that, other things being equal, the terms of agreements will be more favorable to the United States with 301 than without.

Thus one determinant of bargaining power identified by the model is the aggressor country's ability to harm the targeted country in the event that the threat is carried out. (This is straightforward enough that we did not really need game theory to deduce it; but it is useful to have it confirmed by theory.) A threat to close market access will achieve a large shift away from the status quo when the targeted country is very dependent on its sales to the aggressor country, for then the aggressor has the ability to cause a large reduction in the target country's well-being. Over a third of South Korea's exports, for example, go to the United States, giving the United States large bargaining power *vis-à-vis* Korea.

The model further says that the bargaining-power effect of the reduction in one player's fallback can be nullified by a countervailing reduction in the other player's fallback. In other words, if the target country is able to worsen the United States' fallback, then the United States obtains no bargaining advantage from the initial aggressive action. If counter-retaliation is expected, there is no point in lowering the other's alternative, for nothing is to be gained from it. The possibility of counter-retaliation shapes the bargainers' expectations in such a way as to nullify the initial effect of the aggressive bargaining strategy. The threat of sufficient counter-retaliation, by affecting the bargainers' expectations, leaves the two parties in the same relative bargaining position

as they were in initially. The possibility of counter-retaliation was probably why the United States did not put the European Community on the
1989 Super 301 list of "unfair" traders, despite its having arguably more
objectionable trading practices than two of the countries actually targeted, India and Brazil. In their inability to harm the United States by
counter-retaliation, India and Brazil were in a weak bargaining position.

The lesson from our simple game, therefore, is that aggressive bargaining actions are likely to be successful in achieving the aggressor's
aims if they are addressed at countries with small counter-retaliation
ability, and at countries that would suffer significant harm from having
their market access limited.

Negotiators like to be seen to be successful. We have observed that the
criteria for success of aggressive bargaining are that the targeted country
have little ability to counter-retaliate and that it would suffer high costs
if the aggressor country invoked its threat to shut off access to its markets. If the United States chooses 301 actions according to these criteria,
will 301 advance social welfare, broadly defined? The stated aim of Section 301 is to prise open foreign markets that are unreasonably closed
to U.S. exporters. But the two criteria do nothing to identify foreign
markets in which there would be large gains to the U.S. economy from
increased access. Thus the two criteria are irrelevant to the existence of
general economic gains from a 301 action. There is no guarantee that
the sectors chosen for 301 action—selected on the grounds of likely negotiating success—are sectors in which potential gains to the citizens of
the aggressor country are high.

The Costs of Aggressive Bargaining

The worsening of an opponent's alternatives by the use of aggressive
bargaining strategies like Section 301 has been discussed so far purely
as a tactic for making one nation—the aggressor country—better off at
the expense of another. In the model, the bargainers calculate their strategic value of both their own and their opponent's alternatives, and then
they immediately agree on an efficient division of the gains. Lowering
one's opponent's alternatives simply shifts the agreement in one's favor,
without causing any loss in overall efficiency.

Is this unduly optimistic? It is, if the use of aggressive bargaining generates an inefficient (prisoners'-dilemma-like) outcome. In this event, using Section 301 could make both the United States and the targeted
country worse off. Game theory identifies three sources of bargaining
inefficiencies.

The simple model of bargaining with fallbacks depicted the bargainers as being fully informed. If, instead, the bargainers have private information, then they will seek bargaining advantage from it. As we saw

in Chapter 6, it is sometimes rational to pursue the strategic gains from private information so far as to risk either a breakdown of the negotiations or a costly delay in reaching agreement.

In trade negotiations, each country is likely not to know exactly what aims the other's decision-makers are pursuing, and therefore not to know the minimum they will agree to. The benefits to the United States from opening the foreign market are likely to be more accurately estimated by the U.S. negotiators than the foreign negotiators; and similarly the costs to the foreign government of complying with the U.S. demands might be better understood by the foreign negotiators than the U.S. negotiators. This source of potential inefficiency is present whether or not aggressive bargaining strategies are adopted; but it is conceivable that aggressive strategies exacerbate the potential losses from the fact that the bargainers have private information about their own costs and benefits from trade liberalization. Aggressive bargaining increases the stakes in the negotiation, and may result in longer delays to agreement or more frequent disagreements, as the negotiators try to squeeze extra bargaining advantage from their private information.

Another source of bargaining breakdown is the pursuit of the bargaining power that comes from the ability to commit oneself to one's demands, described in Chapter 5. This can be a dangerous tactic, however, if both negotiators use it simultaneously, generating a game of brinkmanship. There are four possible outcomes in a game of simultaneous commitment. If the two bargainers have committed themselves to positions that are consistent, agreement is reached; in particular, if one is committed while the other is not, the committed bargainer gets all he or she demands. But if both are committed to demands that are incompatible, an impasse occurs. Rational behavior by both bargainers creates a positive probability of breakdown, even though there exist feasible agreements that both bargainers would prefer to the impasse: the bargainers can be stuck in something like a prisoners' dilemma. Thus everyone could be made better off if the use of these strategies were eschewed.

The foregoing is relevant to Section 301 if the United States' commitment evokes a counter-commitment from the targeted country. What is the nature of the bargainers' commitments in the trade-negotiations context? The targeted country can write its position into legislation, so that acceding to the United States' demands would require the passage of new legislation. Politicians can further commit themselves by stirring up domestic protectionist sentiment. Their cost of backing down is the loss of their political capital. It is plausible that they do not know at the outset how strong the public's feelings over the foreigners' trade practices will become, and therefore what the political cost of backing down on the trade demands will be; moreover, the size of this cost is likely to be more accurately known to the home government than to the foreign negotiators. This would seem to fit the facts, for example, of the U.S.-Brazilian 301 negotiations over Brazil's computer-industry policy. If both countries attempt commitment, a chance exists that, even if everyone behaves rationally, the United States will be forced to carry out its threat to introduce punitive trade restrictions.

A further consideration is the effects of aggressive bargaining on the stability of the trading system. In our analysis of the bargaining-power implications of aggressive strategies, we have assumed that an agreement, once reached, will be maintained: there exists some mechanism for enforcing contracts. As discussed earlier in this chapter, however, international agreements have only weak enforcement mechanisms. The main guarantee that an international agreement will be maintained comes from the ongoing nature of international interactions. The cost of reneging now is suffering future sanctions from the affected trading partners. In other words, cooperation arises because the players are in a repeated game. As we saw in Chapter 3, repeated games generally have many equilibria, only some of which involve the players behaving cooperatively. Other equilibria are inefficient. Any cooperation that arises from the repetition of a game is fragile. The system can instead be stuck in a low-level equilibrium.

A change in strategy by one of the players, such as implementing aggressive bargaining, will upset an existing equilibrium. There is no guarantee that the new equilibrium that emerges, after all the players have chosen their new strategies in response, will be efficient, even if the old one was. And the bigger the initial change in strategy, the more likely it is to upset the system's stability. There is a danger of retaliation breeding further retaliation. A danger from aggressive bargaining strategies is that they risk upsetting the delicate balance on which the very ability to make international agreements rests.

These three sources of bargaining inefficiencies—generated by private information, commitments, and counter-retaliation—do not, of course, necessarily occur. Sometimes a new agreement is made immediately after Section 301 is invoked. Examples of this are Taiwan's 1986 agreement to change the basis of its customs-duty calculations one week after the President directed the U.S. Trade Representative to propose Section 301 retaliation; and South Korean's 1986 agreement to reduce its barriers on importing U.S. motion pictures and television programs in order to avoid a Section 301 investigation. Bargaining inefficiencies did arise in the case of the European Community's subsidies of canned peaches, over which there were lengthy Section 301 negotiations. The 1985 Section 301 action against the Brazilian computer industry produced acrimonious negotiations. In the Section 301 action against various European countries' subsidization of specialty steels, the United States' threat was carried out: the United States imposed quotas and higher tariffs. Thus there are bargaining costs associated with the use of aggressive bargaining strategies.

Summary

The sanction upon which the ability to make international agreements rests comes from the ongoing nature of international interactions. The penalty for one country's breaching an agreement by raising its tariffs is that its trading partners raise their own tariffs in retaliation.

International trade negotiations illustrate the role of focal points in coordinating the bargainers' expectations and therefore allowing agreement to be reached. Given that many different mutually acceptable potential agreements exist, the fact that the negotiations do not break down is more important to the bargainers than a definitive weighing of the gains to each from the agreement. It follows that there is an advantage to phony precision in negotiations. For agreement to be reached it helps that there is some way of measuring concessions exists, so that an equal division can be made. But the method of measurement need not be a true computation of the gains from the agreement. All that is necessary is that the measure can be defined simply and unambiguously, so as to provide a focal point upon which agreement can coalesce. The norm of reciprocity in trade negotiations—under which countries swap tariff reductions that affect equal amounts of trade—is one such arbitrary measure.

Game theory suggests that the aggressive bargaining such as that involved in Section 301 will tend to shift the terms of agreement, as it is intended to do. This shift will be larger the greater the harm to the targeted country from having its access to the aggressor country's market limited; and the smaller the targeted country's ability to harm the aggressor country in retaliation. But these determinants of the success of aggressive action do not identify the areas where the social gains from freer trade are largest. Thus there is a tendency to direct aggressive actions at the wrong targets. Aggressive bargaining increases bargaining frictions: attempts to exploit the bargaining power that comes from either private information or commitments can lead to costly delays to agreement or even the possibility of a complete breakdown in the negotiations. And the use of retaliatory strategies can upset an existing global equilibrium and lead to counter-retaliation.

What do international bargaining strategies teach us about bargaining in other settings? First, it is important to understand what aims other players are pursuing. Understanding their aims might suggest how to find mutually beneficial agreements. Second, agreements can work well even without formal contracts, provided relationships are ongoing so that the threat of retaliation is available as a sanction. Third, establishing a focal point, at which there is a perceived balance of concessions, is an effective way of achieving agreement in complex negotiations. In defining the focal point, it does not matter much that the units by which the concessions are measured are not very meaningful; what is more important is that the units allow concessions to be measured precisely. Fourth, alternatives to a negotiated agreement are an important source of bargaining power. Aggressive bargaining strategies aimed at worsening opponents' alternatives can produce an outcome that is, from the aggressor's point of view, improved; but they also increase the likelihood of bargaining breakdown.

III

CONTRACTING

THE NEGOTIATIONS that we have analyzed so far have been about simple exchange: once the terms of the agreement have been established, the game has ended. Often, however, the purpose of a negotiation is to establish the rules under which one party is to act on behalf of the other. In Chapters 8 and 9 we look at how to structure the terms of a transaction so as to induce desirable behavior from your trading partner. Then, in Chapter 10, the theory is applied to the design of managerial incentive schemes.

III

CONTRACTING

8

Creating Incentives

How can you make it in another person's interest to behave as you want? How can you create incentives?

The word "incentive" comes from the Latin *incentiuus*, which means "setting the tune"; in this chapter we will ask how best to set the tune. We will explore the uncontroversial, even bland proposition that people must be rewarded if they are to be induced to do something they would prefer not to do. The whole question of incentives arises because of some divergence of interests. An insurance company wants its salespeople to be out looking for customers, but the salespeople might prefer to sit around playing poker. An author, seeking fame, wants her book priced low so as to achieve a large sale; while the publisher, seeking profit, prefers a higher price. A firm operating on borrowed capital, whose liability is limited in the event of bankruptcy, engages in more risky ventures than the banker desires. If a subcontracting firm is able to pass on part of its production-cost increases to the prime contractor, it will be less careful to hold down its costs than the prime contractor wants (it might carry excessive inventories, or use more workers than necessary, or fail to seek the most efficient techniques). A car-owner, after buying theft insurance, becomes less careful to prevent theft than the insurance company would want.

The point of this chapter is that these examples all have the same underlying logic, illustrating yet again the usefulness of game theory in highlighting the common elements in apparently diverse situations. To bring out the common features of such situations, it is convenient to have some general terminology. Let us call the person or organization designing the terms of the transaction the *principal,* and the person or organization performing the task the *agent.* (We will, for the sake of definiteness, refer to the principal as "she" and the agent as "he.")

Differences in Aims

The essential feature of any incentives issue is differences in the aims of the people involved. If people are perfectly in agreement, there is no need for one to create incentives for the other; the desired actions will be chosen.

An ideal solution to the incentives problem, then, is for you, as the principal, to find an agent whose aims are not in conflict with yours. If you want a ditch dug, it is a good idea to hire a fitness fanatic, who will do the work eagerly, regarding it as a workout. You are likely to get good treatment from a physician who finds it an interesting intellectual puzzle to diagnose your illness. Hong Kong entrepreneurs setting up production facilities in China commonly hire a relative from the mainland to run the factory because the incentive problems are smaller.

Realistically, it is often impossible for you, as the principal, to find someone whose aims are perfectly aligned with your own. The laborer you hire to dig your ditch typically does not enjoy the work. Your physician normally regards you as just another patient. Even relatives are not always trustworthy. For these reasons, the principal must either try to change the agent's preferences, or offer the agent some form of reward to induce the agent to do what he or she really does not want to do.

Much of what is done as motivation in organizations amounts to changing people's goals. Fostering a corporate culture, belief in the organization's goals, pride in teamwork, and so on can be thought of as ways of reducing differences between the objectives of the agent—the employee—and the principal—the employer. People are moved in complicated and subtle ways. This is stating the obvious, but it must be stressed here, because in most of this book we consider one particular motivating device, monetary rewards. While money is a motivating device of great practical importance, it is not the only one: others include peer pressure, pride in craftsmanship, the work ethic, and so on. Game theory does not specify what aims the players have; in principle any sources of motivation can be incorporated. But we will focus on monetary rewards because they are important, and because they are the simplest to think about and therefore serve best to illustrate the game-theoretic method.

To get people to do things they would prefer not to do, you must offer some kind of reward. Hidden in this unremarkable assertion are some wildly controversial questions not only of economics but also of politics and philosophy. Some of the fiercest political debates involve beliefs about the importance of incentives (although these assumptions are usually left unstated). Conservatives tend to believe that incentives have large effects, while those on the left minimize the power of individual incentives. From Marx's slogan, "From each according to his ability, to each according to his need," we can infer that Marx thought incentives to be relatively unimportant; that taxing the earnings of the most productive people would not cause them to cease to be productive.

William Safire, with tongue only partly in cheek, once wrote a *New York Times* column advocating that greed be delisted from the seven deadly sins. "Greed," he wrote, "is finally being recognized as a virtue. Dressed in euphemism—'the profit motive' or 'growth incentives' or 'the entrepreneurial spirit'—our not-so-deadly sin turns out to be the best engine of betterment known to man. The world has learned that to concentrate on divvying-up diminishes us all, while scrambling to help ourselves helps others; without Greed, there is no wherewithal for generosity." The greatest of all economists, Adam Smith, writing in the auspicious year of 1776, made the case for self-interest more elegantly: of the individual investor, he wrote: "by directing that industry in such a manner as its produce may be of the greatest value, he intends only his own gain, and he is in this, as in other cases, led by an invisible hand to promote an end which was no part of his intention. Nor is it always the worse for the society that it was no part of it. By pursuing his own interest he frequently promotes that of society more effectually than when he really intends to promote it." A less reputable source, the stockmarket speculator Ivan Boesky, said "Greed is good for you."

As game theorists, we can be agnostic about such sweeping statements about the benefits for society of self-interest. Adam Smith himself was ambivalent: exchanging the hat of the economist for that of the moral philosopher he asked resignedly, "To what purpose is all the toil and bustle of this world? What is the end of avarice and ambition, of the pursuit of wealth, of power, and pre-eminence?" Our more modest interest here is in the effectiveness of incentives as a determinant of people's behavior. One way to get people to act as you want is to structure their rewards so that it is in their interest to do so.

How important are monetary incentives? This question need not be left to the ideologues. It can be answered by observing how the economy actually works; it is a question of fact, not faith.

Piece Rates, Commissions, and Royalties

We find performance incentives everywhere. Consider how production workers are paid. The most clear-cut incentive scheme is payment by output or piece rates. Although this tends to be associated with the sweatshops of the Industrial Revolution, it is surprisingly common in modern industry. In U.S. manufacturing, more than a quarter of the workers receive at least part of their income in the form of piece rates, bonuses, or commissions. The use of such incentives varies greatly from industry to industry: it is most common in the clothing and footwear industries, and least common in the chemical and food industries. Piece rates are not an anachronism: they are used as commonly now as at the end of last century. Paradoxically, the Soviet Union has relied more on direct monetary incentives than U.S. industry: in Stalinist times, almost two-thirds of production workers were paid piece rates.

Performance incentives are, of course, not confined to the production floor. Executives' pay is linked to their firm's performance, both directly via bonus clauses in their contracts and indirectly via stock options. (In Chapter 10 we examine the design of managerial incentive schemes.) Also analogous to piece rates in making pay depend on performance are commission and royalty schemes. Salespeople, for instance, receive some fraction of the sales they generate; and musicians receive a proportion of the revenues generated by their records.

Incentives operate conspicuously in professional sports: the stars earn far more than the ordinary players. But, more subtly, an individual player's pay is also sensitive to variations in performance. In baseball, it has been computed that, on average, with age and number of years in the major leagues held constant, the incremental effect on annual income for batters of each hit is $1300, each run batted in $1500, each run scored $1100, each stolen base $700, and each home run $400. (These are incremental effects, so a home run is worth $1300 + $1100 + $400, or $2800.) For pitchers, each extra victory is worth $2900, each strikeout $400, and each save $900.

Even in the gentle world of academe, where professors are supposedly motivated by their desire to push forward the frontiers of knowledge rather than by the crass concerns of the marketplace, pay is, and long has been, related to performance. In the eighteenth century, in some universities a professor's income came in the form of fees he collected directly from his students, so his income was higher the more students he attracted into his classes. In other universities professors were paid, as now, salaries that were independent of how many students attended their lectures. Adam Smith remarked that the quality of teaching was higher when pay depended on performance: as he put it, "It is the interest of every man to live as much at his ease as he can; and if his emoluments are to be precisely the same, whether he does, or does not perform some very laborious duty, it is certainly his interest, at least as interest is vulgarly understood, either to neglect it altogether, or if he is subject to some authority which will not suffer him to do this, to perform it in as careless and slovenly a manner as that authority will permit." Smith believed professors needed incentives: "In the university of Oxford, the greater part of the public professors have, for these many years, given up altogether even the pretence of teaching." In modern universities, a corollary of publish or perish is that professors are given monetary incentives to produce research. A study of U.S. professors' earnings found that, in the physical sciences, the first article an individual publishes typically increases salary by 6.0%. Thereafter, the increases occur more slowly: the fifth article results on average in 1.3% more pay;

and the fiftieth in 0.5% more. In the social sciences, the effect is smaller but still noticeable: the first article is worth 2.0%; the fifth, 0.9%; and the fiftieth, 0.4%.

Weather forecasters in the city of Kursk in the Soviet Union are paid bonuses tied to the percentage of accurate forecasts they make. Analogously, Wall Street brokerage firms like Merrill Lynch and Shearson Lehman Hutton pay their analysts bonuses based on how well the stocks they recommend actually perform.

More unusual examples of incentive contracts include those once offered to policemen in Orange County, California: for every 3% decline in rape, robbery, burglary, and auto theft, salaries were increased by 1%. Of some historical consequence was the share contract negotiated between Christopher Columbus and the Spanish Crown, under which Columbus, from any "islands and mainlands in the Ocean Sea" that he discovered, was entitled to 10% of "all gold, gems, spices or other merchandise produced or obtained by trade within those domains, tax free". And Louis XIV sold the rights to collect France's taxes to "tax farmers," who enriched themselves on what they collected. The tax farmers kept each dollar they collected beyond their quota; thus they were given much more powerful incentives than the typical public-servant tax official, whose pay is the same regardless of the tax revenue collected. Louis XIV's incentive scheme generated such zeal in tax collection that the tax farmers were universally loathed and often murdered.

A situation that is superficially different but logically equivalent arises if the principal, instead of wanting output to be large, wants some task to be done for as low a cost as possible. This arises, for example, in government contracting. When the Defense Department wants a fighter aircraft to be built, it writes one of three kinds of contract: a fixed-price contract, under which payment is fixed regardless of how high or low the costs turn out to be; a cost-plus contract, which fully covers realized costs, or an incentive contract, which is an intermediate contract form, sharing cost overruns and underruns between the government and the contracting firm. The firm that is awarded the contract must be motivated to pursue the government's aim of keeping production costs low. The firm can do this by, for example, ensuring that it does not hold excessive inventories, or searching conscientiously for low-priced inputs, or not using too many workers on the project. This cost-reducing effort is itself costly to the firm, and so the firm must be rewarded if it is to undertake it. It does not require any sophisticated reasoning to see that the fixed-price contract gives the firm a powerful incentive to limit its costs: each dollar's increase in costs is a dollar's reduction in profit. Under the fixed-price contract, the firm bears fully the consequences of its effort decision. It therefore chooses the effort level that maximizes the total gains from trade. The fixed-price contract puts the full responsibility onto the firm for its cost-saving actions. The cost-plus contract, by contrast, gives no such incentive: cost increases are passed on to the prin-

cipal, and the firm bears no responsibility for the costs it incurs. The
incentive contract, being in between the other two, gives the firm partial
incentives for cost control.

Incentives and the Chinese Peasant

How effective are performance incentives? How much can be gained
from paying a production worker according to output or an executive
according to the firm's profits? Evidence on the effectiveness of performance incentives comes from the biggest economic experiment in history, the reforms that occurred in China in the early 1980s. The lives of
China's 800 million peasants were radically changed when Deng Xiao-
ping abolished the commune system and replaced it with what he called
the "household responsibility system," with each family farming land
that is essentially its own. How much anyone had to eat no longer depended on the commune's success; suddenly people's well-being depended entirely on their own efforts. The political pendulum had swung
from emphasizing ideology and social sanctions to relying on economic
incentives; the Maoist slogan, "Smash selfishness and establish collective
order" was replaced by the Dengist slogan, "To get rich is glorious."

Under the commune system, peasants were organized into production
teams. Each team member was assigned work points, which attempted
to measure both how many hours and how effectively he or she had
worked. Income depended on the number of work points accumulated.
Income was not perfectly related to effort, however, because it was impossible to observe how conscientiously each individual worked: this
would have required each peasant to be continually monitored. Moreover, there was a tendency to spread the commune's earnings across the
individual commune members: those with larger families were given
more income, regardless of effort. Thus the link between individual effort and reward was weak.

Under the responsibility system, in contrast, each peasant family is
given a long-term lease of a plot of land. The household must deliver a
certain quota of produce to the government each year, and may keep
anything it produces beyond the quota. The household members con-
sume it themselves, sell it to the government, or sell it in the newly instituted rural markets. With the exception of the special case of rice, they
may decide for themselves what crops to sow and what animals to raise.
The peasants know that, after the quota is exceeded, they own the entire
extra output resulting from any extra effort they choose to make.

A direct link, therefore, exists between effort and reward under the
responsibility system, but only a partial link under the commune system.
The following chart (Fig. 8.1) shows the effects of these different incentive systems on agricultural productivity. By productivity we mean the
amount of output for a given set of inputs; the efficiency with which the

Figure 8.1. Productivity in Chinese agriculture. *Source:* McMillan, John, Whalley, John, and Zhu Li Jing (1989). "The Impact of China's Economic Reforms on Agricultural Productivity Growth," *Journal of Political Economy* 97: 781–807; and Tang, Anthony M. (1980). "Food and Agriculture in China: Trends and Projections, 1950–77 and 2000" in *Food Production in the Peoples Republic of China,* by B. Stone and A. M. Tang. Washington D.C.: International Food Policy Research Institute.

inputs are used. The period in question saw substantial output increases because inputs of labor, capital, and fertilizer increased: but what we are concerned with here is the extent to which outputs kept pace with inputs. Through the Maoist period, according to the chart, productivity fluctuated randomly, though the net effect was negative—by 1977, according to these estimates, productivity had declined to about 90% of its 1952 (precommune-system) level (despite technological advances such as improved rice strains during that period). In 1978 and 1979, under Deng, the government increased the prices paid for agricultural outputs, while leaving the structure of the commune system unchanged. The chart indicates that productivity increased, showing that the commune system was not completely devoid of efficiency: the communes could respond to the incentive of higher prices. Then, from 1980 to 1984, the commune system was gradually replaced by the responsibility system: the chart shows the productivity growth as the peasants began to respond to the strengthened individual incentives. In marked contrast to the apparently random alternations between positive and negative growth in the pre-1978 picture, productivity increased in each year from 1978 on, with the most spectacular growth, 11%, occurring in 1984. Output increased by 67% between 1978 and 1985. In part this was caused by an increase in inputs. But mainly it was due to the strengthened incentives: productivity increased by nearly 50%. The effective quality of labor was much higher under the responsibility system than in the communes. Individual workers in the commune had an incentive to shirk, since they were paid only a fraction of the return from the effort they exerted. Chinese agriculture provides, therefore, a dramatic experiment in the effectiveness of incentives.

Marginal Incentives

If the principal is able to observe how conscientiously the agent works, there is no incentives problem: the principal simply links payment to effort. But usually it is either impossible or too costly for the principal to measure the agent's activities. To know how hard your ditch-digger was working, you would have to monitor constantly. To know whether your physician was investigating all the possible causes of your illness, you would have to understand medical science at least as well as the physician. To learn how efficiently a manager is running a factory, you would have to spend all your time there watching. Usually, payment cannot be effectively linked to the agent's inputs, because not all of the relevant inputs can be observed. The best that can be done is to link payment to performance.

If there is a constant, predictable relationship between inputs and outputs, it does not matter that inputs are unobservable: by seeing the output, the principal can deduce the size of the inputs, and can reward the agent appropriately. But usually life is not so simple: random events destroy the principal's ability to infer how hard the agent was trying. The principal does not know the hardness of the soil in which the ditch is being dug. The recovery of the patient may occur naturally and not be attributable to the physician's diagnosis and prescription. The factory's output is only partly the result of the manager's decisions; it also depends on the availability of raw materials, the skill of the workers, the reliability of the machinery, and so on. The agent can take advantage of the principal's lack of knowledge by being less than diligent. This brings up the second crucial element that makes incentives questions interesting: in addition to the divergence of interests between principal and agent, the agent's actions are not perfectly observable or deducible, and therefore not completely controllable by the principal.

We will call the agent's decision a choice of *effort* level. The most obvious interpretation is that the principal wants the agent to work hard; the agent dislikes effort and therefore must be monetarily compensated to do any work. But we want the word "effort" to bear flexible interpretation; to be shorthand for whatever causes the divergence of interests between principal and agent. Effort can be interpreted literally as a measure of the agent's distaste for and fatigue from work; or it can be interpreted more broadly as a measure of the desirable things the agent foregoes to pursue the principal's objectives. For example, we will later (in Chapter 10) represent a firm's stockholders as the principal and the manager as the agent. Managers are notorious workaholics, so literally inducing effort is not the issue. But there is still a principal-agent problem, because a divergence of interests exists. The stockholders invest in the firm to make money: they want the firm's profits to be as high as possible. But managers may be pursuing other aims, for which they might sacrifice some of the firm's profits: seeking the perquisites of office, or securing their own long-term job prospects. The stockholders must devise incentives to counter this self-seeking behavior of managers.

Payment schemes such as those discussed earlier in this chapter, involving piece rates, royalties, commission schemes, or other performance provisions, get their incentive effect from the variability of the payment and not from its level. The incentive effect is determined, in economics jargon, by the agent's *marginal* payment. A salesperson who is paid by commission, for example, receives some fraction of the value of any sales he generates. Sales depend on how much effort the salesperson chooses to exert. This effort involves some costs for the salesperson, consisting of both direct costs—fatigue, wear and tear on the car, etc.—and indirect costs—time spent selling is time not spent on other income-earning activities or on recreation. What determines the salesperson's choice of effort is not the size of his fixed salary, for he receives this regardless of his results. Rather, the salesperson bases his effort choice on how much extra payment a little extra effort would produce; in other words, on his marginal rate of payment.

What is the best amount of effort for the salesperson, given the commission rate he is offered? The answer comes from comparing marginal benefits with marginal costs. Suppose the commission rate is set at 30%. Suppose also that, at some particular contemplated level of sales, the salesperson evaluates the cost to him of generating $100 more sales to be $20. With these numbers, the contemplated effort level is not the optimal effort level, for the effort to generate $100 extra sales would earn the salesperson a net gain of $10 (for it would cost $20 but earn 30% of $100 or $30). Extra effort is therefore warranted. Usually there are diminishing returns to effort: it becomes harder and harder to sell extra units: that is, the cost of generating $100 extra sales increases with the level of sales. Thus, as the salesperson increases his effort level starting from the hypothesized initial level, the cost of extra sales increases above $20. The optimal effort level is that at which the cost of $100 extra sales has risen to $30, so that it just equals the benefit. Further increases in effort beyond this would cost more than the extra commission payments they would generate. If the commission rate were set at 40% instead of 30%, a higher effort level would be elicited (namely, the effort level such that the cost of $100 extra sales is $40). It follows from numerical examples such as this (or from the more general model in the Appendix) that it is marginal payment rates that determine incentives. The size of the commission rate determines what effort level the salesperson will choose: where his cost of extra effort becomes equal to his gain from extra effort. The higher the commission rate, the more selling effort it will generate.

The identical logic of effort choice applies to a worker paid by the piece or a manager offered performance bonuses: what matters for the effort decision is how much extra payment a little extra effort will generate. In Chinese agriculture, the replacement of the commune system by the responsibility system in effect changed the incentive scheme under which the peasants worked: from the peasant's marginal rate of payment being less than 100% (since in the communes peasants who produced more by working harder received as extra income only a fraction of their extra output, the rest going to other commune workers) to the peasant's marginal rate of payment being equal to 100% (since under the responsibility system peasants, working their own plots, own any extra output they produce beyond their quota). It was this increase in the marginal payment rate that caused the increase in China's agricultural productivity.

Carrots and Sticks

Incentive schemes need not be as finely tuned as piece rates or commission schemes, which are, in the mathematical sense of the word, continuous: any increase in output yields a comparably sized increase in payment. Incentive schemes are often discontinuous: changes in performance generate no change in pay until some threshold of either good or bad performance is reached; at this point there is a drastic change in remuneration. An example of a discontinuous incentive scheme is the threat of firing a worker if output falls below a minimally tolerable level. Fines and legal liabilities are other discontinuous performance incentives. In Stalinist Russia, a powerful incentive scheme operated: perform or be sent to the Gulag. Voltaire observed a similar incentive scheme: in England "it is thought well to kill an admiral from time to time to encourage the others." An incentive for a chip manufacturer producing under contract to IBM to maintain high quality is provided by IBM's threat not to renew the profitable contract. Having the same effect is the opposite kind of discontinuous incentive scheme: a prize for exceptionally good performance, as is sometimes offered to salespeople. Promotion to a better job is another such prize.

Discontinuous incentive schemes can be used in place of continuous schemes. Often, whatever can be achieved by one can be achieved by the other. For production workers, payment by time worked offers no continuous incentives. Discontinuous incentives are present, however, if the workers are monitored and threatened with a punishment if they shirk, such as firing. In addition, the workers can be promised promotion to better-paying jobs following sustained good performance. Thus the incentive effect of a continuous incentive scheme—payment by piece rates—can be mimicked by a discontinuous incentive scheme—fixed payment rates combined with the threat of firing or the prospect of promotion.

Incentives for Quality

A danger of incentive schemes is not that they do not work, but that they work too well. People may concentrate on the goal for which they are given explicit incentives to the detriment of other goals. A worker offered piece-rate payments may produce quantity at the expense of quality; a manager paid on the basis of the firm's current profits might neglect long-term investment opportunities. Thus incentive schemes must be carefully targeted. If pay is to be related to performance, performance must be defined appropriately. This principle is easy to state but often hard to implement, because some crucial component of performance is difficult or impossible to observe.

That badly designed incentives can be worse than no incentives is illustrated by the experience of a U.S. manufacturer of jet engine blades. The company introduced a plan that rewarded workers for increased output. The workers responded by producing a vast number of blades; but some of them broke apart once inside an engine. The company's customers, aircraft-engine manufacturers, required the company to do expensive replacement work. Because the incentive plan did not take quality into account, it ended up as a costly failure.

Consider how to design incentives for production-line workers. Continuous incentives, piece-rate payments, provide a clear relationship between output and reward and so can be expected to generate a high output. But piece rates create their own potential for shirking: not by reducing output, as under fixed wages, but by reducing quality. This explains the relative predominance of piece rates in the clothing industry: it is easier to check the quality of workmanship in a shirt than in, say, a car. A typical garment factory has a policy of paying all workers by the piece except the quality-control workers, who receive a fixed wage; it is difficult to control the quality of quality control. Thus, in general, piece rates will tend to be used when it is easy to check the

quality of the work; and fixed wages when shirking on quality is prob-
lematic to control.

Even when payment is by time worked, monetary incentives can still
be offered, via discontinuous incentives. Quality is eventually observed:
for example, when irate customers return defective merchandise. Over
time the firm learns how conscientiously its employees have worked.
The incentive effect of piece rates can be mimicked by using delayed
rewards like promotions and end-of-year bonuses. Annual salary increases based on the past year's performance allow firms to build incentives into what appear to be unresponsive salary schemes. The prospect
of firing generates an analogous discontinuous incentive.

Discontinuous incentives can usefully be employed, therefore, when,
because the principal observes crucial variables such as quality imperfectly or with a delay, continuous incentive schemes do not work well.

The Principal's Ideal Payment Scheme

"The shortest and best way to make your fortune is to let people see
clearly that it is in their interests to promote yours," wrote the seven-
teenth-century French author Jean de la Bruyère. We have seen that the
principal, by her choice of how to pay the agent, determines the agent's
actions. Can the principal devise a payment scheme that perfectly aligns
the agent's interests with the principal's? In other words, can the agent
be induced to promote the principal's interests?

The answer yes, and the payment scheme is surprisingly simple. Recall
that the incentive effect of a payment scheme comes from the marginal
rate of payment that it offers: the higher the marginal rate of payment, the more effort it will elicit. Provided the only consideration is the
agent's effort incentives (an important caveat that we shall return to in
the next chapter), the principal fully solves the incentive problem by
setting the agent's marginal payment rate (commission, royalty, piece
rate, etc.) at 100%.

To see this, let us return to the example of the salesperson. What, from
the point of view of the principal, is the ideal amount of effort for the
agent to exert? Imagine that the principal, the sales manager, is able to
do the work herself, at the same cost as the agent. (Although presumably
this is not the case, or there would be no reason to hire the agent.) Suppose, as before, that returns to effort are diminishing: the cost of getting
$100 extra sales increases with the level of sales. The principal, doing
the work, gets 100% of the benefits and incurs 100% of the costs. The
principal therefore exerts effort up to the point where the cost of $100
worth of extra sales has risen to $100. (Once again, the logic is: if $100
extra sales would cost $80, then extra effort is warranted; if, on the other
hand, $100 extra sales would cost $110, selling less would produce a net

gain). Thus, from the principal's point of view, the ideal amount of effort is such that the cost of $100 more sales is $100.

Return now to having the agent do the work on the principal's behalf. As we saw earlier, with a commission rate of 30%, the agent exerts effort up to the point where the cost of $100 extra sales is $30; with a commission rate of 40%, the agent exerts effort up to the point where the cost of $100 extra sales is $40; and so on. In these cases, the effort the agent chooses is, from the principal's point of view, too little. To induce the agent to exert effort up to the point that is best for the principal, where the cost of $100 extra sales is $100, the principal must offer the agent a commission rate of 100%. The agent, regardless of the commission rate, bears the full cost of any extra effort; with a 100% commission rate, the agent receives the full benefit from the extra effort. Thus the 100% commission rate serves to make the agent fully responsible for his effort decisions. By setting the commission rate at 100%, the principal succeeds in perfectly aligning the agent's interests with her own. The gain from trade—the amount that is to be shared between principal and agent—is made as high as possible.

If the agent is keeping the full returns from extra sales, how does the principal earn anything from the transaction? The principal, in designing the contract, sets two numbers: as well as the commission rate, there is the fixed part of the payment schedule. The principal uses the commission rate to induce appropriate incentives for the agent, as we saw; and she sets the fixed part of the payment schedule so as to return some of the gains from trade to herself. (What limits how much of the gains from trade the principal can retain is the agent's ability to veto the contract: if the contract does not offer the agent a net return that is at least as high as the agent could earn elsewhere, the agent will reject the contract.) If the agent is to keep 100% of the value of sales, and the principal is to earn something, the fixed part of the payment schedule must be a payment from the agent to the principal—in effect a negative salary. Thus the best contract from the principal's point of view consists of an initial fixed payment from agent to principal, after which the agent keeps the entire output.

The contract that best succeeds in eliciting effort from the agent, therefore, involves the principal, in effect, selling the right to be the agent; and then the agent is left to act independently and retain all of the fruits of his actions. The agent is fully accountable for the results of his actions; in effect, the agent is self-employed.

Firms sometimes use independent sales agents to do their selling. China's household responsibility system, as noted, gives peasants a marginal payment rate of 100%. In the case of the principal hiring the agent to perform a task for which effort means lowering the cost of doing the work, a marginal payment rate of 100% is achieved by offering a simple fixed-price contract (for then the agent knows that for each dollar saved in production costs, his profits increase by one dollar). A 100% marginal payment rate, in other words, corresponds to a simple arms-length market relationship between principal and agent.

Marginal payment rates of 100%, therefore, are regularly observed. But often contracts do not do what the foregoing analysis says they should do and set the marginal payment rate equal to 100%; instead they are less sensitive to variations in output, having a marginal payment rate that is less than 100%. A salesperson working under a contract with marginal payment rate of 100% would receive no pay unless he achieves some target level of sales; but he would be paid the full value of his sales beyond the target. Salespeople often in fact receive a salary regardless of their success, and earn less than the full value of beyond-target sales. Unlike Chinese peasants under the responsibility system, tenant farmers often work under sharecropping contracts, under which they keep only a fraction, typically 50%, of the value of the output they produce. Contracts between manufacturing firms and their subcontractors often have provisions allowing the subcontractor to pass on some fraction of cost increases as price increases.

The arms-length contract, paying the agent at a 100% marginal rate, has two flaws, which account for the frequent use of less extreme contracts. First, if the principal does not know exactly how productive the agent is, it may, as we will see, be in the principal's interest to offer a variety of contracts, with different marginal payment rates, so as to induce the agent to reveal his productivity. Second, the agent does not have full control over the output; output depends on random outside events as well as the agent's effort. Marginal payment rates of 100%, in making the agent fully accountable for his actions, mean that the agent bears all of the risk of any output fluctuations. If, as is often the case, the agent is risk averse, it may not be in the principal's interest to force the agent to bear all of the risk; a contract with a marginal payment rate of less than 100% shifts some of the risk onto the principal. Contracts, in other words, are designed to do more than simply elicit effort; this we turn to in the next chapter.

Summary

The incentive question has two components. The first is a divergence of interests: what the principal wants the agent to do is not exactly the same as what the agent himself wants to do. The second is the principal's inability to disentangle the effects of the agent's effort from random factors independent of the agent: the agent's output is an imperfect measure of his effort.

The principal's task is to design the agent's reward structure so as to align the agent's interests as closely as possible with her own. The key element here is the *marginal* incentive: the fraction of the return to extra effort that the agent is allowed to keep. The higher the marginal rate of payment, the more effort it will elicit. The contract that best succeeds in eliciting effort has a marginal payment rate of 100%: with such a contract, the agent's interests are aligned with the principal's.

Discontinuous incentive schemes can substitute for continuous schemes; and can work better than continuous schemes if information about performance becomes available only after a delay.

9

Designing Contracts

WE ARRIVED in the last chapter at a remarkably simple solution to the problem of creating incentives. By suitably designing the contract, you can induce your agent to do exactly what you want. You achieve this, as we saw, by allowing the agent to keep the full value of any incremental outputs produced, beyond some pre-set quota. By designing the contract in this way, you succeed in perfectly aligning the agent's incentives with your own.

Needless to say, this is unduly optimistic: differences in interests are rarely resolved as easily as that. Incentive schemes that are used in practice usually do not pay the agent the full value of any incremental output. The contracts are designed, evidently, to address other concerns in addition to effort incentives. Salespeople, while paid in part by commissions, receive in addition a salary that is independent of their success; and the commission rate is less than the value of extra sales to the employer. In subcontracting, fixed-price contracts are not always used; instead, contracts often have provisions for price adjustment in the event of unforeseen increases in the subcontractor's production costs. In these cases, the agents are not paid the full return from any extra effort, and so they are not induced to exert as much effort as the principal ideally would want.

The reason why we often see departures from simple arms-length contracting is that contracts often must do more than simply generate effort incentives. This chapter examines two further purposes that are served by the provisions in contracts. First, if the agent has some private information relevant to the performance of the contract, then, as we will see, the bargaining power the agent gets from this information interacts with the effort incentives, resulting in the principal's offering contracts that give less than full effort incentives. Second, if the agent is risk averse, it may be in the principal's interest to take over some of the risk that the agent is facing; but we will find that this can be done only at the expense of weakening the agent's effort incentives.

Contracting with Private Information

If the agent knows something relevant to the performance of the contract that you, the principal, do not know, how should you specify the terms of the contract so as to reduce your informational disadvantage?

Many deals have this character: the incentives for performance must be set when one party is ignorant of the determinants of performance. You do not know your employee's capabilities, for instance, and you must specify a remuneration package without knowing exactly what level of performance it is reasonable to expect. Or you are the patent-holder for a new biotechnology process negotiating a licensing agreement with a manufacturing company. The manufacturer is better able than you to predict the demand for the new product. What combination of royalty rate and initial payment is best for you? Or you are a government official negotiating the terms for the building of a nuclear submarine. The shipbuilding firm has a more accurate estimate than you of what production costs are likely to be. How do you set a price? And so on. To give this question a specific context, consider again a sales manager designing the compensation plan for a salesperson. Salespeople are paid a combination of salary (independent of performance) and commissions (varying with performance). What is the best possible combination of salary and commission rate?

How successful salespeople are in generating sales depends, as was discussed in the last chapter, on their own efforts. But it also depends on the inherent potential of their particular sales territories: in some, sales are made with little or no effort from the salesperson; in others the salesperson must work hard for each sale. Typically the salespeople, through experience, have more accurate and more up-to-date information about their own territories than the sales manager who sets their remuneration. This lack of information creates pitfalls for the sales manager. If the inherent sales potential is poor, the manager might set a remuneration package that is too demanding, inducing the salesperson to resign and costing the company a valued employee. If the sales potential is good, on the other hand, the manager may set too generous a remuneration schedule, thus paying more than necessary to motivate the salesperson and cutting into the firm's profits. How should the sales manager balance the risk of these opposite mistakes?

The aim is to design the remuneration package so that salespeople working in better territories are paid differently from those in poorer territories. Since only the individual salesperson knows the sales potential of any particular territory, the information must come from the salesperson. Simply asking the salesperson, however, is not guaranteed to produce reliable answers. Salespeople, being only human, might be tempted to understate the territory's potential, for they know that payments based on a report of a low sales potential will result in their receiving bonuses for sales that are not in fact attributable to their efforts.

Can the sales manager devise a payment scheme that succeeds in inducing salespeople to reveal correctly their territories' potentials? The answer is, surprisingly enough, yes. The trick is to make the salespeople accountable for what they say. By making remuneration depend not only on actual performance but also on predicted performance, it is possible to make self-interested people report honestly. (If this is starting to sound like something that has come up before, then it should: what follows is closely related in its theoretical structure to the inheritance game of Chapter 2 and the game of negotiating with an informational disadvantage of Chapter 6.)

To illustrate how to design payment schemes that induce people to tell the truth, suppose that the sales manager knows that the value of a particular sales territory is either high or low, say $100,000 or $200,000 per year, but does not know which it is; only the salesperson knows. (We will temporarily ignore the fact that the sales that will be realized also vary depending on how hard the salesperson tries.) The manager tells the salesperson that both his commission rate and salary will differ depending on whether he reports his sales potential to be high or low. Specifically, the salesperson is offered an annual payment of $20,000 plus 10% of the value of his sales if he reports the lower sales potential ($100,000); and $5000 plus 20% of the value of sales if he reports the higher sales potential ($200,000). (The manager, in setting these numbers, would have to take account of any alternative employment opportunities open to the salesperson. Alternative opportunities are, as discussed in Chapter 5, a source of bargaining power; the salesperson's alternatives put a floor on the amount the manager offers.)

With the stated remuneration package, it is in the salesperson's interest to give an honest report, regardless of whether or not he is by nature honest. To establish this, let us do the salesperson's arithmetic. Let us assume what is, from the manager's point of view, the worst case: the salesperson is not inherently honest, and cares only about money. If the salesperson correctly reports sales potential to be low, he earns $20,000 plus 10% of $100,000, or $30,000. If the salesperson correctly reports sales potential to be high, he earns $5000 plus 20% of $200,000, or $45,000. There is nothing to stop the salesperson, however, from misreporting his sales potential. (After the fact, when sales are revealed to be different from what he predicted, the salesperson can claim innocence by attributing the discrepancy to some unexpected blip in demand.) Could it pay the salesperson either to exaggerate or to understate his sales potential? Reporting the potential to be high when it is in fact low means the salesperson is given the remuneration package for the high-sales case, but actually sells only the smaller amount of $100,000. The total remuneration that results is $5000 plus 20% of $100,000, or $25,000. This is less than the $30,000 he would earn if he were honest. Reporting the potential to be low when it is in fact high, on the other hand, means the salesperson is given the remuneration package for the low-sales case, but actually sells the larger amount of $200,000. The total remuneration that results is $20,000 plus 10% of $200,000, or $40,000. This is less than the $45,000 he would earn if he were honest.

Thus the payment scheme works. By making both the commission rate and the base salary depend on the information supplied by the salesperson, the sales manager succeeds in inducing the salesperson to reveal his information. The numbers defining the payment scheme were not, however, chosen arbitrarily. One requirement for the payment scheme to work is that the total payment to the salesperson be higher when the potential is correctly reported to be high than when it is correctly reported to be low. In addition, the commission rate must be higher, and the base salary lower, for a report of high potential than for a report of low potential. Reporting potential to be high, in other words, must result in a low fixed payment (or else it will pay to report high when it is actually low) and a high performance-based payment (or else it will pay to report low when it is actually high). (The need for this can be seen by experimenting with other numbers, which will show that any remuneration package that does not satisfy these requirements will not induce honest reporting. In the Appendix, this is established algebraically.) Under a judiciously designed payment scheme, satisfying these conditions, it is in the salesperson's interest to reveal his information.

The payment scheme just described succeeds in inducing the salesperson to reveal his information correctly. We have said nothing, however, about how well the scheme works from the principal's point of view: how successful it is in generating revenue for the firm in excess of the payments to the salesperson. To find the best payment scheme, the principal must search over the range of payment schemes that meet the above requirements. Realistically, the principal must also allow for the fact that the sales that will be achieved depend not only on the territory's inherent potential but also on the salesperson's efforts. Variations in the commission rate affect not only information revelation but also, as discussed in the last chapter, the salesperson's effort level. The manager, in seeking the best remuneration scheme, must put herself in the salesperson's shoes and predict his response to alternative remuneration schemes. (An example of finding the best remuneration scheme is developed in the Appendix.) The commission rate must, unlike in last chapter's analysis, do double duty: eliciting information as well as effort; thus it often must be set at less than 100%. The contract that is the best from the firm's point of view has the features just described: it bases payment both on predicted performance and actual performance; and if the agent reports higher potential, he is given stronger performance incentives and a smaller fixed payment.

As a by-product, payment schemes incorporating the agent's forecasts give the principal valuable information: the revealed information about territories' sales potential is useful for the company's production planning.

Many companies use salespeople's forecasts: a survey of some California corporations found that, of those companies that set quotas for their salespeople, about a half ask their salespeople what they think their quotas should be. IBM has successfully experimented with salespeople's remuneration packages that are based on their own reports of their territories' sales potential. IBM found that such payment schemes, incorporating the salespeople's own knowledge, generated more effective incentives than payment schemes that do not make use of the salespeople's knowledge.

The foregoing analysis, as noted, is relevant to many situations other than sales incentives: we need simply change the names of the characters. Production-line workers in some industries can choose between working in a plant that pays piece rates and one that pays fixed wages. The analysis just developed applies to this choice, with the inherent skill of the worker—which the worker knows more accurately than the employer—taking the place of the sales potential of the salesperson's territory. The more productive workers can be expected to opt for the piece rates. How marked is the incentive effect? A study of the earnings of workers in 500 U.S. firms manufacturing footwear and clothing found that, after controlling for sex, union status, and other variables, piece-rate workers earned on average 14% more than workers on fixed wages. There are three sources of this difference in earnings. First, as in the foregoing analysis, the more skillful workers tend to opt for a firm offering piece-rate payments while the less skillful workers choose to work for fixed wages, because the more skillful earn more from output-based pay. Second, there is the effort effect discussed in the last chapter: people work harder when they are directly rewarded for the results of their effort than when they are not. Third (and this leads us onto our next subject), the piece-rate workers' pay is not only higher but also more volatile than the fixed-wage workers' pay: to some extent, the higher earnings are compensation for the greater risk borne by the piece-rate workers.

Risk Sharing versus Incentives

A disadvantage of any performance-based payment scheme is that it subjects the agent to risk. The output produced is usually not completely under the agent's control. A salesperson's performance depends not only on the territory's potential and the salesperson's diligence, but also on random fluctuations in demand. A production worker's output depends on, as well as the worker's skill and effort, variations in the quality of the raw materials. Incentive payment schemes push the risk of unforeseen eventualities onto the agent.

Our discussion of game-playing under uncertainty has not, so far, fully faced the issue of risk. We have not so far (except in Chapter 4) taken account of the fact that, in many circumstances, people dislike risk per se. People are risk averse (in the precise sense that they would be willing to give up some of their anticipated earnings if it would result in a reduction in the potential variability of those earnings). Just how much money people are prepared to give up in exchange for being sheltered from risk depends (as we saw in Chapter 4) on the size of the particular risk—the amount of the potential gains and losses—and their attitudes toward risks in general—their inherent cautiousness or adventurousness.

Behavior toward risk, as we will see in what follows, often affects the way transactions are organized. Because of the risk aversion of the participants, contracts often are designed, in effect, to provide some insurance. Risk aversion shapes many economic transactions. The agent is often more averse to risk than the principal. A firm is better able to bear risks than the individual salespeople or production workers it employs. A large firm like General Motors can absorb risks better than the small subcontracting firms from which it procures parts. In these case there is the potential for gains from trade in risk. Any performance-based payment scheme, as noted, imposes risk on the agent doing the work. The agent, being risk averse, would be willing to accept a smaller average payment from the principal in exchange for having the principal absorb some of the risk. The principal, being less risk averse than the agent, would find this a worthwhile trade. Since this trade in risk potentially benefits both parties, we might expect the contract to accommodate it.

But a trade in risk inevitably weakens the agent's incentives. An employer can remove the risks her workers face by changing their payments from piece rate to fixed wage: but this also reduces their incentives to work hard. A manufacturing firm eliminates its subcontractor's risks by offering a cost-plus contract instead of a fixed-price contract, reducing the subcontractor's incentives to limit production costs. Any contract that simultaneously tries to solve the two problems of risk sharing and incentives inevitably compromises and fully addresses neither. How can the principal find the best possible compromise between these two contradictory aims?

Let us return to our analysis of salespeople's compensation (although, as before, the ideas will be applicable to many different contracting situations). We put aside the possibility that the salesperson is better informed than the sales manager about the factors determining performance. Instead, we focus on the fact that sales depend not only on the agent's effort but also on unpredictable factors such as fluctuations in demand or in the strength of the competition; factors which are, at the outset, unknown to both principal and agent. Since the manager cannot disentangle the effects of these random events from the salesperson's effort, the manager cannot directly reward the salesperson's effort; payments must be based on sales, which only partly depend on the salesperson. The salesperson bears the risk of any fluctuations in sales caused by things that are beyond his control.

The principal's key decision, as before, is over the marginal rate of payment, the commission rate. The relationship between the firm's profit and the salesperson's commission rate depends on two things: how sensitive sales are to the salesperson's effort; and how averse to risk the salesperson is (that is, how much it costs to compensate him for bearing risk). The sensitivity of sales to the salesperson's effort is measured by asking the question: how much higher would sales be if the salesperson were given a commission rate of 100% than if his payment were unrelated to performance? The salesperson's risk premium is measured by asking the question: if the salesperson were responsible for the entire risk of fluctuations in sales (that is, had a commission rate of 100%), how much pay would he be prepared to give up in exchange for having all of the risk removed (that is, being given a perfectly predictable payment).

The following chart (Fig. 9.1) shows, for a particular case, how the profit the firm earns on average from this contract (sales minus payment to salesperson) varies with the commission rate that the firm sets, taking into account that the firm optimally adjusts the salary portion of payments along with the commission rate. (The details of these computations are given in the Appendix.) The chart depicts the case in which the salesperson is able to vary sales by up to 20% (more precisely, sales would be 20% higher if the salesperson were given a commission rate of 100% than if he were on a fixed salary); and the salesperson's risk premium is 30% (that is, if the salesperson bore all of the risk, he would be prepared to give up 30% of his payment in exchange for having all of the risk taken away from him). The chart shows that, as the commission rate is increased starting from zero, the firm's profit increases, because of the strengthening of the salesperson's incentives (as discussed in the last chapter). Eventually, however, further increases in the commission rate become counterproductive: beyond 25%, increases in commission decrease the firm's profit (even with compensatory reductions in the base-salary portion of payment). The chart illustrates how costly mistakes in contract design can be. With the numbers as stated, the computations in the Appendix show that the 25% commission rate results in 5% more profit for the firm than a pure salary contract would; and 43% more profit than a 100% commission rate would. (Notice that the latter comparison shows the importance of risk-sharing in contract design; if the salesperson were risk neutral, 100% would be the best commission rate.)

How is it possible for the commission rate to be, from the firm's point

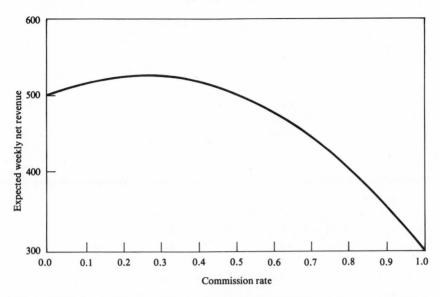

Figure 9.1. Varying the commission rate of the salespersons. *Source:* Computed from the example in the Appendix.

of view, too high? The answer is that, while a high commission rate has the advantage of giving strong performance incentives, it has the disadvantage of imposing risk on the salesperson. Since the salesman has the option of working elsewhere, the firm is forced to compensate for high risk by offering a relatively high salary. At high commission rates, the risk effect outweighs the incentive effect: the salesperson must be given such a high salary to compensate him for the risk he is bearing as to outweigh the gains from the strong performance incentives. The optimal commission rate is found by balancing the risk-sharing effect against the incentive effect; in this case, it is 25%. Just where the optimal compromise between risk-sharing effect and incentives depends on the relative size of the two effects (as is discussed in the Appendix). If the salesperson's risk premium were 40% and the incentive effect 20%, the best commission rate from the point of the sales manager would be 20%; if, instead, the risk premium were 10%, the best commission rate would be 50%.

Commissions are often not the only performance incentives that salespeople are offered; often there are, in addition, carrots and sticks—bonuses, prizes, and promotions for unusually good performance, demotion or loss of job for poor performance. Discontinuous incentives, as noted in the last chapter, reinforce the effect of continuous incentives. To the extent that such rewards and punsihments are present, the commission rate is less needed to provide incentives and can be more used to share risk; the commission rate can therefore be set lower.

The same principles apply to other principal-agent relationships. The contract designer must ask two questions. First, how much discretionary scope does the agent have to produce variations in performance; how responsive is performance to the agent's choice of effort? Second, what is the agent's risk premium: how much money would the agent be prepared to give up to have the risk associated with the task removed from his shoulders? The optimal marginal payment rate depends on the relative size of these two numbers.

The principal, in designing the contract, does not take risk away from the agent out of altruism: she does it to increase her profits. The agent, we have assumed, is more risk averse than the principal (perhaps because the principal is engaged in many different activities with diverse risks, and so she does not worry much about the risks associated with any single activity). A deal under which the principal takes on some of the risk in exchange for a price concession by the agent looks good to both. By the principal's in effect giving the agent some insurance, both principal and agent gain. As long as the principal is less risk averse than the agent, sharing risk is a win-win proposition.

Risk-Sharing via Contracts

Some market institutions whose existence is otherwise a puzzle can be explained as adaptations to risk. Consider, for example, Japan's general trading companies. These are large firms that operate as intermediaries between manufacturing firms. Some activities of the trading companies are easy to understand: obtaining market information, organizing transactions, and so on. But other activities are more mysterious. Sometimes the manufacturer and buyer negotiate the price between themselves and the item is duly delivered without any direct involvement by the trading company. All the trading company does to earn its commission (typically 1% to 3% of the value of the transaction) is to act as a financial intermediary: the manufacturer extends credit to the trading company (rather than the buyer), and the trading company (not the manufacturer) is owed money by the buyer. Viewed in risk-sharing terms, what the trading company offers to the manufacturer is insurance against default of payment. The purchasing firms are subject to the vagaries of the economy: when times are hard, they will sometimes default. The trading company, being large and diversified (dealing with perhaps 100,000 firms), is less risk averse to the possibility of a single default than the manufacturing company, which specializes in a few product lines. Thus a mutually gainful trade in risk exists.

Contracts for the extraction of natural resources such as oil must be designed to reflect both risk and incentives. The most effective contract in giving incentives to the extractor has the extractor paying the owner of the resource a fixed fee and retaining the rights to all that is extracted: then the extracting firm incurs all the costs and receives all the

returns from any effort it undertakes to extract extra units of the resource. Since neither the amount of the resource there to be extracted
nor the price it will sell for are at all predictable, this contract burdens
the extractor with considerable risk. If the extractor is less risk averse
than the owner, such a contract is efficient. This is the case, for example,
if the owner is the government of a poor country, dependent on the
natural resource for its export earnings, while the extractor is a large,
diversified multinational corporation, whose overall profits would drop
by only a small fraction if this particular project is a failure. But if the
owner is, say, the U.S. government and the extractor a small, specialized
(and therefore risk-averse) firm, then the government should share
some of the risk by offering a contract like that derived in the model
above, with some consequent weakening of the incentives for thorough
extraction.

The trade-off between incentives and risk-sharing affects the government when it contracts with a firm to do some work—for anything from
mundane tasks like snow clearing, through more complicated tasks like
roadbuilding, to highly sophisticated work like manufacturing a new
fighter aircraft. The principal—the government—wants costs to be low;
the agent—the contracting firm—bears the costs of keeping costs low.
(A similar relationship exists between a manufacturing firm like General
Motors and the subcontracting firms from which it procures parts; more
on this in Chapter 13.) A fixed-price contract, as already noted, gives
the agent—the contracting firm—the incentive to choose the effort level
that maximizes the total return from the transaction; but it also leaves
the agent bearing the full brunt of any unforeseen cost fluctuations. A
cost-plus contract, on the other hand, puts the risk on the principal, as
it should if the principal is less risk averse than the agent; but it has the
disadvantage of giving the agent no incentive to limit production costs.
An incentive contract is an intermediate form: the agent is permitted
to pass on some fraction of cost increases in the form of price
increases.

Consider, for example, the government's contracting with a firm to
build a nuclear submarine. Table 9.1 shows the history of the construction of the SSN 688 class nuclear attack submarine. The contracts were
of a significant size: each submarine cost about $140 million in 1978
dollars, and each contract was for an average of four ships. Only two
shipyards, Newport News and Electric Boat, were equipped to build this
type of submarine. As the table shows, the cost-share parameter (the
proportion of cost increases that is permitted to be passed on as price
increases) varied considerably over the eleven years of production contracts, from 50% to 85%. (The table also indicates an additional aspect
of the military incentive contract: the ceiling price, expressed as a percentage of target cost. If costs go beyond this ceiling, the contract effectively becomes fixed-price, so the firm is fully responsible for any unusually large cost overruns.) It is to be expected that, as experience

Table 9.1. Incentive Contracts in a Series of U.S. Navy Shipbuilding Contracts

Date	Cost-Share Parameter	Ceiling Price	Contractor
02/70	70%	125%	Newport News
01/71	70%	116%	Electric Boat
01/71	70%	111%	Newport News
10/73	70%	123%	Electric Boat
08/75	85%	133%	Newport News
09/77	80%	135%	Newport News
04/79	80%	135%	Electric Boat
08/81	50%	130%	Newport News

Source: P. DeMayo, "Bidding on New Ship Construction," in R. Engelbrecht-Wiggans et al., eds., *Auctions, Bidding and Contracting: Uses and Theory* (New York: New York University Press, 1983).

accumulates, the cost uncertainties should decline. If everything else is unchanged, this would imply that the firm's risk premium should fall and therefore the cost-share parameter should become smaller. Table 9.1 shows that this is in fact what happened over the latter half of the contract history; but, puzzlingly, the trend was for an increasing cost-share parameter over the first half of the contracts. (This is puzzling if we wish to reconcile the government's behavior with what is theoretically optimal; a cynic might suggest that there is no reason to expect the government to write a cost-minimizing contract.)

What contract should the government, seeking to get the job done as cheaply as possible, offer the firm? The government, having a diversified portfolio of risks, is risk neutral toward this particular contract: that is, it cares only about its predicted cost, and not about the potential variability around that prediction. The contract that is best from the government's point of view depends on the firm's attitude toward the risks associated with this contract (from rising costs of raw materials, new labor contracts, etc.) as well as the size of the incentive effects (i.e., the responsiveness of production costs to the firm's effort). The government, by its choice of contractual terms, determines how much of the risk of unpredictable cost increases the firm faces. Knowing the size of the incentive effect—the extent to which production cost under a cost-plus contract exceeds production cost under a fixed-price contract—and the firm's risk premium, the government official can predict the decision process of the firm's manager, and thereby predict how much effort the firm will exert for any given contractual terms. The firm's predicted effort will fall as the contract hypothetically moves from fixed-price, through incentive contracts with increasingly large passing on of costs, to the extreme of the cost-plus contract. That is, cost-limiting effort will fall as the firm's responsibility for the costs it incurs declines. But simultaneously, as we move through these contract forms, the amount the firm must be compensated for risk falls, as more of the risk is being borne by the government.

The U.S. Department of Defense recognizes that the firms it deals with are often risk averse. A fixed-price contract imposes the risk of unforeseen cost increases on the contractor; a cost-plus contract leaves the government bearing all of the risk and the firm none. Average negotiated profit rates for defense contracts are 11% for fixed-price contracts and 6% for cost-plus contracts. The 5% difference presumably represents the government's estimate of the contracting firms' average risk premium.

The optimal resolution of the trade-off between risk sharing and incentives is for the government to assign a cost-share parameter somewhere between zero and 100%; that is, to impose an incentive contract. The government allows the firm to pass on some, but not 100%, of its production-cost increases. The fraction of cost increases that optimally can be passed on is bigger the larger the firm's risk premium, and the smaller the responsiveness of cost to the firm's effort. The following chart (Fig. 9.2), analogous to that given earlier for the salesperson's contract, simulates how the government's payment to the firm varies with the cost-share parameter, for a case in which the firm's risk premium is 5%, as suggested above, and the firm's discretionary ability to vary production cost (that is, the difference between what production cost would be under a cost-plus contract and what it would be under a fixed-price

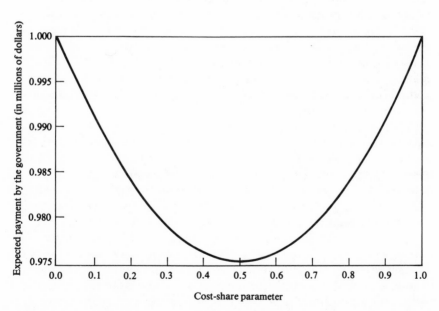

Figure 9.2. Varying the contractual cost share of firms. *Source:* Computed from Question 9.3, page 214.

contract) is arbitrarily assumed to be 10%. The chart shows that, starting with a fixed-price contract, the expected government payment falls as some cost-sharing is introduced by increasing the cost-share parameter: the government gains more from taking some of the risk away from the firm than it loses from the firm's weakened incentives to limit costs. Once the cost-share parameter becomes large enough—beyond 50%— the weakening of incentives outweighs the risk sharing; further increases in cost-share parameter are not in the government's interest. With these numbers, the optimal cost-share parameter is, as in the last contract in the series of nuclear submarine contracts in the above table, 50%.

Relative Performance Evaluation

Incentive problems, as we have seen, are essentially informational problems. With perfect information about the agent's actions, the principal could easily design a contract to elicit the desired actions. It follows that inefficiencies resulting from incentive problems can be reduced by improvements in information. Our modeling so far has presumed that the only information the principal has from which to infer the agent's action is the agent's output. Realistically, further information might be obtainable. If so, the contractual terms should be based on whatever information, direct or indirect, the principal has about the agent's effort.

A commonly available source of extra information is the performance of other agents doing similar tasks. Suppose our insurance company has several salespeople working in a particular city. They have different sales territories, so simply comparing their sales successes does not provide perfectly reliable information on their relative effort levels. The vagaries of the insurance business may affect one more than the other; one may have large sales not because of effort but because of luck. Often, however, the factors that affect sales and are beyond the salespeople's control are not specific to one salesperson's territory: if demand is low this month in one market, it tends to be low in other markets as well. Thus there is some correlation in the randomness the different agents face— there is a tendency, at least partially, for one salesperson's sales to be high when the other's are high. If this is the case, the principal can glean useful information by comparing the different agents' performance. It is in the principal's interest to use this information in the contract, by linking an agent's pay not just to his own performance, but to his performance relative to that of similar agents. Simple ways of achieving this include making the agent's payment depend upon the difference between his own output and the peer-group average; or awarding a prize or a promotion to the best performer. Analogously, when a company such as Toyota subcontracts the production of some component, it usually uses more than one supplier. One supplier's success in generating cost or quality improvements provides a check on how hard the other supplier is trying, and vice versa. The buyer can give extra incentives for cost-reducing or quality-improving effort by making the price to be paid to each supplier dependent on relative performance.

This provides a general lesson for principals: information problems, and therefore incentive problems, can be reduced by comparing the agent's performance with that of other agents doing similar tasks.

Summary

Contracts perform multiple functions; the terms of a contract are set as a compromise between, on the one hand, providing performance incentives and, on the other hand, eliciting information and sharing risk.

If the agent is more risk averse than the principal, there is a mutually gainful trade in which the principal shoulders some of the agent's risk in exchange for the agent's making a concession on the price. A side-effect of this risk-sharing, however, is that the agent's incentives to exert effort are reduced. The optimal contract is a compromise between these two opposing effects, with the principal setting the marginal payment rate less than one.

If the agent has some private information relevant to the performance of the contract, the principal can choose the contractual terms so as, in effect, to induce the agent to reveal his or her information. Again, this means that the optimal contract is a compromise: it does not give the agent full effort incentives.

If the principal can observe several agents doing similar tasks, she can reduce the agents' scope of discretionary action by using one agent's performance as a check on another's; that is, by using relative performance evaluation.

We next look, in Chapter 10, at how to apply the logic of incentives: we use the ideas developed in this and the previous chapter to think about designing managerial incentive systems. The ideas about contract design will also be applied, in Chapter 13, to the design of incentive systems in subcontracting.

10

Setting Executives' Incentives

As is obvious to anyone who has worked in a firm, or to readers of the business pages of any newspaper, firms do not always operate at peak efficiency; and the degree of efficiency varies from firm to firm. What determines how efficient a firm is?

The firm's owners, its stockholders, regard the firm as a source of income. Thus they want the firm to make high profits. This means producing at minimum cost. If production is carried out with higher-than-necessary costs, then it must be that, for some reason, the stockholders' interests are not being fully realized. Why?

Most large modern corporations are not run by their owners but instead by salaried managers. Ownership and control are separated. The stockholders have only a limited influence; most decision-making is delegated to the executives. The control of a corporation is subject to a principal-agent problem, with the stockholders collectively being the principal and the management being the agent. In this chapter we will use the ideas developed in the last two chapters to discuss the extent to which managers' incentives are aligned with with shareholders' interests.

The Separation of Ownership and Control

Adam Smith, writing at about the time of the origin of the modern corporation (the London stock exchange opened in 1773 and the *Wealth of Nations* was published in 1776), described the divergence of interests between owner and manager with his customary vividness:

> The directors of such companies, however, being the managers rather
> of other people's money than of their own, it cannot well be expected,
> that they should watch over it with the same anxious vigilance with

which the partners in a private copartnery frequently watch over their own. . . . Negligence and profusion, therefore, must always prevail, more or less, in the management of the affairs of such a company.

Smith was unduly pessimistic about the ability of corporations to give their managers incentives to advance the corporation's interests. But he did focus on an issue of some importance. Executives have their own agenda, which often conflict with the stockholders' goal of making the stockmarket value of the company as high as possible. A manager might arrange perquisites such as a luxurious office, a chauffeur-driven car, and a team of personal assistants. Corporate jets are used to fly executives to baseball spring training, golf matches, and Superbowl games. Especially venal examples of Adam Smith's "negligence and profusion," of managers pursuing their own interests at the expense of the stockholders' interests, are periodically reported in the newspapers. Managers have been known to give high-paying jobs to family members, use company funds to purchase resort condominiums for their own use, and award themselves low-interest-rate loans from the company. We read of two chief executives who flew separately to Spain in their companies' planes for a red-legged partridge shooting expedition; their trips, each costing tens of thousands of dollars, were regarded as legitimate business expenses. We read of a large advertising company's executive dining room that consisted of a Colonial New England house, transported to New York and rebuilt inside the firm's Lexington Avenue office. With butler service and gourmet food, the two executive floors cost this firm $4 million a year to run; one of the executives had a peeled orange delivered daily, at a cost later estimated to be $300 per orange. We read of the chairman of a major manufacturing company who took a traveling companion named G. Shepard on all his business trips, but in a separate private plane. After the company was taken over and new management installed, it was discovered that G. Shepard was the chairman's dog, traveling separately because of its tendency to bite people.

Fraudulent uses of corporate funds are rare; but the divergence of interests between stockholders and managers is inescapable. Managers might see their careers as being more secure or their prestige as being greater if they push their firms to grow at a faster rate than would be consistent with profit-maximization. It has been estimated for U.S. firms that, for each 10% more in sales, firms pay their executives, on average, 3% more. For this reason managers might indulge in empire-building, reinvesting the firm's profits in growth-promoting projects that yield a lower return than the stockholders could earn if the profits were paid out as dividends and then invested in other firms. Managers sometimes indulge themselves by investing in pet projects that promise lower rates of return than alternative available projects. They might, for the sake of an easy life, be more willing to give in to workers' demands for higher wages than the stockholders would want them to be. Since they are likely to be blamed for any investment projects that fail, they might make cautious decisions, shunning risky but potentially profitable ones. The principal-agent problem—the fact that executives are "the managers rather of other people's money than of their own"—can result in firms' operating at less than peak efficiency.

Little is gained from becoming indignant about self-seeking behavior by managers. It is only human for managers to have their own goals and ambitions: to seek security, prestige, power, income. A more productive response is to take as given the managers' aims, and ask how to design institutions that work as well as possible. The contract-design theory of Chapter 9 gives us a framework within which to pose this question.

Despite the difficulties caused by the separation of ownership and control, corporations thrive. An indicator of the success of the publicly owned corporation is that the market capitalization of the equities listed on the world's ten largest stock markets in 1989 was equal to 73% of the combined gross domestic products of their countries. If the corporate form of organization were too inefficient, it would long ago have succumbed in the competitive marketplace to alternative forms of organization—firms run by a single owner, partnerships, nonprofit firms, or even government-run firms. Individual investors willingly buy corporate stocks, expecting—and usually receiving—from the managers to whom they entrust their money a healthy return on their investment. Evidently the principal-agent inefficiencies can be overcome—at least partially. How?

Managers' Contracts

In 1986, Lee A. Iacocca was America's highest-paid executive, earning $20.5 million as chairman of Chrysler, most of it in the form of bonuses and stock options. "No individual can possibly be worth that much to a corporation," protested Owen F. Beiber, president of the United Auto Workers. What is an executive worth to a corporation? How is executive remuneration established, and is it dependent on the executive's performance?

What can the stockholders do to create incentives for their managers to pursue the stockholders' interests? They can directly address the principal-agent problem by offering their managers contracts that give them a stake in the corporation's profits. Such contracts, like the contracts in our theory of Chapters 8 and 9, have the effect of making the managers' interests more closely aligned with those of the shareholders. This is what is often done in modern corporations: over 90% of medium-sized and large U.S. manufacturing firms link executives' pay to some measure of the firm's performance.

How effectively do managerial contracts link pay with performance? Executives' contracts are usually complicated, involving bonuses, deferred payments, and stock options. But one of the highest-paid executives in the United States in 1987, Reebok chairman Paul Fireman, earned $15.5 million from a contract that was as simple as any piece-rate contract: $350,000 plus 5% of the amount by which the company's annual pretax profits exceeded $20 million (that is, in terms of Chapter 8's model, the marginal rate of payment was set at 0.05).

Such simple and direct links between pay and performance are rare. In some cases it is, to say the least, difficult to see the link. The chief executive officer of Citicorp, John S. Reed enjoyed more than a doubling in his compensation—it rose from $1,143,000 in 1986 to $2,679,300 in 1987—at the same time as Citicorp lost $1.1 billion. This is an extreme example, but it is not uncommon for a chief executive's pay to rise while the firm's profits are falling.

Particular cases prove little. What is the situation overall? In general, do executives' earnings move with the firm's value, so as to have the desired incentive effects? Contrary to popular belief, which depicts executives' pay as being not only unreasonably large but arbitrary, the most thorough existing study, by economists Michael C. Jensen and Kevin J. Murphy, finds that the executive-compensation policies of large U.S. corporations do in fact provide some incentives.

In a smoothly functioning stock market, the competitive forces of supply and demand ensure that the stock price incorporates the best current estimates of the firm's future stream of profits. Thus the corporation's stock-market value provides a measure of the firm's performance. Jensen and Murphy find a statistically significant relationship between the stock-market value of a corporation and its chief executive's salary plus bonuses. The data indicate, in other words, that chief executives are given direct monetary incentives to increase stock-market value. The relationship between pay and performance is, however, typically very small: Jensen and Murphy estimate that the salary plus bonus of a chief executive officer (which on average amounts to over $600,000) increases by only 2 cents when the market value of the firm increases by $1000. (Thus, in terms of the model we analyzed earlier, the marginal rate of payment averages 0.002%.)

The direct link between pay and performance understates the incentives of chief executives, however. In addition to the direct rewards of salary and bonus, there are two indirect incentives. First, there is the threat of being dismissed by the board of directors if performance is below par. The data show that top managers are more likely to leave their firm following unsatisfactory firm performance, so dismissal is not an empty threat. But the data also show that the likelihood of dismissal for poor performance is rather small. Second, executives and their families often hold stock or stock options, giving executives a stake in the company's performance. Stockholdings in fact provide the strongest performance incentives for chief executives. There are good reasons for this. Stockholdings tend to align managers' incentives with the owners'.

But to the extent that owning a large block of the companies' stock prevents managers from diversifying their investment portfolios, the standard risk-bearing disadvantage arises. In fact managerial stockholdings are in most cases quite small, so the incentive effect is muted; but it is still large by comparison with the direct pay incentives. Adding these two effects—the threat of dismissal, and the manager's own stockholdings—to their estimate of the pay-performance relationship, Jensen and Murphy estimate a stronger but still small relationship: on average, a U.S. chief executive's remuneration rises by $3.25 for every $1000 increase in the stock-market value of the company. (In other words, in terms of our earlier notation, the marginal rate of payment is 0.325%.) Variations across firms exist, with managers being given stronger incentives in smaller firms.

Nonsalary earnings account for over 50% of total executive compensation in the United States. Thus, on the face of it, bonuses and stock options make up an important part of executives' remuneration. But the reality of performance bonuses is inconsistent with their appearance. In practice the bonuses paid to executives do not vary much with the firm's performance. Despite its name, much—though not all—of the "bonus" is awarded automatically and is effectively part of the fixed salary.

Are Executive's Incentives Strong Enough?

Chief executives do receive performance rewards; they are in fact given monetary incentives. But their marginal rates of pay seem to be relatively low: the estimated average is 0.3%. How should we interpret this number in the light of our contract theories of Chapter 9?

According to Chapter 9's model the optimal contract is defined by just two parameters: the risk premium that the manager would have if he or she faced a marginal payment rate of one (that is, the amount of money the manager would be prepared to forego rather than bear the entire risk of fluctuations in the firm's value); and the amount of difference in the firm's value that the manager could make by varying his or her value-increasing efforts from minimum to maximum. The marginal payment rate is optimally set small if the risk premium is very much larger than the incentive effect. Is it conceivable that the optimal marginal payment rate for chief executives could be as low as 0.3%?

The manager's risk premium with respect to fluctuations in the firm's value can be expected to be very large, given that the firms' year-to-year variations in value would typically exceed the manager's wealth. The stockmarket value of a firm worth on average $1 billion can easily fluctuate by hundreds of millions of dollars. The manager would be willing to give up a lot to be sheltered from such fluctuations. For this reason, the marginal rate of pay should be far below the benchmark of one (at which the manager's incentives would be perfectly aligned with the stockholders'). A marginal payment rate of anywhere close to one would impose an intolerable amount of risk on the manager.

The fact remains, however, that at about 0.3%, while the executive is undoubtedly given some incentive to refrain from non-profit-maximizing activities, the incentive effect does not appear to be very strong. How important are incentives: how much discretionary ability do chief executives have to cause variations in the firm's performance?

Before pursuing this question, we should note an additional incentive effect omitted from the foregoing discussion of optimal contracting. The stockholders suffer from an informational disadvantage, as they know less than the chief executive about the firm's productive capabilities; they do not know how much the firm's profits could increase in response to changed managerial policies. Managers have better information than stockholders about what investment opportunities exist and how profitable they are likely to be. According to the analysis of Chapter 9, this reinforces the risk-sharing effect in pushing the optimal marginal payment rate below one.

The Limits of Managerial Discretion

The effectiveness of the pay-performance relation as an incentive device depends, as noted, on the size of the incentive effect. The smaller this is, the smaller the marginal payment rate should be. How large is the incentive effect? How much difference to profits can chief executives make by refraining from activities that detract from firm value but increase their own well-being?

It is difficult to estimate directly how much discretionary ability managers have. But there is reason to believe it is usually relatively small. Several sources of discipline work to limit the range of the manager's discretionary actions (that is, work to make the incentive effect small), thereby ameliorating the principal-agent problem. Given that the manager is very risk averse, this means that the optimal marginal payment rate is closer to zero than to one (though not, of course, necessarily as small as 0.3%).

To the extent that the stockholders monitor the manager, the manager's discretion is limited. In most corporations, however, the dispersion of stockholdings means that no individual stockholder has a big enough stake in the firm to justify the time and expense needed to understand the details of the firm's operations. A free-rider problem exists: one stockholder's monitoring would provide benefits to the other stockholders. Each stockholder has an incentive to let the others do the work; as a result, none does it. Most individual stockholders do not own a company in the way that they own, say, their house; they are powerless to affect it.

The board of directors exists, in principle, to monitor the managers on the stockholders' behalf. But the directors cannot be as well informed as the manager about the routine details of the firm's activities. Nor do they necessarily have as much expertise as the manager. And the question arises of who monitors the monitor. Anecdotal evidence indicates that the directors often are beholden to the management and are reluctant to criticize the management's performance. The data show that poor stock-market performance is followed by higher-than-normal turnover of chief executives, indicating that boards of directors do in fact do some monitoring. But the amount of monitoring seems to be small, at least if we believe eyewitness accounts like that of the corporate raider Carl Icahn, whose description of the board meetings of an unnamed company is instructive, even allowing for a little hyperbole:

> Literally, half the board is dozing off. The other half is reading the *Wall Street Journal*. And then they put slides up a lot and nobody can understand the slides and when it gets dark they all doze off. The chief executive officer at that time was a very intimidating sort of guy. A big, tall guy, strong personality, and he was in control of that board. I mean nobody could say anything. I was the only one who owned any stock so I had an interest. I wanted to know what the hell was going on.

The Japanese and German patterns of firm ownership differ from those of most other countries', in a way that results in less discretion for the managers. Banks typically own significant fractions of a corporation's stock and sit on corporate boards. They are also the main source of loans for the corporation. Because each bank/stockholder has a significant stake in the firm, it is less subject to the free-rider incentives. It is in its individual interest to devote some resources to monitoring the managers, and it takes an active role in the company's decisions.

As well as the discipline that monitoring provides, a further constraint on the manager comes from the fact that the firm must be efficient enough to produce an attractively priced product. This product-market discipline works for some firms but not for others: it is more effective the more competition the firm faces from other producers. To quote Adam Smith once again, monopoly is "a great enemy to good management, which can never be universally established but in consequence of that free and universal competition which forces everybody to have recourse to it for the sake of self-defence." The Nobel economist Sir John Hicks puts it more pithily: "The best of all monopoly profits is a quiet life." The manager of a firm that faces little competition is relatively free to pursue objectives other than profits. But a firm that faces strong competition is forced to produce at minimum cost in order to survive. An experiment that provides an empirical test of this proposition comes with the lowering of barriers to international trade, opening a national market to foreign competition. Anecdotal evidence indicates that formerly monopolistic firms that are suddenly faced with competition from imports react by lowering their production costs. This implies that the firms were enjoying their quiet life as monopolists, for if they had been operating with full efficiency, there would have been no room for cost improvements.

A powerful external source of discipline on managers is the threat of takeover. When a firm's stock price drops too low, the firm becomes a tempting target for corporate raiders. (There are several reasons why takeovers occur, but the failure of the existing management to maximize the firm's value is clearly one of them.) If managers fear they will lose their jobs following a takeover, they have an incentive to keep profits high so as to pre-empt any takeover attempt. The managers' fear is quite justified—one study finds that that, in the two years following a take-over, 37% of the top-management team leaves the firm, compared with a normal attrition rate of 13%. The prospect of a takeover means that, in effect, the stockholders are asked to choose among competing managerial teams, the incumbent team and the raider's team. This competition in the financial market gives the incumbent managers an incentive to promote the stockholders' aim of profit maximization. However, the colorfully named defensive tactics available to the management of a raided firm—greenmail and poison pills—often serve to entrench the existing managerial practices and blunt the beneficial incentive effects of the takeover threat.

Executives' long-term career concerns generate self-disciplining. The knowledge that good performance in the current job might lead to offers of more lucrative and prestigious jobs provides an incentive to maximize the firm's value.

How well designed, then, are existing executive compensation schemes? We have argued that executive pay plans do indeed give some, albeit small, performance incentives; and that the need for such incentives is limited by certain constraints on managers' decisions: monitoring by stockholders and directors, competition in the product market, the threat of takeover, and executives' career concerns. In the end, however, there is a good reason to expect the executive compensation scheme not to be ideal from the stockholders' point of view; that is, not to match fully the theoretical model of Chapter 9. This is, at least in part, because there exists yet another principal-agent problem: this time, over who designs the compensation plan. The executives' pay is set not by the principal, the stockholders, but by an agent, the company's compensation committee. This committee is composed of outside directors and, as noted already, directors cannot be relied on to reflect perfectly the stockholders' interests. To the extent that the compensation committee reflects the executives' interests rather than the stockholders', it will set compensation that is both higher and less responsive to the firm's performance than the stockholders would want.

Divisional Managers' Incentives

Analogous to the stockholders' problem of motivating the top manager is the top manager's problem of motivating divisional managers. And so on down the hierarchy: a theoretically similar issue arises for supervisors in motivating the workers (as was discussed in Chapters 8 and 9).

One of the major practical problems in designing incentive schemes, as we noted in Chapter 8, is finding good measures of performance. The design of incentive schemes for divisional managers is more difficult than for chief executives. Stock-market prices reflect the market's prediction of the corporation's future profits, so the firm's market value is probably a reasonable measure of the chief executive's performance. For lower-level executives, however, it is difficult to find appropriate performance measures. The division's performance is only partly under the control of the divisional manager; it also depends on decisions made by others. The divisional manager is part of a team; the firm's performance is the aggregation of its divisions' activities, and it is often difficult if not impossible to assess each individual division's contribution to the whole. The firm's stock-market value is not an accurate measure of performance of a divisional manager, for it is only indirectly linked to his or her own decisions. Basing the divisional manager's pay on the firm's value would generate weak incentive effects and impose a large amount of risk on the divisional manager.

The divisional manager's incentives are usually based on accounting measures of the division's performance such as sales, earnings, or return on investment. These measures are designed to reflect the division's contributions to the firm's overall goals. Rarely, however, are these exact and complete measures of the division's contribution to the firm, so they run the risk of directing the manager's attention at the wrong targets. Incentives can work too well: if the wrong variables are targeted, the incentive plan becomes counterproductive. The divisional manager is often given year-to-year goals, tending to induce short-sighted decisions. Also, accounting measures are susceptible to manipulation by the divisional manager. If current earnings are given too much weight in the manager's compensation, the manager is tempted to boost current earnings by cutting research-and-development expenditures, eroding product quality, and paring investments in new equipment and worker training.

Mitigating the problem of assessing divisional managers' performance is the fact that a source of incentives for lower-level managers exists that is not available for motivating chief executives. Over a period of several years, by informal observation, the top management is able to accumulate reasonably accurate data on a lower-level manager's genuine contribution to the firm. Thus the manager can be offered delayed rewards of the sort modeled in Chapter 8 as discontinuous incentives: the prospect of being promoted to a better job within the firm. Corporate vice-presidents, according to one study, receive average pay increases of 19% upon promotion, compared with average pay increases of 3% in years when they stay in the same position. Promotions, being based on relative merit, have the additional advantage of automatically incorporating relative performance evaluation (as discussed in Chapter 9): performance is not judged in a vacuum, but by comparison with other managers of similar rank doing similar jobs. Thus the continuous rewards based on accounting measures of performance are only a part of the lower-level executive's performance incentives.

Summary

The designer of managerial-incentive schemes faces the archetypical principal-agent problem. Since the manager is more risk averse than the firm, it is mutually beneficial to shift risk from manager to firm. But risk-shifting comes at a cost: removing risk from the manager also removes the manager's incentives to maximize the firm's value.

The partial linking of executives' earnings to the firm's and the industry's performance mitigates the effect of, though far from entirely eliminates, the divergence of interests between stockholders and management. In addition, constraints on the managers' activities—monitoring by stockholders and the board of directors, the threat of takeover, and competition from firms selling similar products—reduce the need for monetary incentives.

IV

BIDDING

WHAT IS the best way to compete in a bidding competition? Faced with bidding competition, what is the best way to exploit it? Chapter 11 develops some ideas about bidding. Chapter 12 then illustrates the ideas by looking at how U.S. television networks compete for Olympic Games broadcast rights.

11

Bidding in Competition

ALL THE GAMES we have so far considered involve only two players. Negotiation games sometimes involve three or more participants. Most of what we learn from two-person games about the possibilities for gains from trade carries over to the case of three or more players. But additional considerations of competition and cooperation arise when there are more than two players: one of the players can try to play the others off against each other; and groups of players can work jointly in coalitions.

Competition, one of the crucial ingredients of business interactions, has so far been omitted from our analysis. In thinking about bargaining, we often presumed that the bargainers were stuck with each other; they had nowhere else to go. In practice, however, one of the main sources of bargaining power is the ability to exploit competition. In this chapter we will look, from one point of view, at how to take full advantage of bidding competition among your potential trading partners; and, from the opposite point of view, at how to compete in a bidding competition. We will also examine conspiracies of bidders that seek to suppress competition among themselves.

Understanding Bidding Competition

Continuing the analysis of bargaining begun in Chapters 5 and 6, we consider the case of a seller who has a unique, indivisible item to sell; but we change things by supposing now that several potential buyers compete for it. The seller, we will suppose, sets the rules that establish who gets the item and how much is to be paid for it.

The essence of any bidding situation is that the bidders value the item for sale differently, but no one knows exactly how highly anyone else values it. If you, as one of the bidders, knew exactly how much your rivals valued it, your decision on how to bid would be very easy. And if the seller knew which bidder valued the item the most and how highly that bidder valued it, the seller could bargain directly with that bidder.

The uncertainty about the bidders' valuations can arise in two distinct ways; and bidding behavior varies depending on which of the two is the predominant source of uncertainty. There may be, on the one hand, inherent differences among the bidders. The bidders for a Van Gogh painting may be collectors who have no interest in reselling the item but differ in how beautiful they think it is. The item may, on the other hand, have a common, true value: winning would turn out to be equally re-munerative for all, although, at the time of bidding, none of the bidders knows for sure what this value is. In the bidding for oil rights, the bid-ders must guess how much oil lies under the tract and what the price of oil will be at the time of extraction. If the bidders for the Van Gogh are speculators who intend eventually to resell it, they must estimate its fu-ture market price when deciding how high to bid. In these cases, the bidders are trying to guess the same number, the true value of winning, but each has different bits of incomplete information.

We will call the case in which valuations are specific to the bidders and differences among the valuations are idiosyncratic to the bidders the *private-values* case. And we will call the case in which valuations at the time of bidding differ because the bidders have access to different in-formation about the item's unique true value the *common-value* case. With private values, each bidder at the time of bidding knows exactly what winning would be worth to him or her, but does not know what it would be worth to others. With a common value, each bidder at the time of bidding guesses the item's true value, and does not know the others' guesses; with the benefit of hindsight, all would agree about the item's value. These two cases are not mutually exclusive: both effects—com-mon value and private values—can be at work simultaneously. But to understand bidding situations, it is helpful to look separately at the two sources of differences in valuations.

Corporate takeovers exemplify the distinction between private values and common value. Financial analysts distinguish two kinds of take-overs. The target of a *disciplinary* takeover is a firm that is not realizing its profit-making potential because of inefficient management. The raider expects that by firing the incumbent managers and hiring more competent managers, or just by strengthening the incentives given to the firm's managers, the firm's profit and share price will rise. In a *synergistic* takeover, in contrast, the raiding firm perceives specific gains to be had by merging with the target firm: from combining marketing or research-and-development facilities, or exploiting new-found monopoly power, or creating tax advantages for the merged firm that are not available to the two firms separately. The case of disciplinary takeover is an instance of common value: nothing particular to the raider creates the takeover opportunity, and any competent managerial team could generate improved performance. Since information is hard to acquire, however, there is no unanimity before the firm is actually taken over about its profit potential. The synergistic takeover is an instance of private values: different potential raiders differ in how much they could increase the target's profits, because the extent of synergy varies from firm to firm.

Deciding a bid is an exercise in decision-making under uncertainty. The bidder may not be sure of the value of the item. And the bidder, not knowing the others' valuations, does not know how high to bid in order to win. This lack of information can cause several kinds of mistakes, as we will see. What is the best way to bid? This question is, of course, of interest to bidders. But it is also of interest to the seller, who, in designing a selling strategy, must put himself or herself in the bidders' shoes to predict how they would respond to alternative selling policies.

A seller must choose how to offer the item to the competing bidders. The seller might inform each bidder of their rivals' offers, and then let them increase their bids to meet the competition. Or the seller might keep the bids confidential. In the context of a formal auction, this is the distinction between, on the one hand, an open auction of the sort used to sell antiques and paintings, in which an auctioneer openly calls bids and the bidding continues until only one bidder remains; and, on the other hand, a sealed-bid auction of the sort often used by governments, in which each bidder submits a single sealed bid, and the highest bidder wins. The seller in an informal negotiation, as opposed to a formal auction, has the same kind of choice: whether or not to tell the bidders what the others' current offers are.

Bidding Strategy in an Open Auction

A piece of undeveloped land is being sold by open auction: all bidders know the current best bid and can, if they choose, bid higher; the last remaining bidder wins and pays the last price called. The bidders know exactly how much they would value owning the item; but they differ in their evaluations of the land because they plan to use the land in different ways. The bidders do not know each others' evaluations of the land, but they have some idea of the range of the others' possible valuations. In other words, the private-values case applies. How should you, as one of the bidders, bid?

This is an easy game to analyze. The best strategy is to remain in the bidding until the price rises to your own valuation of the land, and to drop out as soon as the price goes beyond this. Remaining in the bidding beyond the your own valuation would mean that, if you win, you pay more than the land is worth to you. Dropping out earlier, on the other hand, would mean foregoing the profitable possibility of winning at a price less than your valuation. (Notice that the simplicity in this argument comes from the fact that each bidder's best strategy can be defined regardless of the other bidders' strategies; as in the prisoners'-dilemma game of Chapter 2, it is not necessary to guess the rivals' plans. As we will see shortly, this simplicity is lost when we move to a sealed-bid auction.)

The rule "stay in the bidding until the price reaches your own valuation" is straightforward, but it has some interesting implications. The winning bidder, having the highest valuation, pays a price equal to (or perhaps slightly above) the second-highest valuation. Thus the winner earns a profit: the winner pays less than the item is worth to him or her (because generally there will be a gap between the second-highest valuation and the highest valuation). This profit is due to the privacy of the bidders' information about their valuations, for if these valuations were known, the seller could extract all of the gains from trade by offering the item to the bidder who most values it, at a take-it-or-leave-it price slightly below that valuation. What are the determinants of the second-highest valuation and therefore of the price? The more bidders there are, the closer the second-highest valuation is, on average, to the highest valuation. Thus we have the common-sense prediction that increasing the number of bidders in the open auction on average increases the price. Another, less obvious consideration also determines the competitiveness of the bidding. The more spread out the different bidders' valuations are, the larger, on average, the difference between the highest and second-highest valuations. Thus the spread of valuations is a second determinant of bidding competition. If there is wide disagreement about the item's worth, the winner will probably get it cheaply.

Suppose now that the bidders, instead of planning to use the land that is for sale, are speculators whose sole reason for buying the land is to resell it later at a profit. All of the bidders, therefore, are trying to guess the same number, the future market value of the land. Since they base their forecasts of the future on different factors, the different bidders have different estimates of the land's worth. This is, therefore, the common-value case. Bidding in the common-value case involves all the issues we examined in connection with the private-values case. But it is more complicated, because all the bidders are trying to estimate the same value.

How should you bid in a common-value auction if the method of sale is an open auction? It is easy to see that the optimal bidding strategy is similar to the private-values case already discussed. The rule for bidders is: stay in the bidding until the price reaches your estimate of the land's value. This is, however, different from the private-values prescription in a subtle but important way. In the private-values case, by definition, you know how much you would value winning; you learn nothing useful from observing the others' bids. In the common-value case, all of the bidders are trying to guess the same thing, the future value of the land. Thus the others' bidding behavior gives you indirect information of their private estimates of the value of winning. Since your own knowledge is incomplete, any extra information is useful to you. By seeing how aggressively the others bid, how many remain in the bidding at any point in time, and when they drop out of the bidding, you can improve your own estimate of the value of winning. Thus to the bidding rule, "stay in the bidding until the price reaches your estimate of the item's value," we must append the recommendation "adjust your estimate of the item's value in the light of your observations of your rivals' bidding behavior." If you win the bidding, you learn that you are the only person who thinks the land is worth the amount you are paying. A good rule in common-value bidding is, before raising your bid, to ask yourself if you would still think the item is worth the price you are contemplating bidding even if you knew that none of the others think it is worth that much.

Bidding Strategy in a Sealed-Bid Auction

Choosing your bid in a sealed-bid auction requires a little more thought than in an open auction. Bidding low risks bidding less than some other bidder and losing a profitable opportunity. Bidding high risks bidding much higher than the next-highest bidder and paying more than needed—leaving money on the table. In the common-value case there is a third kind of risk: the risk of bidding more than the item turns out to be worth. The optimal bid in the sealed-bid auction balances these three risks.

Consider an auction for the exclusive rights to a patent to a new computer chip. Bids are sealed and there is a single round of bidding, with the highest bidder winning and paying the price bid. The bidding firms differ in how much profit they could generate from using the new chip, and this is private information to each bidder; in other words, this is a private-values case. What is the best way to bid?

To begin with, let us simplify things by supposing that you know exactly how much each of your opponents would value winning. If your valuation is the highest, then your best bid is slightly above the second-highest valuation. This is because, if you bid lower than this, below the second-highest valuation, you leave your opponent room to bid higher than you and still make a profit. Bidding the second-highest valuation pre-empts this, and still gives you a positive net return, for you pay less than winning is worth to you.

Returning to the more realistic case in which none of the bidders know their competitors' valuations, we see that the optimal bidding strategy is similar to the case of full knowledge. What is the lowest you can successfully bid? You begin by presuming your valuation is the highest of all the bidders'. If it is not, this presumption is costless to you because losing bidders pay nothing. You do not know exactly how far below yours the next-highest valuation is; but, knowing the number of competitors you are facing and the range of their possible valuations, you can estimate what the second-highest valuation is most likely to be. You submit a bid equal to this estimated second-highest valuation. Bidding higher than this risks foregoing some profits in the event of winning; bidding lower makes the probability of losing too high.

Suppose you know that the each of your competitors evaluate the patent as being worth somewhere between zero and $10 million, such that all values in between these extremes are equally likely. Each of your competitors, similarly, perceives your valuation as lying between these bounds; only you know exactly what it is, say, $6 million. What should you bid? It is shown in the Appendix that, if there are, say, 2 bidders (so you have only one competitor), then bidding consistent with the foregoing bidding rule ("bid your estimate of the next-highest valuation") means shading your valuation by one-half: you bid $6 million minus $3 million, for a bid of $3 million. If there are 3 bidders in total, you shade your bid by one-third, for a bid of $6 million minus $2 million, or $4 million. If there are 10 bidders, you shade your bid by one-tenth, for a bid of $6 million minus $0.6 million, or $5.4 million. If there are 100 bidders, you shade your bid by one-hundredth, for a bid of $6 million minus $0.06 million, or $5.94 million. Bids increase with the number of bidders, therefore, but at a diminishing rate. As the number of bidders becomes large, bids become close to valuations. Thus competition matters. If the number of bidders is small, our model suggests that the winning bidder typically earns a surprisingly large amount of profit: the winner pays only half of what winning is worth. Increasing the number of bidders forces the price up, as the profit built into the bids declines.

Insolvent U.S. banks and savings and loans become the property of the U.S. government. As a result of the savings-and-loan crisis, in the late 1980s the Federal Deposit Insurance Corporation (FDIC) found itself in control of hundreds of financial institutions, which it then had to sell. What price should be attached to a bank? Faced with the difficulty of valuing the assets of a bank, the FDIC lets competition establish each bank's value: it offers the banks at sealed-bid auctions. As we have seen, bids reveal bidders' valuations, but only imperfectly: bidders bid below their valuations, especially when there are few bidders (most of the bank auctions have four or fewer bidders). For the 1988 FDIC failed-bank auctions it has been calculated (using a method based on the foregoing theory of bidding behavior) that, on average, the firm that won the bidding bid $4 million below its valuation of the bank for sale; that is, the typical winner left the auction with a tidy $4 million profit.

The Winner's Curse

In one actual use of sealed-bid common-value auctions, for the rights to drill on U.S. offshore oil leases, winning bids are huge. Oil companies bid $590 million, for example, in March 1990 for the rights to drill in U.S. waters of the Gulf of Mexico. One single lease attracted a winning bid of $11.1 million; two losing bidders bid over $8 million for that lease and a third $6 million. With sums like this, we can presume that considerable thought is put into deciding bids. A bidder deciding how high to bid has a complicated decision, based on the results of geological surveys and an assessment of their reliability; a prediction of the future world price of oil; a judgment of how this tract would interact with other tracts to be bid on; and so on. One of the key issues for the bidder in a common-value, sealed-bid auction is highlighted by the following stylized game.

A television game-show host offers as a prize a suitcase full of money, for which five game-show guests are invited to bid out of prize money they have accumulated previously. The players are not permitted to look inside the suitcase, but they are each privately given an estimate of how much money is in it. They are also told that the five estimates, all different and all being multiples of $1000, range between $2000 below the actual amount in the suitcase and $2000 above it. (In other words, the estimates are not precise but are on average correct: if the amount of money is $$X$, the five estimates are $X - 2000$, $X - 1000$, X, $X + 1000$, and $X + 2000$.) If you, as one of the players, are given an estimate of, say, $10,000, and you are told that bids must be in multiples of $1000, how high should you bid?

If you knew all five estimates then you could infer the value of the prize. You know only one number, however, the estimate you have been given. All that you know is that your estimate, $10,000, is one of the numbers $X - 2000$, $X - 1000$, X, $X + 1000$, $X + 2000$. In other words, based on your $10,000 estimate, the true value of the prize, X, could be anything from $8000 to $12,000. What is your best bidding strategy faced with this ignorance?

Since your estimate is on average correct—it has an equal chance of being too high and too low—you might infer that the most likely amount of money in the suitcase is what your estimate says, $10,000. A natural way to bid, then, might be to a bit below this—say $1000 below, since bids must be in $1000 multiples. Then, if you won, you might expect on average to gain a $1000 profit. Or would you?

Suppose everyone does that. Then the person who bids the most is the person with the highest estimate, which we know is $2000 above the actual value of the prize. The "winner" gets an unpleasant surprise after "winning," finding that he or she has bid more than the value of winning. This phenomenon is common enough to have a name: it is melodramatically called the "winner's curse." Although, on average, the estimates are correct, the winner is not selected at random. Bidding based only your own estimate is dangerous, for winning conveys bad news: the winner is the bidder with the highest estimate, so winning means that the winner's estimate is the most optimistic of all the estimates and therefore likely to be too high.

You can overcome the winner's curse by anticipating its effects before bidding. You do this by presuming that you have the highest estimate and therefore you are going to win. When incorrect, this assumption is costless because someone else wins and you pay nothing. When correct, this assumption guards you against the winner's curse. With your estimate of $10,000, this means that you presume that the highest estimate is $10,000. You know that the highest estimate is $X + 2000$, where X represents the unknown true value of the prize. Hence, if your presumption of having the highest estimate is correct, $X + 2000 = 10,000$, which implies the true value X is $8000. If you build some profit into your bid by bidding somewhat below your modified estimate, say $1000 below, and every other bidder adopts the same way of avoiding the winner's curse (namely, subtracting $3000 from estimate to determine bid), then you make $1000 profit when you do in fact have the highest estimate, and zero otherwise. Rational bidding in the face of the winner's curse, therefore, means discounting your own estimate.

The same principles of rational bidding apply in less artificial bidding games. Any actual common-value bidding situation is of course more complicated than this stylized game. In the bidding for offshore oil rights, for example, the bidders do not know exactly who they will be bidding against in any particular auction; the information about the tract's value is not evenly distributed; the bidders must make a prior decision about how much to invest in geological surveys; and they may decide to bid jointly with some other firms in order to share the risk. When a corporation is put up for auction, the bidders do not know exactly how much potential there is for improving its profit performance. But no matter how complex the situation, the principles of common-value bidding remain the same as in our stylized game. The way to avoid the winner's curse is to anticipate it; to presume that your estimate is the most optimistic and as a result to bid more cautiously than the estimate in itself would indicate.

The bidder's decision rule is similar to that given in the last section for bidding in the private-values case: presume your own estimate of value is the highest; under this presumption, estimate what the second-highest valuation is; then bid this amount. The winner's curse, however, gives the common-value case another layer of complexity beyond the private-values case. The precise size of the winner's-curse correction, the amount you shade your bid, depends on how many competitors you expect to be bidding against you, and the amount of uncertainty over the item's true value.

The winner's curse, it has been suggested, accounts for the rash of corporate takeovers that occurred in the 1980s. In a corporate takeover there are (at least) two "bidders." The first "bidder" is the stock market as a whole, which sets a going price for the firm's shares. The second bidder is the takeover raider. Raiders who have only participated in a few takeovers may be duped; they may have not yet learned the fallacy of putting too much weight on their own value estimates and not enough on the market's. If corporate raiders do, in fact, fall victim to the winner's curse, then more takeovers will be attempted than are warranted by the (hidden) objective facts of the raided firms' potential for improved performance.

The winner's curse can also arise in situations where competition is absent. Cost overruns in major construction projects are notorious. The Alaska pipeline, estimated in 1970 to cost $900 million, by 1977 had cost nearly nine times as much, $7.7 billion. Nuclear power plants have often ended up with cost overruns of ten times or more. Even in routine construction, it is common for costs to be over twice the initial estimate. Cost estimates are subject to large uncertainty, especially when new technologies are involved. Even if estimates are just as likely to be too high as too low, there is a tendency for cost overruns if the decision-maker does not understand the winner's curse. A project is accepted if predicted revenues exceed predicted costs, and rejected otherwise. Projects are more likely to go ahead, therefore, if their costs are underestimated; these are the very projects for which cost overruns are likely.

Are winners in fact cursed? Is there a tendency for people to bid more than the item being bid for is worth? In unique situations, it is likely that people sometimes lose by overestimating values. But if the bidding occurs over a long series of similar auctions, it seems reasonable to presume that bidders learn from experience and begin to anticipate the winner's curse. Bidding experiments with student subjects tend to confirm that, as the bidders gain experience, they become less prone to overbid. Although the expression "winner's curse" originated in oil-rights bidding, it is questionable whether in fact the oil companies fall victim to the winner's curse. As noted, spectacular sums of money are bid for wells that may turn out to be dry. With millions of dollars at stake, the oil companies have a powerful incentive not to make systematic errors in bidding; skepticism about pervasiveness of the winner's curse is justified. Statistical evidence suggests that at least a normal rate of return has been earned from offshore oil tracts. But the interpretation of the data is complicated by such events as the OPEC-induced fluctuations in oil prices, so that reasonable people can disagree about whether the oil companies did in fact overbid. In any case, the rate of return to bidders to some investigation of the techniques of bidding looks high.

The Seller's Strategies

Now that we understand something about bidders' strategies, we can look from the other side and ask about the seller's best strategies. Notice that the seller, in choosing how to sell the item, must do the game-theoretic trick of putting himself or herself in the bidders' shoes and predicting how they would respond to alternative selling devices. Like the bidders, the seller must make decisions without full knowledge: the seller does not know exactly what the item for sale is worth to the bidders.

If you are a seller faced with competing potential buyers, what can you do to make the bidding as competitive as possible? We have already seen that the more competition the better (for the seller, though not for the bidders). Competition can be stimulated by encouraging extra bidders to enter. What else can you do to make the bidding more competitive? Should you impose a minimum price? Should you offer the item by open or sealed-bid auction? Should you release to the bidders any information you have relevant to assessing the item's value?

Sellers sometimes impose minimum or reserve prices, refusing to sell the item if no bid exceeds this minimum. It is, in fact, in the seller's interest to set a minimum price. The disadvantage of the minimum price is the risk that all bids will come in below the minimum and the item will not be sold. Weighed against the risk of no sale is the gain from setting the minimum price: the possibility that the minimum price will force a bidder to bid higher than would otherwise have been made necessary by the competition. This gain can be potentially large enough to outweigh the risk of no sale, so it might be in the seller's interest to impose a minimum price that exceeds what the item would be worth to the seller if unsold.

It follows from our discussion of avoiding the winner's curse that, provided there is some common element to the bidders' valuations, on average the winning bid will be higher in an open auction than in a sealed-bid auction. Let us suppose the bidders understand the winner's curse and correct for it appropriately when they make their bids (as is likely if they have a lot of experience in similar bidding situations). Because all bidders are guessing the same true value of the item in a common-value auction, any information about the others' estimates, direct or indirect, is useful to a bidder. The open auction conveys more information than the sealed-bid auction because a bidder can see the prices at which his rivals cease bidding. This provides indirect information about their private estimates. The more information the bidder has, the less he or she rationally distrusts his or her own information, and so the smaller is the winner's-curse correction that is to be applied to the bidder's estimate. Thus, if there is some common-value character to the situation, the seller should impose an open auction rather than a sealed-bid auction. In fact, open auctions are by far the most common in practice: according to one estimate, 75% of the auctions in the world are open auctions. Experienced auctioneers know what they are doing. Our theory has given us an argument, however, that the U.S. government is using the wrong selling method when it sells oil rights by sealed-bid auction. The government could generate more revenue by holding an open auction (or, equivalently, holding several rounds of sealed bidding, with the government informing the bidders of each others' bids at each stage).

The observation that, in a common-value setting, improving the bidders' information generates more aggressive bidding suggests another strategy for the seller seeking a high price. Sometimes the seller has some information about the true value of the item. Should the seller publicize any such information? The winner's-curse logic says that the seller should. When extra information is released, the bidders rationally fear the winner's curse less; as a result, they usually bid higher. Of course they do not always bid higher; sometimes the seller's information indicates that the value is unexpectedly low. But, on average, the policy of publicizing information induces higher bidding, because it makes the bidders less wary of the winner's curse. The extra information mitigates the effect of the winner's curse in holding down the bids. The seller could not, of course, maintain a policy of releasing information only when it was good news, for then the withholding of information would be tantamount to releasing the bad news. Auction houses do, in fact, estimate in advance the price at which artwork and antiques will sell. This is an expensive process, as it requires high-priced expertise. Not only do the auction houses release this information before the bidding, as our theory says they should, but the predictions are remarkably good: they are highly correlated with the prices actually fetched. For over 2000 Impressionist paintings auctioned by Christie's and Sotheby's in London and New York between 1980 and 1982, the average difference between the predicted sale price and the actual sale price was small: only 2.4% above or below.

Does Price Measure Value?

Does price measure value? This philosophical question can be given a precise answer for auction markets. Bidders submit bids that are below their valuations; thus prices underestimate value. But if there is a large number of bidders then, as we saw earlier, the competition drives bids up to close to valuations. Thus, with sufficient bidding competition, the winning bid is close to the valuation of the bidder who values the item the most; price does measure value.

Oscar Wilde defined a cynic as someone who knows the price of everything and the value of nothing; but what we have argued is that, if the competitive process is working smoothly enough, price is the same as value.

That auction prices measure values shows why auctions are used: they are a way of establishing the value of the item when no one knows what that value is. Consider, for example, fine wines. What is a bottle of 1953 Chateau Margaux worth? The usual method of judging wine is to rely on the subjective opinions of a few self-acknowledged experts. An economist's approach is to look at the data; to see what price the wine sells for in auctions. This is a valid measure of the wine's quality, for the auction price aggregates the opinions of all who are interested enough in wine to bid their own money in wine auctions. Orley Ashenfelter, as well as editing the *American Economic Review,* publishes a newsletter for wine enthusiasts, punningly called *Liquid Assets,* that uses auction prices to infer the quality of particular vintages. Measuring the quality of a particular vintage by what people are willing to pay for it produces different rankings from those espoused by the wine columnists.

That auctions reveal value is further illustrated by an auction of airport gates and takeoff and landing slots that occurred in February 1991. At busy U.S. airports, more landing slots are wanted by airlines than are available. Thus these slots are valuable. But since they are normally allocated by airport authorities to airlines by means of a bargaining process, in which each airline argues to the airport authorities why it is the most deserving to receive the slot, there is no market price to use as a benchmark against which to estimate the value of the slots. When Eastern Airlines was shut down, in January 1991, the bankruptcy judge responsible for selling Eastern's assets in order to repay its creditors was faced with the problem of how to attach a price to the slots. The judge's initial approach was to negotiate with individual airlines; but then the judge decided to hold an auction, cancelling the previous agreements. Competition had the desired effect: where the uncontested negotiations with individual airlines had yielded total offers of $155 million, the auction prices totalled nearly $260 million, an increase of over 70%. One spectacular price increase was for three gates at Los Angeles International Airport, for which United Airlines initially offered $6 million. When the gates were auctioned, the competition drove the price up to $21.7 million (bid by Delta Airlines). The auction prices were generally higher than the noncompetitive prices for two reasons: the auction (unlike the noncompetitive negotiations) ensured that the buyer was the airline that expected to get the most value out of using the slot; and the presence of competing bidders meant that the winning bidder could not get away with bidding too much below valuation.

A more unusual application of the idea that auction prices measure value has been developed by computer scientists working at the Xerox Corporation's Palo Alto Research Center, who have designed a system in which computers bid against other computers for the use of still other computers' capacity. In large computer networks, linking thousands of different types of computers, the assignment of computing jobs to individual computers is highly complex. A good allocation of jobs requires a huge amount of knowledge about the relative urgency of the different jobs and the capacities of the different computers. As a substitute for the expensive and time-consuming process of gathering all this information centrally to make an optimal decision, the Xerox team has designed a scheme in which the individual computers are given a "budget" and are programmed to bid for time on other computers. Willingness to pay signals a user-computer's urgency of need; and willingness to sell signals how much capacity a computer has available.

Bidding Conspiracies

We have seen that competition is a source of bargaining power: a seller can seize a large share of the gains from trade by encouraging competition among potential buyers. The buyers, however, may have a countervailing strategy: they might conspire to refrain from competing. If it works, such a conspiracy spares the buyers the discomfort of high prices.

Any attempt by game-players to form a coalition suffers from a possibly fatal weakness: the bidders are tempted to defect from the coalition. To succeed in colluding, the bidders must overcome a prisoners' dilemma. If the collusion is effective, then the bidding will stop at a lower price than would be reached if the bidding were genuinely competitive. Thus one or more of the unsuccessful bidders values the item for more than its selling price; such bidders would be better off paying more and getting the item than not getting it at all. They have an incentive, therefore, to bid above the pre-agreed collusive price. If the collusion is to be successful, this incentive must somehow be countered.

A common way for a collusion to be maintained is to use the fact that the same bidders meet each other over a long series of sales. Then the repetition of the game can be used, as we saw in Chapter 3, to generate incentives for the bidders to cooperate. In antiques auctions in Britain, for example, antique dealers use the threat of retaliation to prevent the emergence of genuine competition. If one of the dealers bids higher than the pre-agreed price, the others respond in kind. According to an observer of these auctions, "When one of the members of the ring goes against his partners, or the ring falls out for one reason or another, then it works very much to the seller's advantage as vindictive competition leads to crazy prices."

It follows that open bidding is more susceptible to collusion than sealed bidding. In an open auction, the bidders immediately see if anyone bids higher than agreed; they can then retaliate by continuing to bid up the price, in the vindictive competition just mentioned. But in a

sealed-bid auction, the bidders only learn of a deviation, if at all, after
the bidding is finished. Any retaliation must come later, in subsequent
competitions. Thus the threat of retaliation carries more force in the
open auction than in the sealed-bid auction. Collusion is more likely to
be successful under open bidding. Hence, contrary to the recommendation we derived above (that open bidding was better for the seller than
sealed bidding), if there is reason to fear collusion, sealed bidding may
be warranted.

Baseball provides a case study of collusion and competition. Before
the 1970s, there was no competition among the owners in setting players' salaries. When free agency was forced on baseball by the courts in
1975, players' salaries were bid up dramatically, providing yet another
illustration of the potency of competition as a way of extracting the gains
from trade. In an attempt to win back some of the money now going to
the players, the owners colluded once again, beginning in 1985. This
time it had to be done surreptitiously, since, unlike pre-1975, it was not
supported by the law. The repeated-game structure was used to enforce
the collusion: if, say, the California Angels were to bid for a New York
Yankees player, the Yankees would retaliate by bidding for an Angels
player.

The conspirators seek an efficient solution, for then the pie to be divided among them is at its largest. In the case of an auction, efficiency
means that the item is awarded to the bidder who values it the most.
Often, however, the bidders do not know the others' valuations. Simply
asking each bidder how much it is worth will not work: the bidders have
an incentive to exaggerate their valuations in order to get the item for
themselves. Conspirators in auctions of such diverse goods as fish, antiques, rare books, timber, and industrial machinery divide their ill-got-
ten gains in an especially apt way: they hold an auction among themselves. This succeeds because, as the theory just developed shows,
auctions reveal information about bidders' valuations—presuming, of
course, genuinely competitive bidding. The conspirators share among
themselves the difference between the price reached in the illicit auction
and that reached in the legitimate auction. This difference represents
the total profit from their collusion: it would have gone to the seller if
the bidding in the legitimate auction had been genuinely competitive.

A collusive technique used in art and antique auctions, reported by a
New York City auctioneer (who naturally disapproves of such behavior),
is notable for its intricacy. A group, or "ring," of seven dealers conspired
in the purchase of a silk tabriz oriental rug which had been put up for
auction. Before the auction, two of the seven were offered $100 not to
participate any further, and the remaining five agreed that one of their
number would bid without competition from the others. That bidder
then "won" the rug in the auction for $5000. Afterwards, the five went
to a nearby coffee house and held their illicit auction. Each secretly wrote
a bid on a slip of paper, after which all bids were listed from lowest to

highest. The five bids were: $6000, $7500, $8250, $9000, $10,000. By prearranged rules, the highest bidder in the illicit auction received the rug upon making payments to the other four, computed as follows. The lowest bidder in the illicit auction bid $1000 more than had been bid in the legitimate auction. One-fifth of this $1000 was allocated to each of the five conspirators. Now the lowest bidder was eliminated from further consideration. The difference between the second-lowest and the lowest bid was $1500; one-quarter of this was allocated to each of the remaining four bidders. The second-lowest bidder was now eliminated and the remaining three shared equally the difference between the third-lowest and the second-lowest bid, or $750. Then the second-highest and the highest bidders shared the $750 difference between the second-highest and third-highest bids. The upshot of these calculations was that the winner of the illicit auction paid $100 to the two who had refrained from bidding; $200 to the lowest bidder; $200 + $375, or $575, to the second-lowest bidder; $200 + $375 + 250, or $825, to the third-lowest bidder; and $200 + $375 + 250 + $375, or $1200 to the second-lowest bidder. Together with the $5000 paid to the seller of the rug, as bid in the legitimate auction, this meant the winner, as a result of bidding $10,000 in the illicit auction, paid a total of $8000 for the rug. This scheme shows, incidentally, that real game-players are capable of concocting mechanisms as complicated as any ever dreamed up by a game theorist.

Procurement Competition

With simple changes (substituting selling for buying, production cost for valuation, lowering price for raising it, and so on) the foregoing analysis becomes a model of a procurement competition. Instead of a single seller and competing potential buyers, there is a single buyer and competing potential sellers. The government, for example, wants to procure a new fighter aircraft from one of several qualified military contractors; or an auto firm wishes to have some parts it needs supplied by another firm.

Procurement corresponds to the private-values case to the extent that bidding firms' production costs differ because of differences in wage rates, capital stocks, and so on. It is the common-value case to the extent that the firms are guessing about, say, a new technology that the winner will have to implement. The conclusions are essentially the same as those we have already seen in the case of selling. The buyer (the procuring firm or the government) can stimulate competition by making it easy for new bidding firms to compete. The buyer can also promote competition by narrowing any inherent differences in production costs: by, for example, helping the bidders to adopt best-practice technology. And, if there are common-value aspects to the work to be done, the buyer can mitigate the winner's curse by accepting open bids and releasing any information he or she has that would help predict production costs.

How much competition matters in U.S. military procurement has been much discussed by the press and pundits. Increased competition is invariably one of the recommendations of the commissions regularly set up to recommend reforms in the Defense Department's procurement processes. The use of competition has in fact been steadily increasing since the 1960s. And there is evidence that taxpayers should be thankful for the attempts to require competition. One study comparing production contracts for various items of military equipment that had first been awarded on a sole-source basis and were later opened up to competitive bidding found that the introduction of competition drove down the price by an average of 12.5%: this provides further evidence of how much bargaining power can come from using competition.

We have been discussing procurement competition in similar terms to the selling games analyzed earlier in this chapter. In one practical respect, however, the procurement game is more complicated than the game of, say, auctioning an antique. The antique is the same no matter who wins the bidding; but a plane produced by McDonnell Douglas is not the same item as a plane produced by Lockheed. In procurement, competition is often over design as well as price; the identity of the winning bidder matters. This complicates the buyer's decision; it is no longer a simple matter to compare bids, for bids must be compared in several dimensions. On one U.S. Defense Department procurement, for example, government personnel spent 182,000 hours evaluating the proposals from four prospective contractors.

Summary

Although we have talked in this chapter about auctions, the recommendations developed here apply beyond the case of formal auctions. Most business negotiations have competition present either explicitly or implicitly. There is usually some alternative trading partner for you to turn to. The auction policies that we have discussed also apply to informal negotiations. The choice between open and sealed-bid auctions, for example, then becomes a decision whether or not to inform the people competing for your business of each other's best offer.

The main lesson from this chapter is that competition among your potential trading partners is a potent source of bargaining power. Competition can be stimulated by increasing the number of bidders or reducing the inherent differences among them. Informing the bidders of their rivals' bids and releasing any information the seller has of the true value of the item are also tactics that can in some circumstances be used to stoke the bidding competition. The benefits of competition are not exhausted when there are a handful of bidders; increasing the number of bidders significantly affects the price.

From the bidders' point of view, rational bidding involves, in the case of the open auction, remaining in the bidding until the price reaches the bidder's own valuation; and, in the case of the sealed-bid auction, guessing the valuation of the next-highest bidder and bidding this amount. The winning bidder earns profit from the difference between his or her own valuation and the next-highest valuation.

In the next two chapters, we look at the use of bidding strategies in practice. In Chapter 12 we describe the spectacular bidding competitions for Olympic Games television rights. Then, in Chapter 13, we combine our analyses of bidding and contracting to think about designing incentives for subcontractors.

12

Bidding in Olympic Competition

THIS CHAPTER tells the story of one real-life, high-stakes bidding game. Three to four years before each Olympic Games begins, a contest takes place that is as fierce as any on the track, in the pool, or in the boxing ring: the U.S. television networks bid for broadcast rights. The creative use of competition, which we analyzed in the last chapter, is illustrated by the games played by the Olympic Games organizers and the television networks. The International Olympic Committee and the local organizing body play strategically against the networks; and the networks play strategically against each other and against the Games organizers.

Winning Bids

The networks bet huge sums of money on their ability to make a profit from televising the Games. The growth in prices since the television rights were first sold in 1960 has been spectacular, as the following tables show (Tables 12.1a and b). (The first column gives actual dollar prices; the second converts prices to 1960 dollars to eliminate the effect of inflation.)

Competition matters. Compare the spectacular sums paid by the U.S. networks for Olympic broadcast rights with the totals paid by Western Europe: $5.7 million for the Calgary Winter Olympics and $28 million for the Seoul Summer Games, or respectively 2% and 9% of the U.S. prices. The broadcast rights are less valuable in Europe than in the United States because commercial television is less widespread there. But much of the price difference exists because the Europeans suppress competition among themselves by having a single body, the European Broadcast Union, negotiate with the Games organizers.

Table 12.1a. Bidding for the Summer Olympics

	Actual Dollars	1960 Dollars
1960 (Rome, CBS)	$0.4 million	$0.4 million
1964 (Tokyo, ABC)	$1.5 million	$1.4 million
1968 (Mexico City, ABC)	$4.5 million	$3.8 million
1972 (Munich, ABC)	$7.5 million	$5.3 million
1976 (Montreal, ABC)	$25 million	$13.0 million
1980 (Moscow, NBC)	$87 million	$31.2 million
1984 (Los Angeles, ABC)	$300 million	$85.7 million
1988 (Seoul, NBC)	$300–500 million	$76.4–127.3 million
1992 (Barcelona, NBC)	$401 million	$90 million*

Table 12.1b. Bidding for the Winter Olympics

	Actual Dollars	1960 Dollars
1960 (Squaw Valley, CBS)	$50,000	$50,000
1964 (Innsbruck, ABC)	$0.6 million	$0.6 million
1968 (Grenoble, ABC)	$2.5 million	$2.1 million
1972 (Sapporo, NBC)	$6.4 million	$4.5 million
1976 (Innsbruck, ABC)	$10 million	$5.2 million
1980 (Lake Placid, ABC)	$15.5 million	$5.6 million
1984 (Sarajevo, ABC)	$91.5 million	$26.1 million
1988 (Calgary, ABC)	$309 million	$78.7 million
1992 (Albertville, CBS)	$243 million	$54.5 million*
1994 (Lillehammer, CBS)	$300 million	$63.4 million*

Source: New York Times, August 24, 1989, p. B12 (from information supplied by the U.S. Olympic Committee). The asterisked (*) numbers are estimates.

Part of the growth in the prices paid by the U.S. networks is undoubtedly due to the increasing size of the TV market itself; but part is due to the increasingly sophisticated selling techniques devised by the successive Games organizers. What has been the secret of their success?

Soviet Capitalists

One of the dramatic price leaps seen in the table is for the 1980 Moscow Olympics: the real price increased almost threefold over the 1976 Montreal Games price. How did the Soviets pull off this coup? The answer is that, being clever capitalists, they skillfully used competition.

ABC had been awarded the Montreal Olympics TV rights without competition, before the other networks even had a chance to submit bids. It was alleged, but never formally investigated by the Canadian government, that some of the organizing officials had accepted bribes from ABC. The failure to use competition was a gift to ABC, which earned over three times the $25 million price in advertising revenue, and costly to the Olympics organizers, already suffering a huge cost overrun on the Games stadium. (The province of Quebec was to make debt repayments of over $1 billion over the next 20 years.)

The Soviets, in contrast to the Canadians, orchestrated a bidding war among the three networks. In Montreal and in Moscow, the Soviets hosted representatives of the networks both separately and together and encouraged them to fight for the contract. They made an outrageous initial demand of $210 million, which they later admitted was three times what they expected to get. Then they played one off against another, letting each know the details of their rivals' current best bids, and encouraging them to raise their own. "They want us to be like three scorpions fighting in a bottle. When it's over, two will be dead and the winner will be exhausted," remarked Roone Arledge, president of ABC Sports, during the bidding. As he described it, "Their plans involved an unending series of bids that went on as long as two guys were able to stand. There was a new sealed bid every 24 hours. The winner would be announced, then the losers could up the ante by a minimum of 5%." After many rounds of this, CBS thought it had struck a deal. But a month later, the Soviets reneged and announced yet one more round of bidding. They even introduced a shill—a phony bidder—in the form of an American trading company with extensive Soviet links called SATRA.

The Soviets failed to keep several promises. They promised to keep bids secret, but did not; and they reopened the bidding with new conditions after what they had announced was the final round of bidding. This may have been unethical, but it was not irrational. The mistake, if any, was made by the bidders: they should have questioned the credibility of the Soviets' statements, realizing that there was little reason to believe the Soviets would maintain their commitments. There was no prospect of dealings between the networks and the Soviet government in the foreseeable future, so the Soviets would suffer few or no consequences upon reneging.

In a further broken promise, the Soviets made a point of informing the competitors of their rivals' bids, although they maintained at the start that bids would be secret. According to a contemporary *Sports Illustrated* report, in the preliminary bidding "NBC was particularly careful about security. It wrote a two-sentence bid on a page of company stationery, sealed it in a film can, sent it by courier to New York's Kennedy airport where it was given to an airline pilot, who carried it in the cockpit to Moscow. There he gave it to the driver for NBC News, who took it straight to the committee." An hour later in New York, CBS knew NBC's bid.

The three networks threatened a boycott in protest to the broken promises. But the Soviets destroyed the networks' solidarity by playing one off against the others. After some more bidding, the deal was finally negotiated with NBC.

The Bidders' Uncertainty

In deciding how high to bid, the networks gamble on the size of the profits to be earned. Large profits can be made. For the 1988 Games, advertising sold for as much as $200,000 for 30 seconds. In 1976, advertising revenue earned for ABC over three times what they bid for the broadcast rights. Sometimes the network has made 100% or more profit. But the gamble can also fail. On a number of occasions, the "winning" network has lost many millions of dollars. (The huge sums of money involved in these decisions emphasize the importance of the ideas about rational decisions under uncertainty discussed in Chapter 4.)

At the time of bidding the networks must forecast revenues and costs three or four years hence. There are many imponderables.

Some of the uncertainty is common to each bidder. Market research can predict advertising revenues, but not perfectly. The size of advertising revenue depends on the number of viewers the advertisers expect, which in turn depends on the effect on audience size of the Games being held in a different time zone (because it means that some events cannot be broadcast live); interest in Olympic sports relative to football and baseball; the number of medals won by Americans; and so on. Changes in technology can change the revenue to be earned from the Games. Part of the reason for the high price bid by NBC for the 1992 Barcelona Games was that NBC hoped to resell some of the broadcast rights to a cable-TV network (which it eventually did, for $75 million). With pay-per-view programming, viewers are charged a fee to watch a specific event; this provides an extra revenue source in addition to the traditional one of advertising, and so increases the value of the Games TV rights. In deciding its bid, NBC gambled that enough U.S. homes would be linked to pay-per-view services by 1992 to make this a profitable revenue source. The cost of producing the broadcast depends on the current salaries of technical staff. Setting the price four years in advance involves a gamble about how much inflation there will be in the meantime and in which direction exchange rates between the U.S. dollar and the host country's currency will move. As the Montreal, Moscow, and Los Angeles Games showed, there is also the risk of some countries' boycotting the Games, with some loss in viewer interest. (This last risk, however, can be shed at a price: for the Moscow Olympics, NBC foresightedly paid Lloyds of London the equivalent of $4.6 million for insurance against nonparticipation by the United States.) In these respects, all three networks are trying to forecast the same things. Their forecasts differ, but only because they have access to different information or have made different guesses about the same numbers. (In other words, these effects tend to make the common-value case of Chapter 11 relevant here.)

As well as differences in information about effects common to all bidders, there are idiosyncratic reasons for differences in the networks' evaluations of the television rights. Broadcasting the Olympics generates extra viewers for the network's other programs, which means more to a network with low overall ratings than one with high ratings. Also, one particular network may be more skilled than the other two at presenting sports broadcasts and would therefore attract a larger audience if it won. Industry experts, for example, credit ABC with having perfected the broadcasting of the Olympics as entertainment, and its sequence of wins in the 1960s and 1970s reflects this. If specific differences such as these dominate the common sources of uncertainty, the highest bidder is likely to be the network for which winning is objectively the most profitable. (In other words, there are reasons why the private-values case of Chapter 11 is relevant here. Since we already argued that Olympic bidding also has some common-value features, we have a hybrid model, with both common-value and private-value aspects present simultaneously.)

The Winner's Curse

Apart from the Soviets' success, another big price increase seen in the above tables is for the 1988 Calgary Winter Games; this was three times the 1984 price, measured in constant prices. In part this was due to a genuine increase in value: more advertising revenue is generated whenever the Games are held in North America. In part, however, the high price was attributable to the logic of competitive bidding. The Calgary Games organizers, like the Soviets, produced a bidding war by having an open-ended bidding process. The bidding went through five rounds. CBS dropped out at $265 million; NBC's last bid was $304 million; and ABC won with $309 million.

In Calgary, ABC lost $65 million, or one-fifth of the bid price. Evidently, it overbid. Further evidence that this was overbidding comes from the prices in subsequent Winter Olympics. The 1992 Games fetched only two-thirds the Calgary price in constant dollars; this is the only case in the history of Games bidding in which the price fell from one event to the next. How can knowledgeable executives bid more than the rights are worth? In Chapter 11 we introduced the idea of the winner's curse. Winning bidders have a tendency to bid too high, finding too late that they have bid more than winning is worth. This is because, as we have seen, all the bidders are trying to estimate the same number, the inherent value of winning. Because they have different information, their estimates differ. The bidder who is willing to pay the most is the one with the most optimistic estimate. Winning conveys bad news, for it tells the winner that everyone else thinks winning is worth less than the winner does; thus the winner's estimate is likely to be too high. Perhaps the ABC executives were victims of the winner's curse when they bid the high Calgary price.

The organizers of the 1992 Winter Olympics in Albertville, France, used a different form of competition from the open bidding used for Moscow and Calgary. They sealed in an envelope a secret minimum price of $200 million, then invited the networks to submit a single sealed bid, telling them that the Games would be awarded to the highest bidder provided the bid exceeded the secret minimum. CBS won with a bid of $243 million; NBC bid $175 million plus 50% of any advertising sales over $325 million; ABC declined to bid.

Are sealed bids or open bids more effective in stimulating bidding competition? The theory of Chapter 11 says that the open auction will tend to generate the higher bids. Rational bidders anticipate the winner's curse. They do this by bidding cautiously, discounting what their own information suggests the value of winning is going to be. But they have more information in an open auction than in a sealed-bid auction, for in the open auction they know the point at which their competitors drop out and how many of their competitors are still in the bidding. These observations give them some indirect information about their competitors' private estimates of the value of winning. Thus they can afford to bid less cautiously than when their only information is their own estimate. Thus theory leads us to expect open bidding to generate higher prices; and in fact it seemed to in Moscow and Calgary.

From the point of view of the bidders, sealed-bid auctions like the Albertville one are more tricky than open auctions like the Moscow one. With open bidding, the bidders only have to decide when to cease bidding. Rational bidders stay in the bidding until the price reaches their estimate of the value of winning; immediately when the price hits this level, they drop out. With a single round of sealed bidding, bidders are faced with more uncertainty: they must estimate not only the value to them of winning, but also what their rivals are going to bid. If they bid too low, they risk losing; if they bid too high, they risk paying more than necessary. In the Albertville bidding, CBS outbid NBC by the not insignificant sum of $68 million, and the minimum price by $43 million. This is called money left on the table. With the benefit of hindsight, CBS had cause to regret the size of its bid: as Arthur Watson, president of NBC Sports, put it, "They gotta be out of their minds."

Minimum Prices

Before the negotiations for the 1984 Los Angeles Olympics, the Games organizers did extensive market research of their own, estimating that advertising revenues would be at least $300 million. On the basis of this information, they asked for a minimum price of $200 million. By using competition, they then drove the price up to $225 million. (The figure of $300 million is listed in the table above because ABC also agreed to provide facilities for other countries' broadcasters, at a cost of $75 million.) In this case, setting a minimum price made no difference to the outcome, for the bidding made it redundant. But in general (as we saw in Chapters 6 and 11) committing in advance to a minimum price is a good negotiating tactic for a seller.

For the 1994 Winter Olympics in Lillehammer, Norway, the International Olympic Committee set a minimum bid of $300 million. ABC and NBC promptly dropped out of the bidding when this was announced, saying that this figure was substantially higher than their estimates of the value of winning. This left CBS unopposed. CBS bid $300 million and was awarded the broadcast rights. CBS's bidding decision was not difficult, given that it estimated the rights to be worth more than $300 million: if there is no competition, bidding the minimum is obviously optimal. (At least, this would be the case if CBS believed the organizers' commitment to the minimum price to be irrevocable. But CBS should have questioned this commitment: what would the committee have done if CBS had called its bluff and refused to bid as high as $300 million?) The International Olympic Committee's decision was more difficult, but appears to have been made sensibly. The seller's aim in setting a minimum price is to set it high enough to induce a high bid, but not so high that no one will bid. The minimum price forced a higher bid from CBS than the competition would have required, and the fact that ABC and NBC thought the rights were not worth the minimum price suggests that it was set near its limit.

Revenue Sharing

The 1988 Seoul Games organizing body followed the Soviets' example of informing each competitor of the others' bids; before accepting NBC's final bid, it asked ABC and CBS if they would bid more. And still another technique for stimulating bidding competition was introduced. NBC won the rights not for a simple price, but for a guaranteed sum of $300 million plus royalty payments that could add as much as $200 million to the fee, depending on the size of NBC's advertising revenues. The schedule of payments was as follows (Table 12.2).

In other words, NBC was to pay $300 million plus two-thirds of any revenue in excess of $600 million to the Games organizers, up to a maximum of $500 million. The theory of Chapters 8 and 9 shows that there are three separate effects of using such a royalty scheme. First, royalties tend to induce high ultimate payments, for they in effect strengthen the competitive pressure that bidders with relatively low estimates of the value of winning can put on bidders with high estimates of the value of

Table 12.2. Contract Between Seoul Olympic Committee and NBC

TV Advertising Revenue	Payment
—	$300 million (minimum)
$637.5 million	$325 million
$712.5 million	$375 million
$787.5 million	$425 million
$862.5 million	$475 million
$900 million	$500 million (maximum)

Source: Chosun Daily News, October 5, 1985.

winning. Bidding is fiercer the smaller the differences in the bidders' evaluations of winning. Using royalties has the effect of reducing the inherent differences among the bidders and thereby stimulating the bidding competition.

Second, the royalty scheme shifts some of the risk of low advertising revenues from the winning bidder to the Games organizers. If the bidders are averse to risk, they will be willing to pay more in return for being sheltered from risk, in effect incorporating an insurance premium in their bids. Thus they bid higher in the less risky case of revenue sharing than in the fixed-price case, when the winner bears all the risk. These two effects work to the Games organizers' advantage because they raise their share of the revenue.

The third effect, on the other hand, tends to lower the total amount of revenue available to be shared between the organizers and the winning network. The royalty scheme alters the winning network's incentives (as was discussed in general in Chapter 8). Suppose that, by routinely selling advertising time, NBC could generate $712.5 million in advertising revenue; but by making an extraordinary sales effort, it could raise the revenue to $862.5 million. With an ordinary fixed-price contract, NBC would keep the entire $150 million in extra revenue. But with the royalty contract stated above, NBC would be entitled to only $50 million, or one-third, of the extra revenue. In either case NBC would bear the full cost of the extra sales effort. Hence the effect of sharing revenues via a royalty contract is to reduce the winning bidder's incentives to take actions generating extra revenue after winning the contract, and so to lower the total revenue to be shared between the network and the Games organizers.

The optimal royalty rate from the point of view of the Games organizers is determined by balancing these three effects. As a general rule, the third effect does not overwhelm the first two: some sharing of revenues by means of royalties is indeed optimal.

During the broadcasting of the Seoul games, it was reported in the press that viewer ratings were lower than expected. One media expert interpreted this as "a continuation of the erosion of network television in general." Another diagnosed it as "a general deterioration of interest in television sports overall and in the Olympics in particular." Thus at the time of the auction for the 1992 Barcelona games, rumors were rife that NBC had lost money in Seoul. The other networks therefore bid cautiously in Barcelona, and along with the media experts and the International Olympic Committee were surprised when NBC bid a record $401 million and won. Later it became apparent that the rumors were disinformation spread by NBC itself. (NBC actually boasted about its outmaneuvering of CBS.) In fact, Seoul had yielded NBC an estimated $40 to $70 million profit on its investment of about $400 million (the $300 million bid plus $100 million in production costs). This emphasizes (as we saw in Chapter 6) that knowledge is power in strategic situations. NBC, being better informed than the other bidders about the likely profits from winning, was in a strong position in the Barcelona bidding. NBC knew the returns were likely to be high, and it knew its opponents believed the returns were likely to be low.

In the initial bidding, the networks offered not fixed prices but formulas sharing revenues, along the lines of NBC's successful bid in Seoul. Unlike in Seoul, however, the International Olympic Committee rejected this type of bidding and insisted on fixed-price bidding, because of the guarantee this offered. Our analysis above suggests that this was a mistake. The sharing of revenues would have reduced the effect of the informational disparities on the bidding, lessening NBC's bidding advantage. More aggressive bidding and ultimately more revenue would have been generated by revenue-sharing bids than by fixed-price bids.

Summary

Bidding for television rights is essentially the same as bidding elsewhere, such as for a government contract, mineral rights, a painting, or the ownership of a corporation. In fact, competition is present, explicitly or implicitly, in most business negotiations, even those not formally organized as auctions. The history of Olympic bidding is instructive for how to behave in many competitive situations.

For competing bidders, the lessons are:

- Estimate the value of winning, taking account of the winner's curse.
- In an open auction, stay in the bidding until the price just reaches your estimate of the value.
- In a sealed-bid auction, set your bid by weighing the possibility of bidding too high (if your bid is not only the highest but also much higher than your nearest competitor's, you have left money on the table) against the possibility of bidding too low (if you bid for too

much profit you may bid lower than a rival bidder and lose a profitable opportunity).

For organizers of bidding competitions, the lessons are:

- Use open bidding rather than sealed bidding, for this encourages higher bids.
- Set a minimum price, high enough to force a high bid but not so high that no one is likely to bid.
- Use revenue sharing to make the bidding more competitive, but be wary of its negative effects on the winner's post-auction incentives.

V

THE STRATEGIC MANAGER

IT REMAINS to bring together the various tools of strategic decision-making. Chapter 13 uses a particular topic—how to organize a network of subcontracting firms—to summarize the ideas of bargaining, bidding, and contracting. Then Chapter 14 distils the book's lessons on how to use game theory in thinking about practical situations.

13

Organizing a Network of Subcontractors

IN THIS CHAPTER we look at how firms set incentives for their subcontractors. This will serve to illustrate and summarize ideas of bargaining, contracting, and bidding from all of the previous chapters.

Japanese industry is characterized by close and extensive links between manufacturers and their parts suppliers. According to the Ministry of International Trade and Industry (MITI), "Japanese manufacturing industry owes its competitive advantage and strength to its subcontracting structure." A U.S. automobile executive estimates that about a quarter of the cost advantage of Japanese firms is due to the superior efficiency of their supplier networks.

Small firms are more prominent in Japan than the United States. Firms with less than 50 employees account for 23% of the value of manufacturing-industry shipments in Japan and only 12% in the United States. This is because of the greater use of subcontracting in Japan: the ratio of the inputs a firm purchases to the value of its output averages 69% in Japan and 58% in the United States.

Through the 1980s, U. S. industry began changing. Increasing use became made of subcontracting in place of vertically integrated production; and suppliers were given extra design and production responsibilities. The U.S. automobile manufacturers, for example, began reassessing their relationship with their suppliers, shifting toward more work being subcontracted, longer-term relationships, fewer suppliers, earlier involvement of the suppliers in design, and more monitoring of suppliers' quality. The U.S. machine-tool industry made increasing use of subcontracting; in part, this was a quest for increased efficiency prompted by import competition. American textile firms began reducing the number of their suppliers and offering longer-term contracts; in exchange for the greater security, the suppliers were expected to time their deliveries to minimize the textile firms' inventory holdings. In response to Japanese competition in the photocopier market in the early

163

1980s, Xerox reduced its pool of suppliers from over 5000 companies to 400, trained the selected suppliers in quality control, and began involving suppliers in the design of new products. Boeing began training its suppliers in statistical quality control, working with them to reduce their costs, and involving them earlier in the development process.

These changes, moving U.S. business practices closer to Japanese business practices, recognized the indubitable success of Japanese methods of organizing production. Imitation is the sincerest form of flattery What are the gains and losses from making increased use of subcontractors? The game-theoretic ideas of bargaining, bidding, and contracting developed in the preceding chapters can be used to help us understand why the practices in use actually work.

Principal-Agent Theory and Business Practice

A buying firm—Toyota or IBM, say—is typically much larger than the firms from which it procures its supplies, so bargaining power is unequally distributed. Principal-agent theory, as we have seen, recognizes this difference in bargaining strength. The principal—in our case the buying firm—is modeled as having most of the bargaining power, in the sense that it is able to design the transaction and set the terms of the exchange. The agent—in our case the supplier firm—has two things going for it, mitigating its bargaining weakness. One is its ability to reject a proposed contract: this it will rationally do if and only if it has an alternative that, taking everything into account, is more profitable. The other is the fact that knowledge is power; and the supplier, being a specialist in the work, is likely to be better informed about the details of production conditions than the buyer. It can use its superior knowledge to its advantage in the negotiations over the price.

Contrary to the stereotype of the exploited subcontractor, Japanese subcontracting firms do in fact have alternatives; they are not forced to accept whatever the large buying firm offers. In Japanese manufacturing industry, only 17% of subcontracting firms deal with a single buyer; 20% have two customers; 26% have three to five customers; and 36% have six or more customers. Not surprisingly, the small firms are aware of the bargaining power they gain from having alternatives (as discussed earlier, in Chapter 5): in a survey of subcontractors, over a half said they wanted to increase the number of buyers with whom they contracted.

Incentives for Cooperation

The first proposition from our earlier analysis that we will use comes from Chapter 3. Ongoing relationships can serve in place of formal contracts in creating incentives for cooperative behavior.

It is a commonplace that the United States is a more litigious society than Japan, and more reliant on contracts. This is sometimes explained by cultural differences. Inter-firm relations work well in Japan, it is said, because the Japanese are an inherently cooperative people. The foregoing proposition takes us beyond such platitudes.

Buyer-seller relationships, like many other economic interactions, can have the character of a prisoner's dilemma: each party's pursuit of immediate gain can lead to an outcome that none of them likes. One way of overcoming this is to write contracts, with each firm promising to refrain from the mutually damaging activity and making itself subject to legal sanction should it break its promise. The above proposition states the game-theoretic idea that repeated interactions, like contracts, permit cooperation to occur. Repetition of a game allows the players to escape the prisoners' dilemma. In an ongoing situation, players cooperate because it is in their interest to do so. Concern for the future may prevent a firm from squeezing the last cent of profit out of its trading partner.

The sociologist Ronald Dore argues that the reason the complex Japanese subcontracting system works is the ongoing nature of the trading relationships: "goodwill and 'give-and-take' is expected to temper the pursuit of self-interest." But it is easy to exaggerate how different the United States is from Japan in this respect: U.S. businesspeople often eschew written contracts, relying instead on exchange relationships, even when considerable risks are involved. When a written contract is used, it often is deliberately vague, with much left to be resolved later by mutual consent. That long-term relationships are not unique to Japanese industry is illustrated by the case of the U.S. automobile frame manufacturer A. O. Smith, which has had a continuous relationship with General Motors for over 50 years.

The point of the repeated-game argument is that players cooperate now for fear of being cut off from profits in the future. Business practice formalizes this notion by the use of numerical ratings. A supplier firm that performs well is given a high rating, which increases the likelihood of being awarded future contracts. Ratings are used both by Japanese and U.S. firms procuring parts.

The proposition that repetition can induce cooperation has, as we saw in Chapter 3, a technical caveat of practical significance. A repeated game has many possible outcomes, only some of which involve cooperation. Repetition means that cooperation can occur; but it offers no guarantee that it will occur. There are also outcomes in which each player rationally seeks all short-run gains. No one player alone can ensure that a cooperative outcome is reached; to move from a "bad" outcome to a "good" one would require a coordinated change in all players' strategies. The significance of this is that the cooperation that can result from ongoing relationships is fragile; the system can instead be stuck in a situation in which no cooperation occurs in the absence of formal contracts.

The maintenance of ongoing relationships is easier in Japanese industry than U.S. industry because Japanese firms deal directly with far fewer suppliers than U.S. firms. But, as noted, U.S. automobile, textile, and electronics manufacturers are now reducing the number of subcontractors they deal with, so cooperation may be becoming more sustainable.

Ongoing relationships in Japan are also cemented by equity ownership and interlocking directorships, so that suppliers are identified as being in the Mitsubishi group, the Nissan group, and so on. The prevalence of such affiliations is sometimes exaggerated, however. Of the 180 suppliers with whom Toyota directly deals, Toyota has a shareholding of 50% or larger in 7, and a shareholding of less than 50% in 25; the remaining 148 are independent firms. Further evidence that linked shareholdings are not the main source of Japanese firms' ability to collaborate successfully is that suppliers do not work exclusively within the group to which they belong. In the auto industry, members of the Toyota group, for example, often subcontract for Honda and occasionally for Nissan. In the semiconductor industry, affiliated suppliers sell to firms that compete with their parent.

Specific Investment

The manufacture of an item requiring some specific investment cannot be contracted to another firm unless short-term profit-seeking can be curtailed, and be seen to be curtailed.

To see the logic of this proposition, imagine an automobile manufacturer negotiating with an electrical manufacturer for a contract to supply some generators. The generator is used only by this auto firm. In order to be able to produce it, the electrical firm must make some specialized investment in equipment. The electrical firm rationally works through forward-looking game logic. "Suppose," it reasons, "we have agreed on a price for the generator and then incurred the expenses of the specialized investment. The agreed price would have been set high enough to cover the investment costs. Now, however, we are in an uncomfortably vulnerable position. The auto firm knows that our new equipment, being specialized, cannot be used to produce anything else. It knows therefore that it could now renegotiate the price downwards: as long as it gives us a profit over our operating costs, but not necessarily over our cost of investment, it is in our interest to accept the lower price rather than have the machinery sit idle."

This awareness of the perverse incentives that would be faced by the purchasing firm after the contract is signed might prevent the supplier firm from agreeing to the contract, even though the transaction, if successfully concluded, would result in gains for both parties. It is not enough for the purchasing firm to promise not to renege. It must somehow be able to make its commitment credible. An inability to make such a commitment would result in an efficiency loss, leaving potential gains from trade unrealized.

An obvious way out of this dilemma is to appeal to the law of contract: to have the auto firm sign a contract that irrevocably commits it not to renegotiate the price for generators. But contracts never specify what would happen in all possible contingencies: that would require impossibly complicated contracts. Thus the buyer can usually find some unspecified contingency to use as an excuse for renegotiation. We have already seen an alternative solution: the incentives in ongoing relationships. The auto firm's reputation for honest dealing is valuable to it; reneging on this contract would diminish its ability to make profitable contracts with this and other suppliers in the future. Another response to situations such as this is to obviate the need for commitment. If the supplier and the purchaser were the same firm, there would be no perverse incentives. Instead of subcontracting the production of the generator, the auto firm could produce it itself.

What are the facts? Some evidence from U.S. industry suggests that the specific-investment argument is not merely theoretical speculation; the evidence shows that the make-or-buy decision is in fact conditioned by specific-capital effects. A study of the make-or-buy decisions of Ford and General Motors finds that components that required considerable engineering development effort tended to be produced in-house. Similarly, an analysis of subcontracting in a U.S. aerospace firm finds that items that were either complex or highly specialized tended to be manufactured internally.

In Japanese industry, the situation is markedly different. Toyota subcontracts to first-tier subcontractors not just parts production, but the entire responsibility for some models' design and manufacture. The specifications of most of the products of the first-tier suppliers in the Japanese automobile industry are designed by the supplier (though this is not the case for lower-tier suppliers). This involves considerable specific investment by the first-tier suppliers. Those supplying firms that undertake the largest amount of specific investment are those that have the most secure long-standing relationships with the buyer.

A more unusual way of achieving commitment not to renege on a deal is seen in the semiconductor industry, where it is common practice for a firm that has produced a new, proprietary product to license its manufacture to some competing firms. At first glance this looks as though the innovating firm is acting contrary to its interest. Why does it give up its potentially lucrative monopoly? One explanation is that this is an efficiency-enhancing form of commitment. With a monopoly producer, users might be reluctant to incur the necessary costs of specialized investment for fear of being subject to price renegotiation. By licensing the technology, the innovator makes an irrevocable commitment not to use such a strategy, because users then have somewhere else to go. This strategy might expand the market for the new technology so much as to make the innovator better off as one of several competing manufacturers than as the sole manufacturer.

Subcontracting versus In-House Production

A firm should contract out the production of a component when outside production costs less than in-house production.

This proposition is less trivial than it seems. The word "cost" should be interpreted here in the Economics 101 sense of *opportunity cost*. Opportunity cost includes not only direct costs, in the sense of things for which money must be paid—labor, raw materials, purchased inputs, etc. In addition, it incorporates indirect costs; specifically, any gains that must be foregone in undertaking this activity. When a firm accepts a contract, its (opportunity) cost is its actual production cost *plus* any profits it could have earned from alternative uses of its resources of capital and labor.

The relevance of the concept of opportunity cost for the make-or-buy decision is that, especially in Japan but also in the United States, a firm is contractually bound to at least part of its labor force: workers cannot be freely hired and fired depending on how much work the firm has. The opportunity cost of in-house production is higher when the firm's labor force is already fully utilized than when the alternative to doing this particular task is for some workers to be idle. In-house production, therefore, is more costly when the firm is operating near capacity than when there is some slack (even though an accountant might measure the cost as being the same in each case). The simple observation that in-house production is less costly when demand falls (when costs are properly measured) explains the often-noted fact that Japanese firms reduce the amount of work they contract out in a recession. Interestingly, this phenomenon is not unique to Japan. The 1972 report of a U.S. commission on government procurement concluded: "When federal procurement expenditures decline, large contractors become concerned about maintaining their work force, and operating their facilities to capacity. As a result, the large prime contractors tend to 'make' rather than 'buy'."

Another reason why the recommendation to contract out when it costs less is nontrivial is that it tersely accounts for the possibility that quality may differ depending on the source of supply. Quality is the inverse of quantity. Low-quality parts can be expensive for the buyer even if they are low-priced: some must be discarded, they cause customer dissatisfaction with the final product, and so on. Thus "cost" is to be interpreted as properly incorporating quality considerations. The ability of a supplier to deliver on time is just another aspect of the quality of what it supplies.

Yet another reason why this recommendation is nontrivial is that the cost of contracting out may vary depending on whether or not the buyer has the capability of producing the item in-house. Having the option of in-house production strengthens the buyer firm's bargaining position, for it can threaten to produce the item itself if the contract price is not low enough. In both Japan and the United States, a subcontracted item is often simultaneously produced in-house. Contrary to the general trend of increasing the extent of contracting out, both Ford and Toyota recently decided to expand their in-house electronics capacity, on the grounds that electronics have increasingly important functions in modern cars.

Evidence from both the United States and Japan indicates the importance of cost comparisons in the make-or-buy decision. A statistical study of the make-or-buy decisions of General Motors concludes that "comparative production costs are the strongest predictor of make-or-buy decisions." Similarly, a MITI survey of Japanese manufacturers that asked procuring firms why they subcontract rather than producing in-house obtained answers that generally amounted to statements about comparative costs. The stated reasons for subcontracting, ranked in order of popularity, were: "subcontractors have expert skills that the parent company does not have"; "the parent company can concentrate in its area of specialty by subcontracting"; "costs of production by subcontractors are low; "the parent company can respond readily to changes in output quantities"; "subcontracting is more efficient since parts are produced in small lots"; and "organizational efficiency falls if the parent company becomes too big."

Why are there cost differences? One important source of cost differences is that a larger firm typically pays its employees more than a smaller firm. This is an aspect of the much-discussed dualism of the Japanese economy. Contrary to common belief, however, it is not unique to Japan. One study finds that the variation between large and small firms' wage rates is on average *larger* in the United States than in Japan. Labor costs are not, however, the only source of a supplier's competitive advantage. Small supplying firms may have a cost advantage over larger buying firms because the smaller firms, having a shorter chain of command, can operate more efficiently. Suppliers' advantages are not confined to labor-intensive processes. Recent advances in computer technology have made computer-aided design and manufacturing systems (CAD/CAM) usable by small firms. As a result of the spread of computerized manufacturing to small firms, large U.S. automobile, aerospace, and machinery companies increased the amount of parts production they contract out.

The cost of external production also depends on how successfully the procuring firm manages its subcontractors. The remaining propositions are about providing supplying firms with incentives to seek cost improvements and to produce at a high quality.

Risk-Sharing versus Incentives

The fraction of production-cost increases that the buyer permits the supplier to pass on in price increases should be higher: (a) the less scope there is for discretionary cost reductions by the supplier; and (b) the more risk averse the supplier relative to the buyer. (This proposition is a direct application of Chapter 9's models.)

In the Japanese automobile and electrical industries, a contract lasts for the life of a model, usually four years in the automobile industry but shorter periods in the electrical industry. The contract agreed to at the start does not specify exact prices or quantities. Instead, the procuring firm specifies target quantities and delivery dates, which it is not, however, bound to meet. The contract also specifies the rules by which price is to be determined. An initial price is established on the basis of detailed cost estimates submitted by the subcontractor and carefully examined by the buyer. Then every six months the price can be adjusted in response to the subcontractor's production-cost changes. In adjusting the price, the subcontractor's labor, materials, and energy costs are considered separately. While the procuring firm will allow an increase in the costs of materials to be passed on as a price increase, it is less ready to agree to passing on increases in labor and energy costs. In addition, there are provisions in the contract for changing the price in response to cost changes resulting from design changes made by the buyer. These rules for changing price generate appropriate incentives for cost control provided the subcontractor has little discretionary ability to vary the cost of its materials inputs, but is able to economize on, or use wastefully, labor and energy inputs; thus the buyer has reason to give the subcontractor incentives to hold down labor and energy costs, but not materials costs.

By contrast, in the U.S. automobile industry, the auto firms traditionally allowed suppliers to pass wage increases on through escalator clauses in the contracts. Thus the contract gives no incentive to supplier firms to hold down wage costs.

A firm is risk averse, as defined in Chapter 4, if it is willing to forego some anticipated profits in order to reduce the risk that comes with these anticipated profits; it is risk neutral, on the other hand, if it always prefers the project that promises the highest expected return, regardless of how much risk the project brings. A large firm, with a diversified portfolio of projects, is likely to be close to risk neutral with respect to any one project: if a single project turns out badly, it makes an insignificant difference to the firm's overall profits. Small firms, in contrast, undertaking only a few projects, care about the risk associated with each. Econometric estimates show that small Japanese manufacturing firms are significantly risk averse, with the amount of risk aversion declining as the size of the firms rises, becoming very small but still perceptible for firms with 200 to 300 employees.

When a risk-averse small firm transacts with a risk-neutral large firm, a mutually profitable exchange of risk can be made (as discussed in Chapter 4). Suppose a simple fixed-price contract is initially considered. This would leave the small firm bearing all of the risk of unforeseen production-cost increases. The small firm, being risk averse, would be willing to accept a reduction in the price it receives in exchange for some of this risk being taken away from it; in effect, it is willing to pay an insurance premium. The large firm, being risk neutral and therefore indifferent to any extra risk from this project, also finds this proposed contract worthwhile. Both firms are made better off by the exchange of risk and price concession.

Thus a contract that allows the subcontractor to pass on a large fraction of its cost increases works well in allocating risk; but has the disadvantage of giving the subcontractor little incentive to limit his costs. An econometric study, using data from Japanese small manufacturing firms, finds that the data are consistent with the hypothesis that contractual provisions are determined by a trade-off between risk-sharing and incentives. The proportion of cost increases that were passed on as price rises averaged between 40% (in the textile industry) and 80% (in the transportation-equipment industry). Over manufacturing industry as a whole, the buying firms allowed an average of about 70% of cost increases to be passed on as price increases.

Japanese auto firms guarantee the amortization charges for any specific investment, such as in jigs and dies, that the subcontractor makes. If demand for the final product is less than predicted, the car maker raises the price paid for the part so as to cover the supplier's full investment costs. In the United States, Ford has a similar policy. Thus the car maker absorbs all of the risk of demand shortfalls on behalf of the subcontractor. For a similar reason, General Motors tends to produce in-house rather than subcontract any items for which there is large volume uncertainty, thus refraining from imposing demand risks on subcontractors.

This risk-bearing argument contradicts the conventional account of Japanese subcontracting, which depicts the procuring firm as using its disproportionate bargaining power to exploit the subcontractor, by forcing the subcontractor to bear the risk of cost and demand fluctuations; the large firm is viewed as using its subcontractors as buffers to shield itself from risk. Our theoretical argument says that a large firm that pushed undue risk onto its small subcontractors would be acting against its own interest; and the evidence indicates that firms do not, in fact, behave in this way.

Multiple Sourcing

When more than one firm is used to supply a particular item, the buyer should make the price paid to one supplier vary with the other suppliers' costs.

Should the buyer use multiple suppliers for any particular part? There is a trade-off. The disadvantage of multiple sourcing is that economies of scale may be foregone: the costs of retooling to enable a new part to be produced must be duplicated if two firms are to supply the part. If the set-up costs are high enough, as they sometimes are with high-technology production, single sourcing is optimal. One of the advantages of multiple sourcing, on the other hand, is that technological knowledge is spread through the supplier industry. This becomes to the buyer's advantage the next time a contract is let, for it ensures there is effective bidding competition (more on this below). The foregoing proposition implies a further advantage to the buyer of using multiple sourcing. The logic was discussed in a slightly different context in Chapter 9. One supplier's success in generating cost or quality improvements provides a check on how hard the other supplier is trying, and vice versa. The buyer firm can strengthen the incentives for cost-reducing or quality-improving effort by making the price it pays to each supplier dependent on relative performance; in effect imposing a contest, with a prize for the best-performing supplier.

According to common belief, Japanese manufacturers use predominantly single sourcing. This is not borne out by careful examination of the data, however. In a sample of 80 parts procured by Toyota, 28% were single-sourced; 39% had two suppliers; 19% three suppliers; and 15% between four and seven suppliers. In a sample of 90 parts procured by Honda, 38% of the parts were single-sourced; 44% had two suppliers; 16% had three suppliers; and 4% had four or five suppliers. (In this tabulation, internal production is counted as one source of supply.) A case study of a Japanese electronics firm finds that the firm seeks at least two suppliers for every component that it subcontracts. This two-vendor policy is designed to protect the firm against interruptions in supply as well as to give the firm a standard for comparing suppliers on cost, quality, and so on.

The Time-Path of Prices

If the supplier's costs are expected to fall during the course of a contract due to learning by the supplier, the buyer firm should not plan to adjust the price downwards in response to cost improvements. Rather, it should announce in advance the time-path of the price, based on its prediction of a reasonable rate of innovation, and then keep to this price path. That is, the procuring firm announces in advance, and sticks to, a price schedule that has the price falling over time, in line with a prediction of an achievable rate of cost improvement.

Once again, the logic of this proposition is similar to arguments we saw in Chapter 8. Let us compare alternative buyer policies. In the first, the buyer monitors closely the supplier's costs and at each point in time sets the price as a mark-up on cost, allowing a reasonable profit for the supplier. In the second, the buyer firm commits itself in advance to the time-path of price. Under the first policy, the supplier knows that it will earn only a fraction of the return from its effort after the price is adjusted downwards following any successful innovation it makes, so it exerts little effort. The second policy induces more innovation, for the supplier is rewarded for its effort by extra profits; it knows that the price path will be the same whether or not it innovates, but its costs will be lower if it does. Moreover, the second policy is better for the buyer firm, for it can capture some of the anticipated extra cost reductions in the price path it sets at the outset.

Japanese car manufacturers seem to follow the policy of committing in advance to a price path. Suppliers are expected to achieve cost reductions as a matter of course. For instance, one manufacturer set target average price reductions for its suppliers of 4% per annum over several years.

Pros and Cons of Bidding Competition

By promising to discriminate in favor of incumbent suppliers at the next contract-renewal time, the buyer can induce the incumbents to undertake cost-reducing innovations or to achieve high-quality outputs. But by doing so, the procuring firm foregoes some of the price-lowering it could get from bidding competition.

At the time of contract renewal, whether it is in the interest of the buyer to favor or to handicap the incumbent supplier(s) relative to alternative bidders depends on which of two effects is the larger. On the one hand, suppose there are actions an incumbent can undertake during the course of the initial contract that improve productivity or quality, but the buyer cannot immediately observe these activities and therefore cannot directly reward them by payment provisions in the current contract. Then the supplier can be encouraged to take these actions by the promise of favorable consideration at contract-renewal time (as we saw in Chapter 8). On the other hand, if the incumbent has a marked cost advantage relative to its competitors as a result of its incumbency, it faces only weak bidding competition and can bid for large profits. The buyer can correct this by favoring the nonincumbents in the contract-renewal bidding, thereby artificially increasing the competitive pressure on the incumbent.

Japanese firms rarely change the subcontractors from whom they procure parts. A 1987 survey of small Japanese manufacturers found that
68% had never changed their parent companies; 15% had changed
once; 10% had changed twice; and 7% had changed three or more
times. Evidently, there is considerable stability in the contractor/supplier
relationship, implying that new contracts are not simply awarded to the
lowest bidder, but that incumbents receive some sort of special treatment. Typically there is competition among a handful of bidders before
contracts are awarded; but the data just cited show that outsiders win
relatively rarely. How can it be in the interest of the buying firm to
forego the lower prices it could obtain by exploiting bidding competition
among potential suppliers (as discussed in Chapter 11)?

The Japanese policy of maintaining long-term relationships with subcontractors is designed to encourage good performance by the subcontractors. In the rating system used by a Japanese electronics firm, suppliers are rated on a 100-point scheme, with points given for quality,
delivery, technological level, cost-reducing effort, and cooperativeness
toward the buyer's requests. Higher-rated subcontractors are rewarded
with more contracts: for example, those contractors given the highest of
five grades made up 22% of the firm's subcontractors, but received 58%
by value of the contracts. A similar system is used in the Japanese auto
industry.

While U.S. industry does make some use of ongoing relationships, as
we have seen, it has traditionally been less willing than Japanese industry
to forego the benefits of bidding competition. Until the beginning of
the 1980s the U.S. auto industry used annual bidding for components
supply. Incumbents and outside bidders were treated equally, out of
considerations of "fairness." Lowering the price was the overriding objective. Anecdotal evidence suggests that this policy provided a disin-
centive for suppliers to produce high-quality outputs or to innovate:
there are instances of a U.S. auto firm appropriating one supplier's
designs and taking them to another supplier who had made a lower
bid. During the 1980s, however, the U.S. auto firms shifted toward the
Japanese method of supplier selection, awarding three-to-five-year contracts and putting more emphasis on rewarding quality and innovation. Similar changes have occurred in the U.S. textiles and electronics
industries.

Despite the close links between Japanese manufacturers and their suppliers, based on ongoing relationships and (in some cases) partial ownership, competitive bidding is in fact used to select suppliers. But it is
not used as rigorously as in the United States: fewer bidders are invited
to compete for any given contract, and bidding competitions are held
less frequently. How can prices that are reasonable from the buyer's
point of view be obtained without making full use of bidding competition?

First, if multiple sourcing is used, competition is not completely absent: the qualified suppliers bid for larger shares of the contract. Whenever a Japanese auto manufacturer makes a model change, for example, there is competition among those firms that have the capability of producing the components—mainly the firms that have already supplied similar items to that auto firm. Suppliers are selected on the basis of their past performance as well as their current bids.

Second, the buyer can reduce the importance of bidding competition by monitoring the suppliers. Given that the suppliers are better informed about their own production costs than the buyer, one of the roles of bidding competition is to reveal cost information. When there are many bidders, the buyer suffers little from this informational disadvantage, for the bidding competition tends to force the bids down close to actual costs. With few bidders, each can bid for a large profit, bidding well above cost. To prevent this, when there are few bidders the buyer must go to the trouble and expense of learning the bidders' costs, so as to be able to recognize and reject bids that are unduly high. In the traditional U.S. method of subcontracting, buying firms did not know the details of their suppliers' production processes; they simply relied on bidding competition to produce reasonable prices. In the Japanese system, with bidding competition downplayed, the buyer must be well informed about suppliers' costs. In fact, Japanese procuring firms regularly inspect their suppliers' production lines and their accounts; and U.S. firms are beginning to do the same.

Third, the fierceness of bidding competition does not depend on just the number of bidders. There is also a more subtle determinant of bidding competition, as we saw in Chapter 11: how different the bidders are from each other. If each of the bidders would be roughly equally efficient at doing the job, the bidding competition is aggressive even if only two bidders compete. For this reason, it is in the buying firm's interest to offer technical assistance to its potential suppliers, ensuring that each of them uses efficient techniques. This has traditionally been a role of procuring firms in Japan, and is increasingly done in the United States.

Fourth, even if only one external supplier seeks a contract, it can effectively be given competition during the bargaining over price by the buyer's option of producing some or all of his requirements in-house. This is recognized by General Motors, for example, which shows a statistically significant tendency to adopt in-house production of items for which there are few competing suppliers.

The Subcontracting Hierarchy

Subcontractors can be organized either in a single tier, with the buyer directly controlling them all, or in multiple tiers, with the buyer dealing directly only with a few first-tier subcontractors, who in turn control second-tier subcontractors, and so on. The benefit of the multi-tier hierarchy is that the buyer need know less of the details of low-level production. The cost to the buyer of operating a multi-tier hierarchy is that some profits that would otherwise go to the buyer are ceded to the first-tier subcontractors.

The classical benefit of decentralized systems is that they economize on the costly activities of acquiring and processing information. A huge amount of diverse information about production technologies, sources and prices of input supplies, and so on is held by subcontractors in any reasonably complex modern manufacturing process. To operate a single-tier hierarchy efficiently, the buyer must understand all of the production processes that are involved. In a multi-tier hierarchy, by contrast, less information need be collected and collated, for control rights are closer to the source of the information.

Weighed against the gains to the buyer from decentralizing the subcontracting system is a disadvantage of decentralization: by implementing a multi-tier subcontracting system, the buyer cedes some profits to high-tier subcontractors. As a general matter, as we saw in Chapter 5 in our discussion of the bargaining power that comes from the ability to make commitments, the right to set contractual terms is valuable: extra profits can be earned by the person who defines the contract. When a first-tier subcontractor sets the rules under which a second-tier subcontractor operates, these rules reflect the interests of the first-tier subcontractor, rather than those of the ultimate buyer. Thus the cost to the buyer of using a multi-tier hierarchy is that the first-tier subcontractors can earn extra profits from their right to set the terms of the lower-tier firms' contracts; these profits would go to the buyer in a single-tier hierarchy.

Japanese subcontracting has a multi-tier, pyramidal structure. The buying firm deals directly with a relatively small group of first-tier suppliers. In turn, the first-tier suppliers control a larger number of second-tier suppliers; and so on down to third-tier or fourth-tier suppliers. A firm's technological sophistication is lower the further down the hierarchy it is. First-tier suppliers in the automobile industry both design and produce entire vehicles; second-tier suppliers have enough expertise to design processes but not products; and third-tier suppliers have still less technological expertise. The size and complexity of this hierarchy is exemplified by Toyota, which in 1980 had 168 first-tier subcontractors, 4700 second-tier subcontractors, and 31,600 third-tier subcontractors.

In the United States, the buying firm traditionally exerted direct control over most of its subcontractors, rather than using a hierarchy. This has changed. For instance, until the early 1980s, General Motors assembled car seats in its vehicle assembly plants, purchasing components—frames, springs, padding, covers, and so on—from eight to ten suppliers. Now it buys complete seats from a supplier, who is delegated the task of procuring the parts from the other suppliers. Thus where there used to be one layer of subcontractors there are now two. This is still less hierarchical than the Japanese auto industry, however, in which seat assembly is the task of second-tier subcontractors, who procure components from third-tier subcontractors.

A measure of the costs of administering subcontractors is the number of people involved in procurement. In 1986, General Motors, producing 6 million cars, employed 6000 buyers to procure goods and services. Toyota, producing 3.6 million cars, employed only 340 people in purchasing. A G.M. plant manages on average 1500 suppliers; a Toyota plant deals directly with an average of only 180 suppliers. With Toyota's multiple-layer hierarchy, much of the procurement is done by the subcontractors themselves. Of course, in a multi-tier hierarchy, the procurement costs are still borne by the buyer, but only indirectly: the costs incurred by first-tier subcontractors in administering lower-tier subcontractors must ultimately be covered by the payments from the buyer to the first-tier subcontractors.

The U.S. commercial-aircraft industry operates a subcontracting hierarchy that resembles the Japanese model. Two-thirds or more of the value of airframes is subcontracted. First-tier subcontractors design some of the components and assemble major sections; below them, thousands of subcontractors compete on price, delivery, and quality to produce systems and components.

A high-tier subcontractor in a multi-tier hierarchy earns extra profits from its right to design the contracts for the lower-tier subcontractors; these profits are attributable to its position in the hierarchy. The buyer can use these extra profits as part of the incentive system. Low-tier subcontractors are promised promotion to a higher tier, and consequently higher profits, should they perform well over a series of contracts. Promotion to a higher tier is explicitly part of the reward system in Japanese subcontracting.

Summary

Our game-theoretic analysis provides several lessons on how to organize interfirm relationships in subcontracting. Whether an item should be contracted out depends on the relative cost—measuring cost as opportunity cost—of in-house and external production; and on the amount of specific investment needed to produce the item. Policies toward suppliers must balance contradictory goals. Pricing policies should be designed to give subcontractors incentives to lower production costs and raise quality; but the pursuit of incentives should be tempered by the fact that it is not in the procuring firm's interest to push undue risk onto the subcontractors. Implementing a hierarchy of subcontractors provides the informational benefits of decentralization, but at the cost of ceding some extra profits to the first-tier subcontractors. Bidding competition is the most effective way of selecting efficient suppliers; but its use should be tempered by the value of maintaining ongoing relationships.

14

Putting It All Together

IF THIS BOOK has been successful, it has persuaded you that game theory is a useful tool for thinking about business situations. It is of course a limited tool. It cannot provide all the answers. The world is more complicated than any game-theoretic model. No real-life decisions can safely be left to game theory to answer. But game-theoretic analysis can be a useful tool, along with other kinds of analysis, in the decision process.

Game theory is a tool for thinking about interactive situations, where what one person should do depends on what others do, and no one individual controls the outcome. Thinking strategically involves recognizing the way in which the your decisions interact with the other players' decisions. It means looking ahead, anticipating the others' plans. And it requires facing up to uncertainty, taking actions before you know all you might want to know about what the consequences of your action will be. Deciding your best action, as we have seen, involves putting yourself in the others' shoes: you must predict the others' actions before you can make an intelligent decision on what action to take.

How do you use the game theory described in this book to think about some particular business situation? The first step is to ask and to answer several questions. (Technically, game theorists *define* a game by the answers to these questions.) Often there will be no unique answer: it will depend on how much detail you want to go into. In analyzing a situation as a game, you face trade-off between realistic complexity and comprehensible simplicity. But by merely answering the following questions you will already gain some understanding of the situation. After they are answered, you can begin game-theoretic analysis.

1. *Who are the players?* In principle everyone in the world is a player in any game. To keep the analysis manageable, it is usually necessary to exclude some players who do affect the situation, but whose

effect is judged to be less important than the central players'. There is also a question of how to define the players. For example, are the players firms; or divisions within firms; or individuals within the divisions? The answer depends on the particular question to be addressed.

2. *What options are open to the players?* Again you must select a few crucial variables from what is often a large number of options. For example, firms may compete using price, or price and output, or price and research-and-development expenditures, or price and quality; and so on.

3. *What goals are the players pursuing?* For example, is it more accurate if you depict a firm as seeking high profit, or sales, or market share, or any of the multitude of possible aims?

4. *What are the sources of gains from trade?* Over what issues can the players possibly agree? Where are there conflicts? To what extent are the the different players' aims complementary with each others'? Can the players create previously unnoticed gains from trade, ways of making all participants simultaneously better off?

5. *Can any of the players effectively make commitments?* The most potent of bargaining techniques is, as we saw in Chapter 5, the refusal to bargain. But for this to work, it must be done credibly; the other players must believe the "or leave it" part of the take-it-or-leave-it demand. Is there anything in the situation that makes it possible for one or more of the players to make credible commitments?

6. *What is the time structure of the game?* Are any of the players' decisions likely to be conditioned by their concerns for their reputations? Games played repeatedly, as we saw in Chapter 3, make cooperation possible in situations where it would not be if the game were played only once. Concern about the future can make it in players' interests to act honorably.

7. *What is the information structure of the game?* Information, as we saw in Chapter 6, is a source of bargaining strength. What does one player know that is relevant that the others do not know? How can that player take advantage of this private information? Conversely, what defensive measures can the other players take to mitigate their informational disadvantage?

Just answering these seven questions is by itself a fruitful exercise: you will learn much about the structure of the situation, even before you use any of the techniques of game theory.

After answering these questions, you can start doing game theory: trying to understand the logic of the situation, finding the players' best actions. The ideas on negotiating, contracting, and bidding outlined in the previous chapters can be used to make educated guesses about how the players are likely to behave.

Game theory brings out hidden links; it shows the common structure underlying apparently diverse situations. We saw in Chapters 8 and 9, for example, that many different contracting situations—involving royalties, commissions, piece rates, managerial incentives, cost-overrun provisions, and so on—can all be understood in terms of the players' responses to incentives, information, and risk. Seeing these links enables you to generalize from your experience: to see how to apply lessons learned in one situation to others.

The Appendix discusses some games in more detail (which necessarily means some mathematical detail) than in the previous chapters. This is followed by a section called More Games that can be used to sharpen your game-theory skills. Finally, there is a Reading Guide to help you find other sources of information on game theory and its applications.

Game theory is not only a powerful tool of business analysis, but also a useful habit of mind: a way of clarifying your thinking in business and in life.

APPENDIX

The Details of the Games

IN USING game theory, it is often helpful to proceed in three stages, with three distinct thought modes. In the first stage, a simplified model of the situation, that is, a *game,* is analyzed. The game is contrived so that it can be thoroughly understood. It is completely self-contained; the exercise is to deduce how the rational players will behave, given their specified aims and the actions available to them. At this stage, we put on blinkers; we must resist the temptation to add any additional features, however realistic they might be. The rigorous model, because it is simplified, prevents woolly thinking; it allows us to sort false ideas from valid ones.

In the second stage, we extrapolate from the game to actual strategic interactions, to see what lessons about the world our simplified model offers. How does the game relate to the world? What actual interactions does our game capture a piece of? What general lessons can be extracted from the game? As was argued in the text, many business decisions have the same basic structure; game theory illuminates the common structure underlying a wide variety of situations.

A third thought mode is also necessary. What are the limits of our analysis? What of importance is left out? Did the process of simplification distort the true logic of the situation? This third stage, while essential, needs to be discussed less than the other two, because it is the easiest. It merely requires the normal kind of healthy skepticism needed toward new ideas of any sort.

Most of the foregoing text has been in the second mode. A thorough understanding of game theory, however, requires working in the first mode as well, as is done in what follows. The English language is not a precise enough instrument with which to solve games of any complexity; we must use mathematics. Game theory's central question—"What is the *best* decision?"—is, after all, inherently mathematical, for it involves quantitative comparisons. Mathematics, it has been said, has no symbols for confused ideas. In what follows, the games discussed in the text are reformulated in more precise terms, in order to check that the ideas are not in fact confused. The mathematics used is of the simplest possible kind; nothing more is required to work through these games than a hazy memory of high-school algebra.[1]

Working through a precisely specified game requires some disciplined thinking. But it turns out to be quite addictive. Solving games is fun.

Chapter 3: Understanding Conflict and Cooperation

A classic game that illustrates best-response reasoning in a slightly richer setting than the games of Chapter 3 is the oligopoly game introduced in a remarkable book published by the French mathematician Augustin Cournot in 1832, anticipating game theory by more than a century (*Researches into the Mathematical Principles of the Theory of Wealth*. London: Macmillan, 1897).

COMPETITION BETWEEN TWO FIRMS

Two firms, called A and B, produce an identical product. The more they produce the further the price is driven down; specifically, the relationship between price p and total output q is $p = 13 - q$. Each unit sold costs $1 to manufacture. The two firms meet each other only once in the market. How much will each firm produce, seeking the highest possible profits?

Represent the output of firm A by q_a and firm B by q_b, so total output q is equal to $q_a + q_b$. The profit earned by firm A is revenue minus cost, or $pq_a - q_a$, or $[13 - (q_a + q_b)] q_a - q_a$. Notice the essential game-theoretic aspect of this: firm A's profit depends on its rival's decision, q_b; therefore its own decision q_a must be based on its conjecture of what its rival will do. A's best action is not independent of what B does, and vice versa. In deciding how much to produce, each firm must put itself in the other's shoes, to calculate what it would be rational for the other to do.

To find firm A's best output, temporarily suppose it conjectures some particular but arbitrary output from firm B, q_b. By rearranging the above profit expression, firm A's profit is equal to $q_a[(12 - q_b) - q_a]$. Hence the output that maximizes firm A's profit is $(12 - q_b)/2$. What we have found is firm A's best response to whatever firm B produces; this is firm A's *best-response function*. The more A believes B will produce, the smaller is A's own profit-maximizing output. If we repeated the analysis on firm B's behalf we would find that firm B's best response to any particular output q_a that it predicts firm A will produce is given symmetrically: $(12 - q_a)/2$ is firm B's best-response function.

So far, we have said nothing to pin down what level of q_b it is rational for firm A to predict. Let us now assume that not only outputs, but also beliefs about rival's output decisions, are rational. That is, let us require that the output that firm A conjectures for firm B is itself profit-maximizing for firm B; and vice versa. At the equilibrium (strictly, Nash equilibrium) of the game, each is being simultaneously rational, given the other's action; each firm is playing its best response. In the algebra, this means that we can replace the q_b in firm A's best-response function by firm B's own best response. Thus firm A's equilibrium output satisfies $q_a = (1/2)[12 - \{(12 - q_a)/2\}]$. Solving this equation, we get $q_a = 4$. Symmetrically, firm B's equilibrium output is $q_b = 4$. The resultant profit for each firm is \$16.

This outcome is a kind of prisoners' dilemma, in that a coordinated decision to maximize joint profits would have each firm producing less: each firm would produce 3 units of output (instead of 4), and earn \$18 profit (instead of \$16). (To see this, notice that total profit is $(13 - q)q - q$ which is maximized by setting the total output q at 6 units, yielding a total profit of \$36; divided equally, this gives each firm an output of 3 units and a profit of \$18.)

REPEATED COMPETITION

Two firms compete as in the previous game, with the difference that, instead of facing each other only once, they meet repeatedly, once in each time-period over an indefinite time horizon. How much will each produce in each period?

Cooperation can be achieved, resulting in higher profits than in the one-shot game, if the firms adopt the following strategy. Each firm begins by producing the output consistent with maximizing joint profits; that is, 3 units each. In subsequent periods, the firm continues to produce 3 units, unless its rival has in some earlier period deviated by producing more, in which case the firm retaliates by producing the one-shot-game output of 4. Will this threat of retaliation serve to discourage deviation? Consider firm A's computation of the costs and benefits of deviating. (Firm B's computations are identical.) Given that firm B is producing 3 units, the highest current-period profit firm A can make is \$20.25. (This is because its profit from producing q_a, given firm B produces 3 units, is $[13 - 3 - q_a]q_a - q_a$, which is highest when q_a is 4.5, resulting in a profit for A of \$20.25.) In subsequent periods, after B retaliates in accordance with the above strategy, the game is the same as the one-shot game, so A earns \$16 in each period. If, on the other hand, A does not deviate, it repeatedly earns its share of the joint-maximum profit, or $18. Which of these streams of profits—an initial $20.25 followed by a perpetual stream of $16, or a perpetual stream of $18—is higher? The answer depends upon how present and future sums are compared. Suppose a sum of money one period in the future is worth a fraction d of the same sum now; that is, the discount rate is d (where d is some number between zero and one). Then the firm values the continuing stream of $18 profits at $18 + 18d + 18d^2 + 18d^3 + \ldots$, which is equal to $18/(1 - d)$. This is to be compared with the profit stream should the firm deviate this period, the present value of which is $20.25 + 16d + 16d^2 + 16d^3 + \ldots$, which is equal to $20.25 + [16d/(1 - d)]$. It does not pay firm A to deviate if the former sum is larger than the latter, which simple algebra shows to be the case if d is not too small; specifically if d exceeds 0.53. The argument applies symmetrically to firm B. Thus if future returns weigh heavily enough—if the discount rate is close enough to one—cooperation can be sustained in the repeated game.

The repeated game has many other equilibria. To see one of these other equilibria, suppose firm A believes firm B will produce the one-shot-game output of 4 units in each period regardless of what A does. Then by the logic given above, A's best response is to produce 4 units in each period. But then it is rational for B to produce 4 units in each period. The beliefs are self-validating; the inefficient outcome is an equilibrium of the repeated game.

Chapter 4: Weighing Risks

To develop the theory of decision-making under uncertainty in more generality, we depict the decision-maker as having a *utility function*. The utility or satisfaction that the individual derives from being able to spend an income (or wealth) of X is $U(X)$, where U is the utility function. We assume that more is better than less, so utility increases with increases in income.

Suppose a particular decision will yield a profit of either $\$X_1$ or $\$X_2$, with probabilities respectively p_1 and p_2. (The extension to an arbitrary number of potential outcomes is obvious.) The corresponding expected utility is computed as $p_1U(X_1) + p_2U(X_2)$. We hypothesize that rational decision-making under uncertainty means choosing the action that yields the highest expected utility.

The expected dollar return from this gamble is $p_1X_1 + p_2X_2$. Imagine offering the individual the choice between receiving this expected return for sure and receiving the result of the gamble. Define an individual to be *risk averse* if he or she strictly prefers receiving the expected return for sure; and define him or her to be *risk neutral* if he or she is to be equally well off in either case.

Suppose that the rate of increase in utility falls as income rises: in common-sense terms, this means that a given individual values an extra dollar less the higher his or her income is. Then the individual is risk averse: the individual prefers the expected income for sure to the gamble. The common-sense of this result is seen by considering an individual faced with a 50–50 chance of losing and gaining $100. The fact that marginal utility is declining means that more is lost in utility terms from the $100 loss than is gained from the $100 win. Thus the individual prefers the certainty of no gain or loss to this gamble; he or she is risk averse.[2]

The risk premium was defined in the text to be the amount the individual would be willing to pay to be sheltered from risk. If Y represents the distribution of possible outcomes, the risk premium R is defined (using E to mean expected value) by $U(EY - R) = EU(Y)$: that is, getting for sure the expected dollar return minus the risk premium is equivalent to facing the gamble. The size of R depends on both the shape of the utility function U (the individual's inherent attitude toward risk), and the size of the gamble (the probabilities p_1 and p_2 and the expected sum of money Y).

In some of the model-building later in this Appendix, for the sake of simplicity of analysis, we will suppose that the uncertainty takes a particular form. We will assume that, while the decision-maker does not know the size of some variable, he or she does know that it falls somewhere between two numbers a and b (1 and 10, for example), and that any number between these bounds is equally likely. This is convenient to assume because it makes calculations involving the probabilities and expected returns conveniently simple. Imagine a computer that can produce at random any number between a lowest number a (or 1) and a highest number b (or 10); the computer is programmed so that any number between these bounds is equally likely. (This is called the *uniform probability distribution*.) What is the probability that the number the computer prints out is less than some given number x (say, 3)? A little algebra shows that this probability is $(x - a)/(b - a)$ (or, in the numerical example, 2/9). This is because the probability of the number being less than x (or 3) is just the ratio of the weight of numbers less than x (or 3) to the weight of all the possible numbers between a and b (or between 1 and 10). Similar reasoning shows that the probability of drawing a number that exceeds x (or 3) is $(b-x)/(b-a)$ (or, in the example, 7/9). As a check, notice that the probability that the number drawn is either above x or below x is $(b-x)/(b-a) + (x-a)/(b-a)$, which equals, as it should, 1 (or, the probability the number is either above 3 or below 3 is 7/9 + 2/9, or 1). We will use probability calculations like these in our game-solving later in this Appendix (specifically, in the games associated with Chapters 8, 9, and 11).

To focus our attention on the particular strategic issue being investigated, most of the analysis in this book sidesteps issues of risk sharing, by representing individuals as being risk neutral. The exception to this is Chapter 9, where the focus of attention is risk aversion itself: how different individuals' having different degrees of risk aversion affects the structure of transactions.

Chapter 5: Gaining Bargaining Power

Alternative opportunities and costs of delay were discussed in Chapter 5 as sources of bargaining power. It is worth checking whether these arguments stand up in rigorous models. One role of theorizing is to separate the wheat from the chaff: to sort correct propositions from plausible but incorrect propositions. As the physicist Arthur Stanley Eddington said in another context, it is "a good rule not to put overmuch confidence in the observational results that are put forward until they are confirmed by theory."

To model bargaining games rigorously, let us extend the notion of rationality: as well as requiring that actions be rational, let us require that the beliefs themselves be rational. For beliefs to be rational, they must stand up to a series of questions of the sort: "Given what I believe he is going to do, what must this mean he believes I will do? But then what must he believe that I believe he will do?" And so on through a possibly infinite chain of beliefs about beliefs. Solving a game involves finding actions for the players that are simultaneously rational for all of them; none has an alternative action that would make him or her better off given the others' plans of action. The players implicitly coordinate their expectations of what each other is going to do: the outcome of the game is such that, to quote Thomas Schelling, "each expects the other not to expect to be expected to retreat." We have already seen, in the two-stage bargaining game of Chapter 2, an example of this kind of reasoning. There we learned that having the right to make the final offer confers considerable bargaining power. In what follows we shall analyze two other deliberately contrived bargaining situations which, remarkably enough, do have unique outcomes if both buyer and seller go through the rational-beliefs chain of reasoning. In these models there is no deadline; in principle, the bargaining could go on forever. These examples highlight two of the sources of negotiating strength or weakness discussed in Chapter 5: the attractiveness of the bargainers' alternative opportunities, and the bargainers' patience (or, conversely, their costs of delay).

We suppose that the negotiation process has the following structured (and artificial) form. The seller makes the initial offer of how to divide the $100, which the buyer can accept or reject. If the buyer rejects it, he makes a counteroffer after a certain time has elapsed; we can think of the delay as one day. The seller then chooses whether or not to accept the buyer's offer; if she rejects it, the process is repeated, indefinitely if necessary.

BARGAINING WITH ALTERNATIVES
TO AGREEMENT

In the bargaining between seller and buyer over the division of the $100
gain from trade, there is a chance that events beyond the control of the
bargainers will cause the bargaining to break down irrevocably: at each
stage of the game, breakdown can occur with probability p. Thus the cost
of delaying agreement is the risk of having the bargaining break down.
Each of the bargainers has some outside alternative to be invoked in the
event of a breakdown in the negotiations; we will refer to these outcomes
as their fallbacks, and represent the value of these fallbacks to seller
and buyer as f_s and f_b dollars respectively. Each bargainer knows the
other's fallback. What division of the $100 will the rational bargainers
agree to?

Before solving this game, notice that for the negotiation to be at least
potentially fruitful, the fallback returns must be small relative to the pie
being negotiated over. Specifically, it must be that $f_s + f_b$ is less than
$100. The total gains to both bargainers from a successful trade are
$100 - f_s - f_b$.

A good negotiator looks several moves ahead. To solve the two-stage
game of Chapter 2, we had to look forward to the second (that is, the
final) stage. The present game, however, has no final stage; the bargainers must predict a potentially infinite future. This would take a long time
to do. Fortunately, it turns out that to find the bargainers' rational actions, we must, on their behalf, look forward only as far as the third stage
to calculate what is the least the other will settle for. The logic is rather
intricate (and as difficult as any we will encounter in this book), but it is
rewardingly elegant. It uses to the full the fundamental game-theoretic
idea that rational behavior in interactive situations requires you to put
yourself in the other person's shoes; and it shows the necessity of thinking several moves ahead.

Suppose the game has reached the third stage without agreement. By
the rules of the game, it is the seller's turn to make the offer. Define z
to be the *most* that the seller can induce the buyer to let her have in the
third stage. Thus, by definition of z, the seller rationally demands z and
the buyer rationally agrees. (We can presume that z is not smaller than
the seller's fallback f_s.) The question to be asked is: what is z?

Now go backwards in time and imagine we are in the second stage.
What can the buyer offer the seller that the seller will accept? The buyer
knows that the seller knows that she, the seller, will get z if she forces the
bargaining into the third stage. But the seller also knows there is a probability of p that the bargaining will break down between her rejection of

the offer and the start of the third stage, in which case she would get only f_s. Hence the seller will be willing to accept something less than z in the second stage. By rejecting the buyer's offer, the seller takes a gamble: she gets z with probability $(1 - p)$ (that is, the probability that there is no breakdown) and f_s with probability p; thus she gets, on average, $(1 - p)z + pf_s$ upon rejecting the offer. The buyer correctly reasons that this is what he must offer the seller in the second stage; this leaves the buyer with the remainder, that is, $[100 - (1 - p)z - pf_s]$.

We go further backwards now to the first stage. By parallel reasoning, the seller deduces that from her point of view the best offer to the buyer is something less than what the buyer would get by waiting until the second stage; the buyer is willing to accept precisely $\{(1 - p)[100 - (1 - p)z - pf_s] + pf_b\}$. So the seller gets the difference between \$100 and this amount, or $100 - \{(1 - p)[100 - (1 - p)z - pf_s] + pf_b\}$.

The final step in the argument is to observe that the third stage, once it is reached, looks exactly the same to the bargainers as the first stage did: there is still \$100 to divide; it is the seller's turn to make an offer; and there is an infinite stream of potential stages still ahead. Thus the best the seller can do in the first stage must be the same as the best the seller can do in the third stage, once the game reaches it. Thus it must be that $z = 100 - \{(1 - p)[100 - (1 - p)z - pf_s] + pf_b\}$. Solving this clumsy but elementary equation we find that, from the \$100, the seller gets an amount $z = [100 + (1 - p)fs - fb]/(2 - p)$.

We learn several things from this formula. Outside opportunities are a source of bargaining power. From the formula, z becomes larger as f_s increases: the better the seller's outside options, the more ready the buyer will be to settle. Conversely, z is smaller the bigger f_b is; if the buyer's options improve, the seller must settle for less. (This effect can be checked by plugging numbers into the formula. For example, if the seller gets \$10 in the event of breakdown and the buyer gets nothing, and there is a 1% probability of breakdown within any stage, then the agreement gives the seller \$55.23 and the buyer \$44.77. If the seller instead had a fallback of \$45, she would get \$72.64 from the agreement and the buyer \$27.36.)

If breakdown is very likely, so that p is close to one, then the seller's payoff z is approximately $100 - f_b$. This is because, with breakdown likely, the first stage is probably the last, so the seller can demand all of the \$100 less what the buyer gets in the event of breakdown. If, on the other hand, breakdown is unlikely so that p is close to zero, then the seller receives a payoff of $z = [100 + f_s - f_b]/2$. In particular, if in addition the bargainers have equally attractive alternative opportunities, so that f_s is equal to f_b, then each gets \$50; the rational agreement is a 50–50 split of the pie.

The bargaining game with costs of delay mentioned in the text is as follows.

BARGAINING UNDER COSTS OF DELAY

Waiting is costly to the bargainers: $1 in the future is worth less to each than $1 now. Specifically, the seller discounts future returns at rate d_s and the buyer discounts future returns at rate d_b, where both d_s and d_b are numbers less than one. (This means that the seller, from the perspective of the first stage, values the prospect of receiving $x in the second stage at xd_s; similarly, $x received two stages in the future is worth $x(d_s)^2$ now, $x received t stages away is worth $x(d_s)^t$ now, and so on.) Each bargainer knows the other's discount rate. Each gets nothing in the event of breakdown. What division of the $100 will the bargainers agree to?

The solution is, as we will see, that the seller, who makes the first offer, gets a sum of money equal to $[100(1 - d_b)]/[1 - d_s d_b]$ and the buyer gets the rest of the $100, or $[100d_b(1 - d_s)]/[1 - d_s d_b]$. In particular, what is the solution if each bargainer has the same discount rate? Calling the now common discount rate d, we see after a little algebra that the seller's return is $100/[1 + d]$ and the buyer's return is $100d/[1 + d]$. Since d is smaller than one, by definition, this means that the seller gets an advantage from making the first offer. (This is because, at the time of the first offer, the buyer knows that his causing a delay would shrink the pie for both of them; and the seller can extract some profit from this.) Finally we consider what happens if we make the delay costs not only equal, but small; that is, set d_s and d_b closer and closer to one. This can be interpreted in two ways: either the bargainers' costs of delay are approaching zero, or the time between offer and counteroffer is approaching zero. Putting d equal to one in the preceding expressions, we find that the rationally agreed settlement gives each bargainer $50. In this case the bargainers agree to a 50–50 split. These results are obtained as follows.

We require that, at the end of the negotiation, each bargainer not only do the best he or she can given his or her assessment of what the other will accept, but also base this on beliefs that are rationally formed. This, as we saw in Chapter 5, involves an infinite chain of reasoning of the form: "If I believe this is the highest price my opponent will accept, what must that imply he or she believes about what I will accept? But then what must my opponent believe that I believe that he or she will accept?" And so on, indefinitely. To deduce what is rational behavior in this setting, it turns out once again to be enough to look ahead to what will happen if the third stage is reached. Suppose $z represents the highest payoff the seller can attain should the third stage be reached; that is, in the third stage, the seller rationally asks for $z and the buyer rationally agrees. Go back now to the second stage, in which it is the buyer's turn to make the offer. If the buyer offers the seller an amount of zd_s (which is less than z since the discount rate d_s is less than 1), then the seller is just as well off as she would be should play proceed to the third stage. (By the nature of discounting, the seller is equally happy with $\$zd_s$ now as with $\$z$ one stage later.) Hence the seller would rationally accept this second-stage offer, leaving the buyer with the remainder of the $100, that is, $\$(100 - zd_s)$ in the second stage. This is the best the buyer can do. Now go back to the first stage. The seller knows that, by the nature of discounting, the least the buyer will rationally accept in the first stage is $\$(100 - zd_s)d_b$; this gives the seller the remainder, which is $\$[100 - (100 - zd_s)d_b]$.

The final step in the argument is to notice that nothing in the structure of the negotiation changes over time. The game in the third stage, viewed from that stage, is the same as the game in the first stage, viewed from the first stage. We started by defining the best payoff the seller could attain in the third stage to be $\$z$. And we showed that the best she could attain in the first stage was $\$[100 - (100 - zd_s)d_b$. Since the game is essentially unchanged, these two sums of money must be equal: that is, it must be that $z = [100 - (100 - zd_s)d_b]$. When we solve this equation for z, we get $z = [100(1 - d_b)]/[1 - d_s d_b]$.

We could now repeat the argument, defining y to be the *lowest* payoff to the seller in the third stage. The details are left for the reader to check, but we would find by a symmetrical argument that $y = z$. The seller's lowest payoff is the same as her highest. Thus the outcome of fully rational behavior by both negotiators is unique. The outcome is as stated above.

Commitment was discussed in Chapter 5 as a source of bargaining power. In actual negotiations, one of the negotiators sometimes has the ability to commit himself or herself to a position. But often neither does. The idea of commitment remains useful as a theoretical device, however, regardless of how realistic it is. As well as being a real-world bargaining strategy, commitment is a game theorist's tool that allows us to dissect strategic interactions. The commitment assumption enables us to look at one issue at a time. Strategic interactions can become highly complex even in stylized models, and more so in real situations. This is especially the case, as we will see, when we introduce private information into our models. By assuming that one of the players can make commitments, even though it is not necessarily justified by the facts of the situation, the game theorist can grasp a part of the problem. Commitment simplifies the analysis because, with commitment, the strategic interaction goes in only one direction. As we have discussed, the essential feature of decision-making in games is that each of the players must put himself or herself in the other's shoes to predict how the other is going to act. If one player can make commitments, then half of this process is cut away. The player who can commit, in deciding what position to commit himself to, must predict the other's responses. But the other player, the one who cannot commit, does not have to go through this strategic reasoning, for the committing player moves first. Thus the assumption of commitment sidesteps the complexities of bargaining that we saw in the two previous games, and allows us to focus on the main issue in which we are interested. We will call the person who can make commitments the *principal,* and the other person the *agent.* The principal can be thought of as the more active party, the one whose decisions we are most interested in. In Chapters 6, 8, 9, and 11, we take advantage of the modeling simplifications that the assumption of commitment offers; we assume one of the parties can make take-it-or-leave-it offers.

Chapter 6: Using Information Strategically

The following model represents the behavior of a seller who is handicapped by a lack of information about how high a price the buyer would be willing to accept.

SELLING IN IGNORANCE OF THE BUYER'S VALUATION

A seller offers an item to a potential buyer. The seller values the item at zero if unsold. The buyer knows exactly how much it would be worth to him to own the item; but the seller does not know this. In the seller's perception, the buyer could value it at anything between zero and $200, with any value in between equally likely. The seller is able to commit to her offer; what price will she demand?

Since the seller can credibly commit to her offer, the entire game takes the form of the seller naming her price and the buyer accepting or declining. Let us represent the buyer's valuation as $\$b$; the buyer knows b, the seller does not. As we have seen, if the seller knew the buyer's valuation, she would demand as high a price as the buyer would be willing to accept, namely b; the seller therefore would capture all of the gains from trade. But the seller cannot do this if she does not know b. The seller is not completely ignorant, however; she knows the range of possible values that b could take.

What is the seller's best strategy? Suppose she asks a price p. The buyer will rationally accept this take-it-or-leave-it offer if p is less than b, and reject it otherwise. If the buyer accepts, the seller receives a profit of p; if the buyer rejects, the seller gets zero profit. The seller cannot predict which will happen, but she can calculate the odds. The probability of acceptance is the probability that p is less than b. Since, in the seller's perception, b is equally likely to be anything between 0 and 200, this probability is $(200 - p)/200$ (as we saw in the discussion of decisions under uncertainty). Hence the return the seller gets on average from asking p is $p(200 - p)/200$. The seller's best price is the value of p that makes this quantity as large as possible. To find this value, notice that the quantity $p(200 - p)/200$ equals zero when $p = 0$ and when $p = 200$; also, its graph is symmetric in between these points (since it is a quadratic function). Hence it reaches its highest point halfway between 0 and 200; thus the best price for the seller to set is $100.

The buyer benefits from the seller's informational handicap. If the seller had complete information, the price would equal the buyer's valuation so the buyer would get no net gain. With incomplete information, if there is no sale the buyer likewise gets no gain; but if there is a sale, the price is less than the buyer's valuation so the buyer receives a net gain. This net gain is entirely attributable to the privacy of the buyer's information.

With this pricing strategy the seller deliberately introduces the possibility that she loses the sale. She would sell the item for sure if she set a price of zero; but then she would get zero profit. By increasing the price above zero, she introduces the possibility of asking more than the item is worth to the buyer and not selling the item; but she also earns positive profit when she does make a sale. Our algebra shows that these two contradictory forces are optimally balanced when the price is set at $100. With this price there is a 50% probability that the buyer rejects the offer. On average, over the range of possible buyer valuations, the profit the seller earns by setting this price is $50 (because she earns $100 with 50% probability and zero with 50% probability, so her expected return is $100 \times 0.5 + 0 \times 0.5$). Compare this with the $100 profit she would get if she knew for sure the buyer's valuation, and that valuation were at its average level of $100. The social costs of informational asymmetries are, in this example, large.

Let us turn now to the other topic of Chapter 6, signaling.

JOB-MARKET SIGNALING

An employer wants to hire a worker. Two kinds of worker exist: highly productive and less productive. If of the high-productivity type, the worker will generate $200 worth of output; if of the low-productivity type, $100 worth of output. Productivity is an innate characteristic of a worker: workers know their own productivity, but the employer cannot observe it before hiring. Both the worker and the employer know that the overall fraction of low-productivity workers is q and the fraction of high-productivity workers is 1 − q. Competition from other employers forces this employer to offer to pay the worker the full amount of productivity as perceived at the time of hiring. Before entering the job market, the worker can choose to receive education. Education has no direct effect on productivity, but is observable by the employer. To achieve E units of education costs a productive individual $E and an unproductive individual $2E. Will the worker's educational level serve to signal innate productivity?

An equilibrium of this game consists of a set of self-confirming beliefs. The worker and the employer begin with beliefs about how signals are to be interpreted. For the system to be in equilibrium means that, after each acts on these beliefs, neither sees anything to indicate the beliefs are mistaken. How much education will each type of individual choose in an equilibrium?

Suppose the employer believes that there is some cut-off level of education E^*, such that anyone educated to more than E^* must be of high productivity, and anyone with less than E^* education must be of low productivity. The employer therefore offers to pay a wage of \$200 if the worker has E^* or more education and \$100 if he has less education than E^*. Since education is costly, the worker faced with this wage schedule will choose either zero education or exactly E^*; any other level of education would involve costs and no additional return. A high-productivity worker who has E^* education therefore earns a net return (wage minus education cost) equal to $(200 - E^*)$. If the same individual remains uneducated, he is hired (given the employer's beliefs) as an unproductive worker and paid \$100. Education is profitable for a productive worker if the former number is the larger. Similarly, a low-productivity worker earns a net return of \$100 if he gets no education. But if he is educated to E^*, he is mistakenly hired as a high-productivity worker, earning a net return of $(200 - 2E^*)$. It pays him not to be educated if the former number exceeds the latter.

The employer's beliefs about the relationship between education and productivity are confirmed in the marketplace if the worker chooses to receive education if he is productive and chooses not to if he is unproductive; that is, both $200 - E^*$ is larger than 100 and 100 is larger than $200 - 2E^*$. Simple algebra establishes that both these conditions are satisfied if E^* is any number between 50 and 100.

Two features of this outcome are worthy of note. First, signaling succeeds in this example: anyone with credentials of E^* is in fact a productive worker. The market does succeed in overcoming its informational difficulties. We call this a *separating equilibrium,* since the market succeeds in separating low-productivity from high-productivity workers.

Second, there is an essential arbitrariness to the level of credentials required. Any E^* between 50 and 100 works. How is E^* established? The model is silent on this, but presumably it is determined by history or custom. E^* is the qualification everyone believes is necessary for this job, because that is the way things are customarily done: it is the social convention about how much signaling is needed to achieve credibility. The customary E^* might be as low as 51, or it might be as high as 99. Given that signaling is education's only role, the former level is more efficient from the point of view of society as a whole. Everyone is better off the lower the accepted credential level, provided it is high enough to work as a signal (that is, in this example, the most efficient credential level is just above 50). But, because of its history, the market can be stuck with higher-than-necessary credentials being imposed. Comparisons across different countries of the credentials required of job applicants suggest that signaling equilibria are indeed arbitrary.

(We can, however, reduce the inconclusiveness of this model by invoking considerations of higher-level rationality. Suppose the social convention has it that a productive individual must get 80 units of education to signal that he is productive. But suppose our worker is more rebellious than most and questions the social convention. He acquires 79 units of education and then tells the employer that, despite the fact that his educational credential is lower than the norm, the employer should realize he is productive. The worker points out that—by similar computations to those given earlier—it could not possibly pay him to obtain the 79 units of education if he were a low-productivity type, even if the employer were fooled into paying him as a high-productivity worker. If the employer is prepared to accept the validity of this point, and therefore to interpret the 79 units of education as signaling high productivity, it is rational for the worker to deviate from the convention by obtaining slightly less than the customary education. Repeated chipping away at the credential level will drive it down to the lowest level consistent with a separating equilibrium, or 50 in the above game. Thus the unique equilibrium to survive out of the previous multiplicity of separating equilibria is the equilibrium that is efficient.)

The separating equilibria do not exhaust all of the possibilities. Because the beliefs upon which an equilibrium is based are essentially arbitrary, there is another kind of equilibrium of this system. Signaling need not work. Suppose the employer begins with the belief that a worker with less than E^* education, for some number E^*, is unproductive with probability q and is productive with probability $1 - q$. A worker with more than E^* education is interpreted by the employer as being a productive worker for certain. To a worker with more than E^* education, the employer therefore offers a wage of $200. A worker with less than E^* education has a productivity of $100 with probability q and $200 with probability $1 - q$. On average, therefore, such a worker's productivity is $100q + 200(1 - q)$, or $200 - 100q$; this is the wage the employer will offer him. Once again, the worker chooses between the education levels zero and E^*. A productive worker who is not educated earns $200 - 100q$; one who is educated earns on net $200 - E^*$. It pays not to become educated if the former number is bigger, or E^* is larger than $100q$. (And if it does not pay a productive worker to become educated, it must not pay an unproductive worker to incur the still higher education costs.) Thus, provided the required educational credential is high enough (specifically, it is larger than $100q$), no worker receives an education. The employer's initial beliefs are confirmed, for the proportion of uneducated workers who turn out to be unproductive is indeed q.

Thus this is an equilibrium in which no signaling takes place. Given the employer's history-determined beliefs about how to interpret educational signals, no one finds it profitable to become educated, and no communication takes place. We call this a *pooling equilibrium,* since low-productivity workers are pooled with high-productivity workers in the job market. That pooling equilibria exist means that it is possible for the market to be stuck in a situation in which no communication occurs.

Chapter 8: Creating Incentives

To make our thinking about incentives more precise, let us model incentive schemes of the sort described in Chapter 8.

In what follows, the principal is modeled as being in a strong bargaining position, in the precise sense of being able to commit to the terms of the contract. Working in the agent's favor, on the other hand, are two limitations on the principal's contract design. First, the agent has veto power: he can go and work elsewhere if what the principal offers is not sufficiently attractive. Second, the agent chooses his own action, which the principal can observe only imperfectly: the principal can determine this action choice only indirectly, via the terms of the contract.

In order that the agent is not comparing apples and oranges when weighing the payment to be received against the effort to be exerted, we suppose the agent measures the cost of effort in dollar-equivalent terms. Further, for the sake of simplicity of analysis in the following games, we will suppose that the effort cost is proportional to the square of the effort level; and we will write the constant of proportionality as $[1/2D]$ where D is some positive number, which looks clumsy but turns out to be convenient for subsequent interpretations. (That effort-cost is quadratically related to effort means—realistically enough—that the cost of exerting some more effort is larger the harder the agent is already working.)

AN AGENT'S RESPONSE TO INCENTIVES

An agent, choosing an amount of effort E, bears an effort cost of $E^2/2D$, measured in dollar terms, and produces an output, which accrues to the principal, of $Q = E + u$, where u represents some random term which is on average zero (so the expected value of Q is E). Neither the effort E nor the realization of the random term u can be observed by the principal. The principal offers to pay the agent according to his performance: the payment P is equal to $s + rQ$, where s and r are numbers chosen by the principal. What effort level will the agent choose?

Notice this game has the elements we have been discussing: the principal's interests differ from the agent's interests, this divergence being represented by the effort cost borne by the agent and not the principal. And the principal cannot disentangle the consequences of the randomness from those of the agent's effort choice, so the principal cannot infer effort from her observation of output. Hence the contract cannot be based on effort, but only output.

The contract is defined by the numbers s and r. The number s shows the amount the agent will be paid regardless of his success or failure in generating output. The term rQ is the variable part of the payment; r is typically a fraction, no larger than one. Depending on the particular application of this model, r can be interpreted as a commission rate or a royalty rate or a piece rate; and s as a salary.

The agent's net return is his payment less his cost of effort: $s + rQ - [E^2/2D]$. The rational agent will choose his effort E to maximize the expected value of this quantity. According to the contract, the agent in effect keeps a fraction r of any extra output he produces. He fully incurs any extra effort costs. Thus (since the expected value of Q is E) the agent's net expected return can be rewritten as $s + rE - (E^2/2D)$. Our rational agent chooses his effort to maximize this quantity. His optimal effort level is therefore $E = rD$. (To see this, either use calculus or note that, since s is independent of E, the agent is essentially maximizing $rE - (E^2/2D)$. This quantity equals zero when $E = 0$ and when $E = 2rD$; since it is symmetric, being quadratic, its highest point is reached halfway between, at $E = rD$.)

We have seen that the agent rationally sets his effort level E equal to rD, and that the expected output level is E. Thus the expected output induced by the contract is proportional to the marginal payment rate r: the commission rate, royalty rate, or piece rate determines the output. Also, the difference in output between a contract that imposes on the agent full responsibility for his actions (that is, $r = 1$) and a contract that gives the agent no incentives for extra output (that is, $r = 0$) is equal to D. The parameter D, which we arbitrarily introduced in the cost-of-effort relationship, therefore turns out to be a natural measure of the effectiveness of incentives. The size of D shows the discretionary power of the agent: how much output can vary as a result of changing the agent's incentives. In practice, how much do incentives matter: how large is the incentive parameter D? It varies from case to case. Estimates of D are hard to come by, but some exist. The analysis of Chinese farmers under the changing incentive systems summarized above implies a D of approximately 60%. A rough estimate of large U.S. military contracting firms' responses to contractual incentives suggests a D of about 10%.

The sequence of events in our model is: first, the principal selects and announces the terms of the contract; second, the agent decides whether or not to accept; third, if he accepts, the agent chooses his action. In designing the contract that is best from her own point of view, the principal must put herself in the agent's shoes and predict two things: what contracts the agent will accept; and how the agent would act in response to alternative contracts. That is, the principal must go through the foregoing chain of the agent's reasoning.

In the game specified above, what contract will the principal rationally set, given that the agent has an alternative opportunity yielding a profit of A that he will take if he rejects the offered contract?

The principal faces two restrictions. One is her inability to observe the agent's actions directly. The other is the ability of the agent to go elsewhere. Thus the principal must offer a contract that yields at least A to the agent. The principal, having done these computations, is able to find the contract that yields him the highest profit. It is convenient to express the principal's profit in a somewhat indirect way. The principal's profit is the total gain from the relationship minus the agent's profit. The total gain from trade is output minus production cost: $Q - (E^2/2D)$. The agent's profit is A, if the principal succeeds in extracting as much as possible subject to the agent's not leaving. Replacing output Q with expected output E, we find that the principal's expected profit is the difference between these two, or $E - (E^2/2D) - A$. A simple maximization exercise on the principal's behalf, similar to that just performed, shows that the principal wishes to elicit from the agent an effort of $E = D$. Thus the effort the principal wants (which we found to be D) and the effort the agent chooses (which we found to be rD) are the same if the principal writes a contract with $r = 1$.

By setting $r = 1$, the principal offers the agent the full value of resulting from any incremental effort by the agent. The principal earns his own profit from the transaction via the other contractual parameter, the fixed term s. The agent's ability to walk away from an offered contract constrains the principal's choice of s. The agent's expected net return, shown above to be equal to $s + rE - [E^2/2D]$, must be no less than his alternative return A. The principal captures the maximum profit by choosing s to make these two expressions equal, having already set $r = 1$. This gives $s = A - [D/2]$. Since the agent is retaining the full value of incremental output, for the principal not to make a loss s must be a negative number. (With $E = rD$ and $r = 1$ the principal's profit is equal to $-s$; so for the principal to engage in the transaction it must be that s is negative.)

As noted in the text, a discontinuous payment scheme can be used in place of a continuous scheme. With discontinuous payment schemes, just as with continuous payment schemes, the effect of payment scheme on effort exerted is determined by considerations of marginal returns. A little extra effort generates a little extra output, which results in slightly higher probability of earning the bonus (or a slightly lower probability of receiving the punishment). The equivalence between continuous and discontinuous payment schemes can be made precise as follows.

A DISCONTINUOUS INCENTIVE SCHEME

The output and cost-of-effort relationships are as in the previous game, but with the additional feature that the random term u varies between two bounds a and b, with all values in between equally likely. The principal wishes to motivate the agent with a discontinuous payment scheme rather than a continuous one. What contract will the principal offer?

The discontinuous payment scheme gives a relatively large payment to the agent if output is satisfactory, and a relatively low payment if unsatisfactory. Let us represent this as: payment is $x + y$ if $Q \geq Q^*$ and x if $Q < Q^*$, with Q^* the performance standard set by the principal. Thus the difference, y, can be interpreted as the size of either the punishment or the reward (depending on whether $x + y$ or x is regarded as the normal level of payment). Because of the randomness the principal sometimes makes mistakes: rewarding a high output that was solely due to good luck or punishing a low output caused by bad luck.

With this discontinuous payment scheme, a change in the agent's effort level does not change the payment unless it moves output from one side to the other of Q^*. Hence the return to extra effort reflects the reduction in the probability that output falls short of the target. For a given effort level, the probability that the target is not met is the probability that $E + u < Q^*$, or $u < Q^* - E$. Under our assumption that all values of u between a and b are equally likely, this probability is $[Q^* - E - a]/(b - a)$. Suppose the agent increases his effort level by one unit. Then the probability that the resulting output is above Q^* increases by $1/(b - a)$. Since success increases payment by y, the agent's expected return from his effort therefore increases by $y/(b - a)$. In the continuous-payment model above, the agent's extra payment following one unit's extra effort was r. By comparison, we can conclude that any continuous payment scheme can be mimicked by a discontinuous payment scheme. To achieve the same effort level as a continuous payment scheme with royalty or commission rate r, the principal sets the size of the punishment y to satisfy the condition $y/(b - a) = r$. If $r = 1$, as it is optimally according to the analysis above, this means that the optimal punishment is equal to the maximum amount of variability in output attributable to luck, $(b - a)$.

Chapter 9: Designing Contracts

Can a remuneration package be designed so as to induce the agent to reveal to the principal information about his potential productivity? We analyzed in the text an example of a payment scheme based on both the agent's prediction of performance and actual performance. Let us now look a little more generally at such payment packages.

INDUCING HONEST REPORTING

A sales territory has either high or low sales potential; sales will either be Q_g or Q_p, with Q_g larger than Q_p. The salesperson knows which is the case, but the sales manager does not. Can the sales manager devise a remuneration package that induces the salesperson to reveal his information?

The manager offers a remuneration scheme under which salary and commission rate vary with report. If the salesperson reports potential to be high, he is paid a total of, say, $r_g Q + s_g$ upon selling an amount Q; if the salesperson reports potential to be low, he is paid an total of $r_p Q + s_p$ upon selling an amount Q. (Thus r_g and r_p are the alternative commission rates, and s_g and s_p are the alternative salaries.) Does honesty pay? It does if the parameters of the payment scheme, r_g, r_p, s_g, and s_p, satisfy two conditions. First, it does not pay to report high when there is the low potential Q_p; and second, it does not pay to report low when there is the high potential Q_g. If high is correctly reported, the payment is $r_g Q_g + s_g$, which we write as P_g. If low is correctly reported, the payment is $r_p Q_p + s_p$, which we shall write as P_p. Suppose the potential is in fact high. If low is (incorrectly) reported, the payment is $r_p Q_g + s_p$, which can be rewritten as $P_p + r_p(Q_g - Q_p)$. For it not to pay the salesperson to misrepresent, it must be that P_g exceeds $P_p + r_p(Q_g - Q_p)$. This implies, in particular, that the payment upon correctly reporting potential to be high (that is, P_g) exceeds payment for correctly reporting potential to be low (that is, P_p). Suppose, on the other hand, the potential is in fact low. If high is (incorrectly) reported, the payment is $r_g Q_p + s_g$, which can be rewritten as $P_g - r_g(Q_g - Q_p)$. For it not to pay the salesperson to misrepresent, it must be that P_p exceeds $P_g - r_g(Q_g - Q_p)$. Combining the two inequalities that insure correct reporting, we find that the contract parameters must satisfy $P_p + r_p(Q_g - Q_p) \le P_g \le P_p + r_g(Q_g - Q_p)$. In other words, the payment offered upon a report of high potential must be high enough to discourage understatement of a high potential; but low enough to discourage exaggeration of a low potential. The first and third terms in this inequality show, since $Q_g - Q_p > 0$, that $r_g > r_p$. Also, the inequality $P_g \le P_p + r_g(Q_g - Q_p)$ can be rewritten (from the definitions of P_g and P_p above) as $s_g - s_p \le (r_p - r_g)Q_p$, which is negative;

this implies that s_g is smaller than s_p. In other words, to induce truth-telling, the payment scheme must offer a relatively high performance payment and a relatively low fixed payment in the event that potential is reported to be high.

The foregoing analysis produced some limits on the contracts that principal could offer. But many different contracts fall within these limits. What is the best remuneration package from the principal's point of view? Let us incorporate, as the text discussed, the fact that the salesperson has some alternative employment (which will put a lower bound on the total payment he will accept); and that sales depend not only on the territory's sales potential, but also on the salesperson's effort (which, as noted in Chapter 8, will vary with the commission rate).

SETTING THE SALESPERSON'S COMMISSION RATE

Sales achieved depend on both the territory's inherent potential, which is either high or low, and the salesperson's effort. Specifically, if the salesperson's effort is E, total sales Q equal $1 + E$ if the territory is good, and E if the territory is poor. As before, the effort of level E costs the salesperson (regardless of whether his territory is good or poor) an amount $E^2/2D$ for some number D. The salesperson has alternative employment, which he can choose to take up instead of the offered contract, yielding a net payment of $1. The salesperson knows the territory's potential, but the manager does not. What contract should the manager offer?

If the salesperson is lucky enough to be working a good territory, he can achieve $1 worth of sales without any effort. The manager, in designing the contract, tries to avoid over-rewarding the salesperson if he has a good territory, and penalizing him if he has the poor territory; but the manager does not know whether the particular territory is good or poor.

Suppose the manager contemplates offering two different contracts, one for each kind of sales territory. If the territory is good, the payment for sales Q will be $r_g Q + s_g$; while if it is poor, the payment will be $r_p Q + s_p$. The manager can predict, as we have seen, that the effort induced by the former contract will be $E_g = r_g D$, and by the latter contract, $E_p = r_p D$. The manager lets the salesperson choose between the two contracts. Moreover (and this is the key point in the firm's contract-design exercise) by being sufficiently cunning the manager can induce the salesperson to choose the contract appropriate to his territory. To see this, we must compute the net rewards that the salesperson would earn under the alternative contracts. If the territory is poor and the corresponding contract is in force, the salesperson's net reward is payment minus cost of effort, which equals $r_p E_p + s_p - (E_p^2/2D)$. Given that the salesperson chooses an effort level of r_pD, this net reward can be rewritten as $(r_p^2D/2) + s_p$, or n_p for short. If the territory is good and the appropriate contract is in force, the salesperson's net reward equals $r_g(1 + E_g) + s_g - (E_g^2/2D)$, which—given the salesperson's effort choice—can be rewritten as $r_g + (r_g^2D/2) + s_g$, or n_g for short.

So far we have presumed that the salesperson opts for the contract appropriate to his territory. Is it in his interest to do so? Suppose the salesperson were to understate his territory's potential, claiming he has a poor territory when in fact it is good. He would then receive the poor-territory contract and exert the corresponding effort E_p, producing sales equal to $1 + E_p$. Thus he would earn a net return of $r_p(1 + E_p) + s_p - (E_p^2/2D)$, which can be rewritten as $r_p + (r_p^2D/2) + s_p$, or (from the definition of n_p) $n_p + r_p$. The manager can make sure a salesperson in a good territory does not understate his territory's potential by cleverly setting the contract terms. The salesperson earns more by correctly reporting his potential than by misrepresenting it if (from the above algebra) the manager ensures that n_g is no smaller than $n_p + r_p$. An important result is implicit here. Provided the contractual parameter r_p is not zero (as will turn out to be the case) this means that n_g exceeds n_p; that is, the salesperson earns a higher net return if his territory is good than if it is poor. In the event the territory is good, the manager must cede some profit to the salesperson in order to induce him not to understate his territory's potential. The private information gives the salesperson some bargaining power, from which he can squeeze some profit.

An additional constraint on the manager's decision comes from the salesperson's outside opportunities. The contract must offer a net return that is not lower than what the salesperson could earn elsewhere, which is \$1. Thus both n_p and n_g must be no less than 1; but since we have already required that n_g exceed n_p, this just means that n_p must be no less than 1. The firm, facing these two incentive constraints, maximizes its profit by ensuring each is only just satisfied; that is, that $n_p = 1$ and $n_g = n_p + r_p$.

Before completing our solution of this game by computing, on the firm's behalf, the best possible contractual terms, notice that by combining the last two equations we see that $n_g = 1 + r_p$. The firm wants the salesperson's net return n_g to be as low as possible, for profits ceded to the salesperson are profits lost to the firm. This equation says that these lost profits are lower the lower the contractual parameter r_p is, so in this respect the firm wants to set r_p low. But the firm faces a dilemma, for (from the analysis of the last chapter) setting r_p low means that the salesperson has weak effort incentives in the event that his sales territory is poor. In other words, inducing the salesperson to correctly reveal his territory's potential in the event it is high can be achieved only at the expense of giving less than full effort incentives in the event the territory's potential is poor.

As in the earlier contracting games, let us write the firm's profit as the total gain from trade minus the salesperson's profit; and the total gain from trade is sales minus the salesperson's cost of effort. In the event the territory is good and the salesperson has revealed this fact, the firm's profit is $(1 + E_g) - (E_g^2/2D) - n_g$. In the event it is poor, the firm's profit is $E_p - (E_p^2/2D) - n_p$. From the firm's point of view, the territory may be either good or poor, each with equal probability. Thus the firm's expected profit is $0.5[(1 + E_g) - (E_g^2/2D) - n_g] + 0.5[E_p - (E_p^2/2D) - n_p]$. We have seen that the salesperson's incentives impose on the firm's contract-design exercise: the salesperson's ability to choose his effort level means that $E_g = r_gD$, $E_p = r_pD$; his ability to veto the offered contract means that $n_p = 1$; and his ability, if he has a good territory, to act as though it were poor means that $n_g = n_p + r_p$. If we impose all of these incentive constraints then we can write the firm's expected profit as $0.5[1 + r_gD - (r_g^2D/2) - (1 + r_p)] + 0.5[r_pD - (r_p^2D/2) - 1]$. The firm chooses the alternative contractual parameters, r_p and r_g so as to maximize this expected profit. The best value of r_p is computed by treating r_g as if it were a constant term; and vice versa for r_g. The optimal parameters so computed are $r_g = 1$ and $r_p = (D - 1)/D$ (which is less than one and—we will find—no less than zero). In particular, r_p is smaller than r_g; the salesperson is given the more stringent performance incentives if he reports his territory to be good. Finally, the other contractual parameters, s_g and s_p can now be found, by expanding the equations $n_p = 1$ and $n_g = n_p + r_p$, using the formulas for r_p and r_g, and doing some simple algebra; in particular, this exercise shows that s_g is smaller than s_p; the fixed part of the payment scheme is higher if the salesperson reports his territory to be poor.

(Two loose ends remain. First, we have ensured that it does not pay the salesperson to claim his territory is poor when it is in fact good. We must also guard against the opposite kind of misrepresentation: claiming it is good when it is poor. But this has been implicitly taken care of. The salesperson's net return from such misrepresentation would be $r_gE_g + s_g - (E_g^2/2D)$, which is equal to $n_g - r_g$. This is to be compared with this salesperson's net return upon correctly revealing his potential, n_p, which was shown above to be equal to $n_g - r_p$. Since we have established that the firm sets r_g to be larger than r_p, the latter net return is the higher, and this misrepresentation does not pay. Second, the firm has the option of contracting only if the salesperson reports his territory to be good. Could this yield more profit for the firm than the foregoing solution? Substituting $r_g = 1$ and $r_p = (D - 1)/D$ into the above expression for the firm's profit (given in the previous paragraph) we find that this profit is $[2D^2 - 4D + 1]/4D$. This is to be compared with the firm's expected profit if it instead sets contractual terms that the salesperson would reject if the territory were poor. A moment's thought shows that the best contract of this type has $r_g = 1$ and gives the salesperson, in the event the territory is good, a profit of only 1; thus the firm's expected profit is $0.5(1 + D - [D^2/2D] - 1)$, or $D/4$. This is the larger profit if D is less than 3.73 (as can be seen with a little algebra). Hence if the incentive parameter D is smaller than 3.73, it pays the firm to distinguish more strongly still between the two possible types of territory, contracting only if the salesperson has the good territory. The solution derived earlier therefore applies only if D exceeds 3.73; incidentally, this ensures that the marginal payment rate $(D - 1)/D$ must be larger than zero whenever it is applicable.)

Nothing in the foregoing algebra required that the firm offer two different contracts; the algebra permitted the firm to set $r_g = r_p$ and $s_g = s_p$ and therefore not to distinguish between the different territories. Since the optimal solution was found to distinguish them, we can conclude that it must pay the firm not to offer a single, nondistinguishing contract. In particular, the firm could, if it chose, set both r_g and r_p equal to one. This would, as we saw in the last chapter, have the advantage of maximizing the total gains from trade to be shared. But it has the disadvantage, from the firm's point of view, of leaving a large share of the gains from trade with the salesperson, in the event that the sales territory is good. The firm retrieves some of these gains by setting r_p less than one, at the expense of lowering the total gain in the event that the sales territory is poor.

This optimal remuneration package can be implemented in either of two ways. The manager can ask the salesperson whether the territory is good or poor, having announced how the contractual terms will vary depending on the salesperson's answer. Or the manager can simply offer the two contracts, letting the salesperson choose the contract he prefers. According to the logic just given, it is in the salesperson's interest to choose the package appropriate to his territory, provided the manager has correctly designed the alternative packages. By his choice of a contract from those offered by the manager, the salesperson in effect reveals his information about his territory.

What we have computed are the optimal combinations of commission rates and fixed payments. If the salesperson reports that he has a territory with high potential, he receives a higher commission rate and a lower fixed payment than if he reports his territory to have low potential. A salesperson working in a good territory gets full effort incentives (that is, $r_g = 1$); but one working in a poor territory does not (that is, r_p is less than 1) because this package must not be made so tempting as to induce a salesperson with the good territory to misrepresent its potential. The firm optimally sets the performance-incentive parameter r_p larger the larger D is. That is (from last chapter's analysis of the meaning of the parameter D), a salesperson reporting his territory to be poor is offered a relatively strong performance incentive if the salesperson, by varying his effort level, has the ability to cause a large variation in realized sales.

Let us change the focus and turn now to risk-sharing issues. Knowledge of the territory's potential is no longer an issue: assume the sales manager knows it. The sales manager offers to pay the salesperson according to output: as before, we represent the payment by $P = s + rQ$, where P is the payment, Q is the value to the firm of the sales, and s and r are numbers chosen by the principal: s is the salary, independent of the agent's performance, and r is the commission rate, linking pay to performance. At the two extremes, r is equal to zero (the salesperson receives a fixed salary regardless of his performance) and r is equal to one (the salesperson receives the full return from any extra sales). In general the manager can set r anywhere between zero and one (but recall that in the model of the last chapter it was optimally set equal to one).

At the time of accepting the contract, the salesperson does not yet know how the uncertainty will resolve itself. In evaluating this job, our risk-averse salesperson discounts its expected return by his subjective evaluation of the risk: that is, by his risk premium. The size of the risk premium depends on both the salesperson's inherent cautiousness and the variability of the possible outcomes: it measures how much the salesperson would pay to be completely sheltered from the risk. Suppose that if the salesperson bears the full risk of the project (that is, if $r = 1$) his risk premium is R. This means that, if f represents the return the salesperson expects to receive on average, his expected return from his risky job, net of the risk borne, is $f - R$. (If the salesperson were risk neutral, his risk-aversion coefficient R would be zero and he would care about the expected return alone.) Now suppose manager proposes that the the firm share some of the risk by setting the commission rate r below 1. The salesperson now bears only a fraction of the risk; thus his risk premium has shrunk. If, for example, the salesperson's risk is halved, the risk premium is quartered. More generally,[3] for any fraction r, the risk premium is r^2R, so that the salesperson's evaluation of the risky prospect is $f - r^2R$.

To anticipate the argument to follow: the salesperson's risk aversion means that his subjective return is lower the more the risk. The firm, being risk neutral, can increase the total gains from trade—the sum of its own return and the salesperson's—by accepting some of this risk. But relieving the salesperson of risk distorts his effort choice. The manager designs the contract by weighing the incentive and risk-sharing effects.

THE RISK-SHARING CONTRACT

The salesperson, with effort E, produces output $Q = E + u$, where u is a random term representing the vagaries of the project, at cost $E^2/2D$. The salesperson's best alternative to accepting this contract yields a risk-adjusted return of A. The firm offers payment $P = s + rQ$, choosing the numbers s and r. The salesperson is averse to risk: if f is his expected *dollar payment, he values this risky contract at $f - r^2R$. The firm is risk neutral. What contract will the manager offer to maximize the firm's expected profit?*

In all respects but one this is the same game as we solved in the last chapter. The sole difference is that the salesperson does not seek to maximize his expected return; rather he adjusts the expected return downwards to account for the risk he faces.

The manager can put himself in the salesperson's shoes and predict how the salesperson will respond to any given contract. Thus he can decide which contract will on average give the firm the highest profit. (The caveat "on average" is needed throughout this analysis because the variability of output is the essential feature of this question.) The firm must offer a contract sufficiently attractive for the salesperson to accept it given the alternative uses of his time: this the firm does by its choice of the fixed payment s. It must also balance, optimally from its point of view, the conflicting objectives of giving the salesperson incentives and absorbing risk from the salesperson: this is the role of the commission rate r.

If the randomness has resolved itself by the time the salesperson chooses his effort level, he faces risk only at the time of deciding whether to accept the contract, not at the time of doing the work. As we saw in the last chapter, the salesperson, retaining a fraction r of the output he produces, rationally chooses an effort level $E = rD$.

Having predicted the salesperson's effort choice, we now move backwards in time to examine his decision on whether to accept the contract. The firm must offer a contract worth at least as much as the risk-adjusted value of the salesperson's best alternative, A. And it maximizes its own profit by offering no more than this much. The firm therefore designs a contract that equates the salesperson's risk-adjusted return from this project to his best alternative: that is, $f - Rr^2 = A$. By rearranging this equation, we see that the lowest expected return that the firm can offer that the salesperson will accept is $f = A + Rr^2$. This equation simply says that the firm offers the salesperson remuneration that covers what he could earn elsewhere plus compensates him for the risk he bears.

The final step in the argument involves going still further back in time and asking what contractual terms the firm should choose. The firm's profit is, as in the model of the last chapter, the total gain from trade minus the salesperson's profit. The total gain from trade is output minus production cost or $(E + u) - (E^2/2D)$. Since the firm is risk neutral, however, it pays no heed to the random term u. Putting itself in the salesperson's shoes, the firm predicts that the salesperson will respond to the contract by choosing the effort level $E = rD$, as we derived in the last chapter. Thus the firm predicts a total expected gain from trade of $rD - [r^2D/2]$. We found the salesperson's net return to be $A + Rr^2$. Thus the firm's profit is equal to $rD - [r^2D/2] - [A + Rr^2]$. (This is what is graphed in Fig. 9.1.) By using the properties of quadratic functions as we have done several times before (or by using calculus) we deduce that the contract that maximizes the firm's profit has a commission rate r defined by: $r = D/[D + 2R]$.

This formula has a common-sense interpretation: the optimal sharing rate is a compromise that depends on both the salesperson's risk premium and the scope for the salesperson's discretion. The firm should make payment more sensitive to output the smaller the salesperson's risk premium and the more responsive output is to incentives. In the extreme case of a risk-neutral salesperson or of no outside uncertainty ($R = 0$), this formula calls for $r = 1$; as in the last chapter, if the firm needs only address the incentives issue, the salesperson keeps 100% of his marginal output. At the other extreme, if the salesperson has no discretionary power to affect output ($D = 0$), the formula calls for $r = 0$, for then the risk-sharing issue is fully addressed. For the non-extreme cases in which the salesperson is risk averse, there is uncertainty, and the salesperson has some discretionary ability, the optimal contract involves partial sharing of output between firm and salesperson: the optimal extent of this sharing can be computed from the formula.

The extent of sharing in the contract depends on the relative size of just two numbers: D, the extent to which output can respond to the agent's effort; and R the risk premium the agent would have if he bore all of the risk in the transaction. Rough estimates of D were cited above: 0.1 for large U.S. military-contracting firms, 0.6 for Chinese farmers. The size of the risk premium is the answer to the question: how much would you be prepared to pay to get a guaranteed return in place of the bearing the entire risk of the activity? What is the maximum insurance premium you would pay? The answer varies from situation to situation, depending as it does on both the objective size of the uncertainty in the particular project and the agent's subjective evaluation of risk. The formula can be rewritten as $r = 1/[1 + 2c]$, where c is the ratio of R and D. Thus if the incentive effect and the risk premium are equal, the optimal sharing rate is 1/3; if the incentive effect is twice as large as the risk premium, it is 1/2.

Similar analysis can be done for the opposite kind of situation: the principal, instead of wanting output to be large, wants some task done for as small a cost as possible, as in the example of government contracting discussed in the text. The payment that the principal promises to make to the agent can be written as $P = v(C - w) + w$, where P represents the amount paid and C is the agent's production cost. The numbers v and w are chosen by the principal. The parameter w is a target price: if C exceeds w there is a cost overrun, whereas if w exceeds C there is a cost underrun. The term v is a share parameter, which determines how cost overruns and underruns are to be shared between the principal and agent. If $v = 0$, the contract is fixed-price. If $v = 1$, the contract is cost-plus. If v is between zero and one, the contract is an intermediate form; the U.S. Department of Defense calls such contracts "incentive contracts." The optimal cost-share parameter v can be solved for by logic analogous to that just given. There is a trade-off between giving the agent incentives to limit costs and shifting risk from agent to principal.

Chapter 11: Bidding in Competition

In a private-values auction, the bidders know their own valuations but not others' valuations. Suppose the bidders know the probability distribution of the others' valuations. It is as if the bidders draw their valuations like numbered balls from an urn. Each bidder knows the fraction of balls in the urn bearing a particular number; only the individual bidder knows his or her own actual draw.

BIDDING IN A SEALED-BID AUCTION

Several bidders compete in a sealed-bid auction. The bidders know their own valuations. But they do not know each others' valuations: all that they know is that the other' valuations lie somewhere between 0 and 1, with all intermediate values equally likely. What is each bidder's best bid?

Consider first the case of two bidders; call them A and B. Bidder A knows her own valuation is v_a and bidder B knows his own valuation is v_b. But bidder B does not know v_a, and bidder A does not know v_b. Suppose bidder A conjectures that bidder B follows the decision rule: bid some particular fraction of k of valuation (k is, so far, an arbitrary number lying between zero and one). Thus A conjectures that B will bid an amount kv_b (although A does not know what v_b is). A believes, therefore, that she will win if she bids an amount p_a that is bigger than this: that is, $p_a > kv_b$, or $v_b < p_a/k$. Given the distribution of possible values for v_b, the probability of A's winning is p_a/k. If A wins, her profit is the difference between the price and her valuation, $v_a - p_a$; if she loses, she gets nothing. Thus on average her profit from bidding p_a is $(v_a - p_a)p_a/k$. This expected return equals zero when $p_a = 0$ and when $p_a = v_a$; since it is a quadratic and therefore symmetric curve, its maximum point is halfway between these values, at $p_a = v_a/2$. This is the bid that A rationally chooses given her conjecture about B's decision rule. Is this a rational conjecture? It is, if $k = 1/2$, because, by the symmetry of the situation, B's best response to A's using this strategy is to bid one-half of his own valuation. Hence A rationally bids half of her valuation; and B behaves similarly.

An increase in the amount of competition would, however, reduce this profit. If there are more than two bidders, say n bidders, the optimal bidding rule is: bid a fraction $(n - 1)/n$ of valuation. In other words, shade valuation by $(1/n)$th.

To solve for the case of any number of bidders, consider one bidder's decision. Suppose this bidder, bidder 1, conjectures that each of his $n - 1$ rivals submits a bid that is some particular fraction k of valuation. If bidder 1 bids p_1 he will then win the item if his bid is higher than all of the others', which occurs if $p_1 \geq kv_i$, for all $i = 2,...,n$ (provided his conjecture about his rivals' decision rules is correct). That is, bidder 1 wins if $v_i \leq p_1/k$, for all $i = 2,...,n$. He therefore wins with probability $[p_1/k]^{n-1}$. Bidder 1's net gain if he wins with the bid p_1 is $(v_1 - p_1)$, so his expected net gain is $(v_1 - p_1)[p_1/k]^{n-1}$, which he maximizes[4] by setting his bid at $p_1 = (n - 1)v/n$. What has been found is bidder 1's best response to the decision rule he arbitrarily presumes his rivals to be following. But, by symmetry, it is rational for each of the rivals to be using this decision rule provided they set $k = (n - 1)/n$. Thus the Nash equilibrium has each bidder, given a valuation of v, submitting a bid of $(n - 1)v/n$. Thus, as discussed in Chapter 11, the bidders choose their bids by shading their valuations by a fraction $1/n$.

Notes

1. Arguments requiring a little calculus or probability theory will be given in footnotes.
2. If marginal utility strictly falls as income rises, then $d^2U/dX^2 < 0$. This means that $U(p_1X_1 + p_2X_2) > p_1U(X_1) + p_2U(X_2)$, or $U(EY) > EU(Y)$, where E denotes expectation and Y denotes income. (To check this, simply draw a graph of a function U which has the property that $d^2U/dX^2 < 0$; that is, is concave to the origin. $U(p_1X_1 + p_2X_2)$ is a point on the graph between X_1 and X_2; $p_1U(X_1) + p_2U(X_2)$ is a point on the straight line joining the points on the graph corresponding to X_1 and X_2.) Thus the individual is risk averse.
3. This is because, under certain assumptions about the agent's preferences and the form of the risk, the risk premium is proportional to the variance of the random term. If the share of the risk for which the agent is responsible is reduced in the proportion r, the variance he faces is reduced in the proportion r^2 (since multiplying a risk by some number multiplies its variance by the square of that number). For more details, see B. Holmström and P. Milgrom, "Aggregation and Linearity in the Provision of Intertemporal Incentives," *Econometrica* 55 (1987): 303–328.
4. To see this, differentiate the net-gain expression with respect to p_1, set the result equal to zero, and solve for p_1.

More Games

GAME THEORY is best learned by doing. What follows are some additional games to test your strategic skills. Most can be solved using only the analyses described in the chapters. A few (marked with an asterisk) require the mathematical tools developed in the Appendix. Solutions to the games are at the end.

Chapter 2: Playing Games as Games

2.1.   Three men (called M_1, M_2, and M_3) and three women (called W_1, W_2, and W_3) seek marriage partners. Marriage is heterosexual and monogamous. Preferences over potential marriage partners are as follows.

$$(M_1): W_1, W_3, S, W_2 \qquad (W_1): M_1, M_3, S, M_2$$

$$(M_2): W_3, W_1, S, W_2 \qquad (W_2): M_2, S, M_3, M_1$$

$$(M_3): W_1, W_3, S, W_2 \qquad (W_3): M_3, M_2, S, M_1$$

The first of these, for example, is to be read as: "the first man prefers marrying W_1 to marrying W_3 to being single to marrying W_2"; and so on.

Any proposed set of matches can be upset if a man and a woman prefer each other to the partners they are currently paired with. With whom will each settle down?

(For a less trivial application of this kind of model, see A. E. Roth, "The Evolution of the Labor Market for Medical Interns and Residents: A Case Study in Game Theory," *Journal of Political Economy* 92 (Dec. 1984): 991–1016, in which a matching mechanism of this sort is used to analyze the allocating of interns to hospitals.)

2.2. An impecunious professor, seeking to earn some money at the same time as teaching game theory, offers to auction a dollar bill to his class. The rules of the auction are unusual: the dollar will be awarded to the highest bidder, but both the highest and the second-highest bidders must pay their bids to the professor. Bids must be in multiples of 5 cents. How much money will the professor make?

2.3. In *A Treatise of Human Nature* (1740), David Hume, starting from the assertion that "nothing is more certain, than that men are, in a great measure, govern'd by interest," gave the following example of the consequences of self-interested behavior:

> Two neighbors may agree to drain a meadow, which they possess in common; because 'tis easy for them to know each other's mind; and each must perceive, that the immediate consequence of his failing in his part, is, the abandoning the whole project. But 'tis very difficult, and indeed impossible, that a thousand persons shou'd agree in any such action, it being difficult for them to concert so complicated a design, and still more difficult for them to execute it; while each seeks a pretext to free himself of the trouble and expence, and wou'd lay the whole burden on others.

Was Hume a good game theorist?

2.4. Two firms, like the firms in the text, compete to sell an identical item. They compete by setting prices, and then producing enough to satisfy demand. Each incurs a constant unit production cost of $5. What price will rule in the market?

Chapter 4: Weighing Risks

4.1. Imagine that you are being tested for cancer. You have read that this test is 98% accurate. If you have cancer, it will show positive 98% of the time, and if you do not it will show negative 98% of the time. You have also read that 0.5%, or 1 in 200, of the population actually have cancer. Now your doctor tells you that you have tested positive. How worried should you be? More precisely, what is the probability you have cancer?

4.2. The Pentagon has the choice of building two kinds of ship: large ships, which operate singly, or small ships, which operate in pairs. A pair of small ships costs exactly the same to build and operate as one large one. The difference between the two is in vulnerability. Under enemy attack, a large ship has a probability of p of surviving to execute its mission, while each of the small ships has a probability of $p/2$. However, a small ship can carry out its mission even if only one survives. (Assume that for each member of the pair the risks are independent; i.e., the probability of one's surviving is unaffected by whether or not the other survives.) If we are interested only in the execution of the mission, which option is superior? (From Barry Nalebuff, "Puzzles," *Journal of Economic Perspectives* 2, Fall 1988, pp. 181–182.)

Chapter 5: Gaining Bargaining Power

5.1.   Modify the bargaining-with-deadline game of Chapter 2 by supposing it can last for at most three stages. The first two stages are as in Chapter 2's game; in the third, A makes the offer, and the sum to be divided has shrunk to $70. What will A propose in the first round?

5.2.   Thomas Schelling is quoted in the text on "the paradox that the power to constrain an adversary depends on the power to bind oneself." Explain the "paradox" in terms that someone who has never heard of game theory would understand, giving examples. What does the "paradox" teach us about bargaining strategies?

Chapter 6: Using Information Strategically

6.1.*   A seller who values an item at zero faces a buyer whose valuation the seller does not know but perceives to lie between $1 and $4, with all intermediate values equally likely. If the seller has the ability to commit himself to his offer, what price will the seller set so as to maximize expected return? Explain why there will not always be a sale, despite the fact that both are better off with a sale than without.

6.2.   Consider the following signaling game. An employer faces two kinds of employees. Group I members have a productivity of 1 and make up a fraction q of the population. Group II members have a productivity of 3 and make up a fraction $1 - q$ of the population. The employer cannot directly observe a potential employee's productivity; he can, however, observe his education level. Group I people incur a cost of $4E$ to earn E units of education; group II people incur a cost E for E units of education. Exhibit, and discuss the significance of,
   (a) A separating equilibrium; that is, an outcome in which group I and group II people are distinguishable by their education levels.
   (b) A pooling equilibrium; that is, an outcome in which group I and group II people get the same education.

Chapter 8: Creating Incentives

8.1.   In 1988 some U.S. states changed the basis for pricing by regulated firms such as telephone companies. The old pricing policy was called "rate-of-return" pricing: a regulated firm is permitted to charge a price that is computed as a fixed percentage mark-up over its production cost. The replacement policy is the "price cap," under which the regulatory agency fixes the time-path of the firm's price in advance, based on a prediction of the firm's costs but not on what the costs actually turn out to be. Compare the incentive effects of the two pricing regulations. Specifically, suppose that the regulated firm can, by incurring some costs that are not recognized as production costs by the regulatory agency, reduce its own production costs. Under which system will the regulated firm operate with lower production costs?

8.2.   A certain professor requires his students to produce team papers, with all members of a team receiving the same grade for their joint paper. The grade can be based only on the team's output, as the professor cannot observe individual team-members' contributions. Teams consist of four students. Since the team's output is essentially the average of its members' inputs, some students are worried that there is an incentive to try to free-ride on teammates, by putting in less than the appropriate amount of effort. Under the assumption (which any professor knows to be correct) that all students are identical both in inherent ability and in aversion to work, can you devise a grading scheme for the professor that overcomes this free-rider problem? Does this have anything to say about how firms should pay members of production teams, given that individuals' contributions to the team's output cannot be observed?

8.3.*   A principal hires an agent to produce some output. Output Q depends upon the agent's effort E according to $Q = E + u$, where u represents the effect of luck; u is a random variable with mean zero. Effort E costs the agent a dollar-equivalent amount of $E^2/8$. Both principal and agent are risk neutral. The principal offers the agent a contract that pays a sum $rQ + s$ for the output Q, where r and s are numbers chosen by the principal. The agent has an alternative occupation, should he reject this contract, which yields a net return of \$1. For any such contract, how much effort will the agent rationally exert? Show that the optimal contract from the principal's point of view has $s = -1$ and $r = 1$.

Chapter 9: Designing Contracts

9.1.   Many Chinese village governments own factories. During the flirtation with capitalism since 1978, the villages have begun leasing the factories to individual contractors. The village government, as owner of the factory, has the power to establish the terms of the contract. In the early stages of the reforms, contractors were required to pay a fixed sum of money each year to the village, and allowed to keep any profit beyond this. Later, after seeing how successful the factories became under private management, the villages wanted a piece of the action and instituted profit-sharing schemes, with 20% to 30% of profit going to the contractor and the rest to the village. [Jean C. Oi (1987), "The Chinese Village, Inc.," unpublished, Department of Government, Harvard University.] Would this change in policy increase or decrease the villages' revenues? Can you think of any other management situations that have this character?

9.2.   Consider a contract between Toyota and a subcontractor for the supply of some parts. Compare, in terms of incentive and risk-sharing effects, a contract that specifies a fixed price with a contract that allows the subcontractor to pass on 50% of any production-cost increases.

9.3.*   Derive the optimal government-firm contract discussed in Chapter 9. Specifically, suppose the government can offer a contract under which it pays the firm an amount $v(C - w) + w$ if its realized cost is C. If the firm's cost-reducing effort is E, let the realized cost be $C^* - E$ for some number C^* (to be interpreted as the maximum possible cost); and let the cost incurred by the firm be $E^2/2D$, for some parameter D. If the firm bears all of the risk of project's costs, its risk premium is R.

9.4.   In the *Principles of Economics* (1920), Alfred Marshall wrote of sharecropping as follows:

> When the cultivator has to give to his landlord half of the returns to each dose of capital and labour that he applies to the land, it will not be to his interest to apply any doses the total return to which is less than twice enough to reward him. If, then, he is free to cultivate as he chooses, he will cultivate far less intensively than on the English plan [i.e., under a system of fixed rental payments]; he will apply only so much capital and labour as will give him returns more than twice enough to repay himself: so that his landlord will get a smaller share even of those returns than he would have on the plan of a fixed payment.

Is Marshall's argument correct? What assumptions underlie it? Sharecropping has persisted for centuries and is still very widely used: if it is inefficient, as Marshall argues, how has it survived?

Chapter 11: Bidding in Competition

11.1.   You are bidding in an auction. You know exactly how much the item would be worth to you if you owned it, but you do not know how any of the other bidders value it. The auction is sealed-bid, with a twist: the highest bidder gets the item, but pays a price equal to the second-highest bid. What would you bid? Compare the outcome of this auction to an oral auction (in which bids are openly called and rise until only one bidder remains).

11.2.* Two firms are competing by sealed bidding for a contract to do a fixed task. The firm that bids lowest wins the contract at the price it bid. Each knows its own cost of doing the work, but not its rival's; each perceives the other's cost as being between 0 and 1, with all intermediate values equally likely. What will each rationally bid?

11.3. According to a *Wall Street Journal* report, the FBI "has launched an inquiry into whether US Sprint Communications Company illegally obtained competitors' confidential bid information and used it to win part of a giant federal telephone-services contract." It was alleged that Sprint employees spied on American Telephone and Telegraph Co. and Martin Marietta Corp., its rivals for the contract, obtaining confidential bid information, and then Sprint used this to adjust its sealed bid so as to win a part of the contract. If the government's sole aim is to get the best possible price, should it be concerned about this behavior?

Solutions

2.1. We can solve by elimination. M_1's absolute favorite is W_1, and vice versa, so they can veto any proposed matching that does not pair them. Now, given that M_1 and W_1 are paired, M_3 and W_3 are best for each other and can ensure they get together. With them eliminated, M_2 prefers being single to being paired with W_2.

2.2. When the dollar is in fact auctioned in class, two students invariably end up competing for the dollar bill, and bidding well over a dollar for it, much to the amusement of the rest of the class. The professor, if he were hard-hearted enough actually to take their money, would earn several dollars' profit. What explains this apparently irrational escalation? The answer is that, once two people have submitted bids, the lower bidder will always want to increase his bid. Suppose, for example, one has bid 50 cents and another 55 cents. Then the first has an incentive to bid 60 cents so as to make 40 cents' profit instead of 50 cents' loss. But then his rival has an incentive to bid 65 cents. The logic remains unchanged even when the bids climb beyond $1; there is no limit to the possible escalation, even though both are acting rationally given that they have begun bidding.

Bidders with foresight might calculate that there is another possibility: the game does have an equilibrium, although it is rarely reached in experiments. One of the bidders (it does not matter which one) submits an initial bid of $1, and no one else bids. Then the winner makes no profit, but no one makes a loss. As soon as more than one person has bid, however, this outcome is ruled out and the escalation begins.

The dollar auction is a peculiar game, and none of the other games we examine in this book have outcomes like this endless escalation. But it serves as a useful warning: games do not necessarily have benign, stable outcomes. One real-world game that, one could argue, has something of the dollar auction in it is the arms race. Once trapped in the competition, each side spends ever more on arms in a self-defeating attempt to improve its position relative to the other side. (For a more thorough analysis of the dollar-auction game and its implications, see Barry O'Neill, "International Escalation and the Dollar Auction," *Journal of Conflict Resolution* 30, 1986: 33–50.)

2.3.   There are (at least) two possible interpretations of this argument. One is that, with only two players, each one's stake is high enough that it is in his individual interest to do the draining himself; whereas, with a large number of players, each one has too small a stake in the outcome to make it individually worthwhile to do the drainage. The two-player case could be represented, for the sake of illustration, by the following payoffs:

	Drain	*Don't drain*
Player A:		
Player B:		
Drain	(10, 10)	(8, 12)
Don't drain	(12, 8)	(0, 0)

With these payoffs, each player's best response to the other's not draining is to drain himself. The game has two equilibria: A drains and B does not; and B drains and A does not.

An alternative interpretation of Hume's argument is that the players are in a repeated game, and it is possible to induce cooperation by retaliatory strategies when there are two players but not when there are very many (because with many players it is difficult to observe individual defections).

2.4.   Each charges a price of $5, just enough to cover production costs. To see this, suppose one charges more, say, $6.00. The other's best response is to charge $5.99 and get all the market; in particular, this is better than matching the $6.00 and getting only a fraction of the market. But then the first firm's best response is to charge $5.98. This best-response reasoning drives the price down to $5.00, from which no further undercutting is profitable. Note, however, that dynamic strategies of the sort described in the text, punishing deviations, might maintain $6.00 (or any other price above $5.00) as an equilibrium.

4.1.   Suppose 10,000 tests are done. Of these, on average 50 people will have cancer. Of these, 98% will test positive and so, on average, there will be 49 positive tests. Of the (on average) 9550 cancer-free people, 2%, or 191 people, test positive. Thus there are a total of 240 positive tests, of which 191 are false positives. So the probability of a positive test indicating cancer is 49/240 or just over 20%, a surprisingly low probability.

4.2. Once again careful thought about the logic of probability yields a surprising answer: the large-carrier option is better. The large carrier executes its mission with probability p. Either one of the small carriers executes with probability $p/2$, so is sunk with probability $1 - (p/2)$. Hence both are sunk with probability $[1 - (p/2)]^2$. The small carriers succeed in executing their mission if at least one is not sunk; in other words, if it is not the case that both are sunk. The probability of this is $1 - [1 - (p/2)]^2$. A little algebra shows this is equal to $p - (p^2/4)$, which is smaller than p, the probability the large carrier succeeds.

5.1. We go through the same forward-looking reasoning as in Chapter 2 and the Appendix to Chapter 5. If, for whatever reason, the game reaches the last stage, then A rationally demands (slightly less than) $70, and B rationally accepts. Thus, if the game is in the second stage, B knows that he must offer A at least $70 to induce acceptance; B there-fore gets at most $20 of the $90 if the game ends at the second stage. In the first stage, therefore, A knows that the least B will accept is $20, so A asks for the remainder, $80. Once again, notice that, although the players must think through this chain of possible actions and counter-actions, the actual playing of the game is much simpler: A asks for $80, B immediately accepts the $20, and the game ends.

5.2. See Chapter 5; or, better yet, see Schelling's original account in *The Strategy of Conflict* (Cambridge: Harvard University Press, 1960, Ch. 2.)

6.1. Let p denote the price the seller demands. There is a sale if the buyer values the item at more than p; from the seller's perspective, this occurs with probability $(4 - p)/3$. The seller's expected profit is there-fore $p(4 - p)/3$, which is maximized when p is $2. No sale is made if the potential buyer happens to value the item at between $1 and $2 (which occurs with a probability of 1/3). With the price at $2, the seller's ex-pected profit is therefore $(2/3) \times 2$, or 4/3. The seller could instead guar-antee a sale by setting the price at $1 and earning a certain profit of $1; but this is 33% less than the expected profit from the $2 price.

6.2.
(a) Let us denote the cut-off level of education E^*. Since education in this simple model serves solely as a signal, rational individuals will choose no other levels of education than E^* and zero. For a separating equilib-rium, high-productivity people must find it in their interest to pay the costs of education, while low-productivity people must not. For a high-productivity person to earn a higher net return from being educated than from not being educated, it must be that $3 - E^*$ (the net return from being educated and being paid as a high-productivity person) must be larger than 1 (the salary from not being educated and therefore being assumed to have low productivity). This implies that E^* is less than 2.

On the other hand, for it not to pay a low-productivity person to incur the cost of education so as to be paid as a productive person, it must be that $3 - 4E^*$ (the net return of an educated low-productivity person) must be less than 1 (the salary of a low productivity person who is recognized as such). This implies that E^* is larger than 0.5. It follows that a credential level set anywhere between 0.5 and 2 works as a signal to separate high-productivity people from low-productivity people.

(b)   Once again, let us denote the required credential level by E^*. If it is high enough that no one incurs the cost of education, then an employer seeing someone with no education learns nothing about the individual, and so can only infer that the individual has low productivity with probability q and has high productivity with probability $1 - q$. The offered salary is therefore $(1 \times q) + (3 \times (1 - q))$. For this to be consistent with the individual's rational decision on whether to incur the cost of education, this salary must be higher than $3 - E^*$, which is the net return to a high-productivity individual who is educated and therefore recognized to have high productivity and paid accordingly. This requirement reduces to E^* being larger than $2q$: in this case the credential level is so high that no one wants to attain it.

8.1.   We compare under the two systems the effects on the regulated firm's profits if the firm makes the effort necessary to achieve a $1 reduction in its production costs. Under rate-of-return regulation, the cost-lowering that successful innovation produces is passed on to the firm's customers in the form of lower prices; since the firm's profit is a fixed proportion of its cost, the innovation actually *lowers* the amount of profit the regulatory agency allows the firm to keep. The firm is not only not rewarded for the innovation; it is penalized. Under price-cap regulation, on the other hand, the price the firm receives is independent of realized production costs. Thus each dollar by which costs are lowered translates into a dollar increase in profit. The firm has full incentives to engage in innovation. (When California introduced price-cap regulation for telephone services in 1989, it imposed a price path that meant that, after adjusting for inflation, prices would fall each year by 4.5%—the 4.5% being the regulatory agency's prediction of a reasonable rate of productivity increase under the price cap. This is to be compared with the actual rate of productivity increase that had been achieved under the old rate-of-return regulation, which was only 2% to 2.5%.)

8.2.   The problem with grading by team output is that, to raise the team's grade by one point, all four team members have to put in one point's worth of effort. If only one puts in this extra effort, the grade is raised by only one-quarter. Thus, each individual receives only a fraction of the return from his or her own effort. As a result, all team members have an incentive to shirk.

One grading scheme that counters this free-rider problem is as follows. Suppose a normal grade, which all teams would get if they put in the proper amount of effort, is 80. The first column below represents the true, objective worth of the project, judged as the work of four people. (As everyone knows, professors are infallible graders.) The second column represents the grade actually awarded.

Objective grade	Grade awarded
.	.
.	.
84	96
83	92
82	88
81	84
80	80
79	76
78	72
77	68
.	.
.	.

This scheme works because it stretches the gap between one grade and the next. A student, contemplating putting in a little extra effort, knows that he or she will be fully rewarded for it; the grade he or she receives will rise by as much as it would if the project were an individual one. The extra effort will also raise the teammates' grades, but this is assumed to be irrelevant to the student's calculation. (For more on this solution, see R. Preston McAfee and John McMillan, "Optimal Contracts for Teams," *International Economic Review*, 32 August 1991, 561–578).

In practice, students object to having this grading scheme imposed on them. Why would people not want to be subjected to it?

Management games that have this structure include: (1) Several firms have formed a joint venture to undertake research and development. How should the costs and benefits of the joint venture be allocated among the cooperating firms? (2) A production process requires the inputs of several workers, and it is not feasible for the employer to measure the individual workers' contributions. What system of remuneration will most effectively give the workers incentives to exert effort?

8.3. The agent's expected net return is expected payment minus cost of effort, which can be written as $rE + s - [E^2/8]$. This is maximized when the agent sets $E = 4r$.

The total expected gain from trade is $E - [E^2/8]$. The principal rationally pushes the agent's net return down to his best alternative of 1. The principal's expected profit equals the total expected gain from trade minus the agent's net return, or $E - [E^2/8] - 1$. Given that the agent chooses his effort rationally, this equals $4r - 2r^2 - 1$, which is largest when $r = 1$; this is the r the principal sets.

The agent's expected net return is payment minus effort cost, or $rE + s - [E^2/8]$, which, as noted, must equal 1. From $E = 4r$ and $r = 1$, this gives $s = -1$.

9.1. Will the village extract more money by sharing in the factory's profits or by requiring a fixed payment? The surprising answer is that sharing in the profits probably reduces the village's earnings. (The equivocal word "probably" is inserted for a reason that will be discussed later.) It costs the contractor something to increase output and profit: he must work harder, and he must get his employees to work harder. Not all these costs of increasing output show up in the accountant's balance sheet. Thus the contractor bears 100% of such costs. With a fixed-payment contract, the contractor keeps 100% of any profit he generates above the required payment to the village; but with the sharing contract, he keeps only 20% or 30% of the return to any extra effort he makes. Under the latter contract, therefore, he will exert less effort and produce less total output. With the fixed-payment contract, the total to be divided between the contractor and the village is greater; the village would earn more by raising the fixed payment than by taking a share of the profits.

This logic must be modified if either the contractor is more fearful of risk than the village government, or the contractor's profit-making potential is known only by the contractor himself. Either of these effects can make it in the village's interest to share the profits; but it seems implausible that these effects would be sizable enough to make it in the villages' interests to set sharing rates as high as 70% or 80%.

The sharing parameter in these contracts between Chinese village governments and factory contractors is 0.2 to 0.3. If we guess at 0.8 for the size of the incentive parameter, then by using the formula in reverse we deduce that the risk premium would have to be 80% in order for the contract with sharing rate 0.2 to have been optimal, or 47% for the sharing rate 0.3. These numbers imply extreme caution: the contractors would give up most of their profits to be sheltered from risk. They therefore seem implausibly large. Either the village government made a mistake in designing the contract, or the village government was taking into account some other effects not considered in our simple model, or our guess of 0.8 for the incentive parameter D is too high. If we were more pessimistic about the force of incentives and assumed D to be 0.2, the implied risk premium assuming the optimality of the contract is 20% (for the sharing rate of 0.2) or 12% (for the sharing rate of 0.3).

Other games that are logically equivalent to this one include: (1) A firm is deciding how to pay its production-line workers. Should it offer a fixed wage or piece rates? (2) A contract for the supply of some equipment is being negotiated between two firms. The costs of producing the equipment are not perfectly predictable. What proportion of cost increases should the purchasing firm allow the supplier firm to pass on to it as price increases?

9.2 The fixed-price contract offers stronger incentives to the subcontractor to limit costs and so results in lower production costs. But it shifts all of the risk onto the subcontractor. To induce the subcontractor to accept the fixed-price contract, Toyota must offer a price high enough to compensate the subcontractor for the risk he is to bear. If the subcontractor is risk averse enough, and the scope for production-cost variations is small enough, the fixed-price contract might be more expensive for Toyota than the incentive contract.

9.3. Once again solving the game by looking at the last stage first, we consider the firm's optimal response to any given contract the government offers, $P = v(C - w) + w$. The the firm's total cost (including its effort cost) if it chooses the effort level E is $C^* - E + (E^2/2D)$. The resultant profit is $[v(C^* - E - w) + w] - [C^* - E + (E^2/2D)]$. The effort E that maximizes this profit is $D(1 - v)$. (This is obtained either by differentiating the profit expression and putting the result equal to zero, or by using the properties of quadratic functions as is done several times in the Appendix.) Notice that, with a cost-plus contract, $v = 1$ and effort is zero (since it is costly to do and it is not rewarded). When the contract is fixed-price, $v = 0$ and the effort level is D. Thus D is the difference between realized costs under a cost-plus contract and under a fixed-price contract.

Going backwards in time, we now consider the government's choice of contract. The government predicts that the firm, if it accepts the contract, will respond as just described. The government also knows that the firm has the option of rejecting the contract. Suppose the firm has an alternative that yields a risk-free profit of A. Then the least the government can offer is a risk-adjusted profit for the firm equal to A. As in the Appendix, represent the firm's risk-adjusted profit by $f - R$, where f is the expected profit and R is the risk premium if it bears the full risk. Since, however, the sharing contract means the firm bears a fraction $(1 - v)$ of the risk, its risk-adjusted profit is $f - R(1 - v)^2$ (as explained in the Appendix). Thus the government is constrained by the firm's threat of exit to offer an expected profit f of at least $A + R(1 - v)^2$; and the government minimizes its own procurement costs by offering the firm just this much profit.

The total gain from trade is value of output minus total production cost, or $Y - (C^* - E) - E^2/2D$, where Y is the value to the government of the output it receives. The government's net gain is this total gain from trade minus the firm's profit, $A + R(1 - v)^2$. Finally, the government knows the relationship between the contract parameter that it sets, v, and the effort E with which the firm responds is as we derived above: $E = D(1 - v)$. Substituting this amount into the expression for the government's net gain, we get that its net gain is $Y - [C^* - D(1 - v)] - [D^2(1 - v)^2/2D] - [A + R(1 - v)^2]$. The government chooses the sharing rate v so as to maximize this net gain; this results in an optimal sharing rate of $2R/(D + 2R)$.

9.4.   Marshall was correct to point out disadvantage of sharecropping: it offers inadequate incentives to the farmer (the argument is the same as that given in Chapter 8 on why salespeople's commissions that are less than 100% produce too little effort.) But Marshall left out of his account the sharecropping's advantage: it shifts some risk from the farmer to the landlord. If, realistically, the landlord has more diversified sources of income than the farmer, or simply has more income than the farmer, then (other things being equal) this risk shifting can be mutually beneficial (as argued in Chapter 9).

11.1.   The answer is that you bid your true valuation. (The logic is identical to that of the inheritance game of Chapter 2.) To see why, suppose you bid something other than your valuation. This does not change how much you pay if you win, for the price is determined by someone else's bid; it can only change the likelihood of your being the winner. Suppose first that you bid less than your valuation. This changes the outcome only in the event that you would have had the highest bid by bidding true valuation, but by bidding lower you go below someone else's bid. But this means that lowering your bid below your valuation can only make you worse off: it is possible you lose when by bidding true valuation you would have won and paid less than your valuation (since the price you pay is equal to a bid lower than yours). On the other hand, compare bidding true valuation with bidding higher than your true valuation. Bidding higher can only change the outcome in the event that you win with the high bid but would not win with the true-valuation bid. This occurs if someone else's bid is between your two possible bids. When you win with the higher bid, the price you pay is equal to this other bid. But this price is higher than your valuation, so you make a loss. We conclude that it cannot be rational to bid anything other than your true valuation; in this second-price auction, bids reveal valuations.

11.2.   Let firm A conjecture that firm B is using the decision rule: if cost is c_b, bid an amount $k_1 + k_2 c_b$, where k_1 and k_2 are constants which we temporarily take to be arbitrary. Firm A wins if its bid b_a is less than B's bid; that is, if b_a is less than $k_1 + k_2 c_b$, or $(b_a - k_1)/k_2$ is less than c_b. Given that costs are uniformly distributed between zero and one, the probability of winning is therefore $1 - ([b_a - k_1]/k_2)$. Firm A's expected profit is thus $(b_a - c_a)(1 - [b_a - k_1]/k_2)$, where c_a is A's cost. Firm A maximizes this expected profit by setting its bid at $(c_a + k_1 + k_2)/2$. Now we reconsider B's decision rule, so far arbitrarily specified. If it is a rational decision rule, it must be derivable by the reasoning just given; this implies the rule initially conjectured must be the same as the rule derived, that is, $(c + k_1 + k_2)/2 = k_1 + k_2c$. For this to hold for any cost c, it must be that $k_2 = 1/2$; it follows then that $k_1 = 1/2$. Hence the equilibrium bidding rule is: if cost is c, bid $(1/2) + (1/2)c$.

11.3.   The theory of Chapter 11 concludes that an open auction generates better (in this case lower) prices on average than a sealed-bid auction because of winners' curse effects. The spying, if it occurred, in effect converted the auction from pure sealed-bid to partially open-bid. But there is no guarantee that the partially open auction works better from the government's point of view. If the spying firm learned that it would have bid much lower than its competitors, it would raise its bid to just below theirs'. In this case the spying makes the government worse off. If the spying firm learns it would have bid more than its rivals, it might lower its bid, making the government better off. But it would presumably bid only slightly below its rival, so the improvement for the government is minimal. In net terms the government is likely to be worse off under the partially open auction than under the sealed-bid auction.

Reading Guide

A book as brief and nontechnical as this must fall far short of even introducing the range of topics in modern game theory and its applications. The following reading list offers some references that guide the reader to deeper and more general treatments, as well as point the way toward caveats to the foregoing results that are too technical for discussion in the text. (To go any further into game theory requires a certain amount of mathematical knowledge, of the level taught in economics graduate schools; many of the following references—those marked with an asterisk—assume such knowledge.) Also listed in what follows are references to applications, and to the sources of facts cited in the text. Some teaching cases are also suggested.

Chapter 1: The Art and Science of Strategy

Game theory was invented in:

*Von Neumann, John, and Morgenstern, Oskar (1944), *Theory of Games and Economic Behavior*. Princeton: Princeton University Press.

The other seminal works of game theory are by the Princeton mathematician John Nash:

*Nash, John (1951), "Non-Cooperative Games," *Annals of Mathematics* 54: 286–95.

*Nash, John (1953), "Two Person Cooperative Games," *Econometrica* 21: 128–40.

Useful expositions of modern game theory's applications in economics, at a level of technicality one step beyond this book's, are:

Kreps, David M. (1990), *A Course in Microeconomic Theory*. Princeton: Princeton University Press.

Kreps, David M. (1990), *Game Theory in Economic Modelling*. Oxford University Press.

Milgrom, Paul R., and Roberts, John (1991), *Economics of Organization and Management*. Englewood Cliffs, NJ: Prentice-Hall.

Rasmusen, Eric (1989), *Games and Information: An Introduction to Game Theory*. New York: Basil Blackwell.

Tirole, Jean (1988), *The Theory of Industrial Organization.* Cambridge: MIT Press.

Mathematically sophisticated accounts of modern game theory include:

*Aumann, Robert J., and Hart, Sergiu, editors (1992), *Handbook of Game Theory with Economic Applications.* Amsterdam: North-Holland.

*Borland, Jeffrey, Creedy, John, and Eichberger, Jurgen, editors (1992), *Recent Developments in Game Theory.* London: Edward Elgar.

*Friedman, James W. (1990), *Game Theory with Applications to Economics.* 2nd edition. New York: Oxford University Press.

*Fudenberg, Drew, and Tirole, Jean (1991), *Game Theory.* Cambridge: MIT Press.

*Luce, R, Duncan, and Raiffa, Howard (1957), *Games and Decisions.* New York: Wiley.

*Moulin, Hervé (1981), *Game Theory for the Social Sciences.* New York: NYU Press.

*Myerson, Roger (1991), *Game Theory.* Cambridge: Harvard University Press.

The techniques of modern mathematical economics and game theory that underlie most of the ideas reported in this book are briefly explained in

Fudenberg, Drew, and Tirole, Jean (1989), "Noncooperative Game Theory for Industrial Organization: An Introduction and Overview," in *Handbook of Industrial Organization,* edited by R. Schmalensee and R. Willig. Amsterdam: North-Holland.

*Myerson, Roger B. (1985), "Bayesian Equilibrium and Incentive Compatibility: An Introduction," in *Social Goals and Social Organization,* edited by L. Hurwicz et al. Cambridge: Cambridge University Press.

Poker is analyzed game-theoretically in

Gillies, D. B., Mayberry, J. P., and von Neumann, J. (1953), "Two Variants of Poker," in H. W. Kuhn and A. W. Tucker, eds., *Contributions to the Theory of Games,* Volume II. Princeton: Princeton University Press.

The works quoted in this chapter are:

Schelling, Thomas C. (1984), "Strategic Analysis and Social Problems," in *Choice and Consequence.* Cambridge: Harvard University Press.

Popper, Karl R. (1976), "The Logic of the Social Sciences," in *The Positivist Dispute in German Sociology,* edited by T. W. Adorno, et al. London: Heinemann.

The anecdotes about von Neumann come from:

Halmos, P. R. (1973), "The Legend of John von Neumann," *American Mathematical Monthly* 80: 382–394.

Heims, Steve J. (1980), *John von Neumann and Norbert Weiner: From Mathematics to the Technologies of Life and Death.* Cambridge: MIT Press.

Regis, Ed (1987), *Who Got Einstein's Office? Eccentricity and Genius at the Institute for Advanced Study.* Reading, MA: Addison-Wesley.

Game theory, incidentally, has found applications in areas other than economics and business; for instance, in biology:

Maynard Smith, John (1982), *Evolution and the Theory of Games.* Cambridge: Cambridge University Press, 1982.

in international relations:

Oye, Kenneth A., editor (1986), *Cooperation under Anarchy.* Princeton: Princeton University Press.

in political science:

Ordeshook, Peter C. (1986), *Game Theory and Political Theory.* Cambridge: Cambridge University Press.

in military strategy:

Allen, Thomas B. (1987), *War Games*. London: Heinemann.

in philosophy:

Campbell, Richmond, and Sowden, Lanning, editors, (1985), *Paradoxes of Rationality and Cooperation*. Vancouver: University of British Columbia Press.

and in linguistics:

Pool, Jonathon (1986), "Optimal Strategies in Linguistic Games," in *The Fergu-
sonian Impact, Vol. 2: Sociolinguistics and the Sociology of Language*, edited by
J. A. Fishman et al. Berlin: Mouton de Gruyter.

Chapter 2: Games as Games

(a) Theory

The prisoners' dilemma is due to the mathematician A. W. Tucker. The standard
account of it is in

Luce, R. Duncan, and Raiffa, Howard (1957), *Games and Decisions*. New York:
Wiley, Ch.5.

and for additional discussion of it, as well as a general history of game theory,
see

Aumann, Robert J. (1987), "Game Theory," in *The New Palgrave: A Dictionary of
Economic Theory and Doctrine*, edited by J. Eatwell, M. Milgate, and P. New-
man. London: Macmillan.

The location game is due to

Hotelling, Harold (1929), "Stability in Competition," *Economic Journal* 39: 41–57.

The idea underlying what I have called the inheritance game comes from Vickrey's classic paper:

Vickrey, William (1961), "Counterspeculation, Auctions, and Competitive Sealed
Tenders," *Journal of Finance* 16: 8–37.

For more on information-revelation games, see

*Groves, Theodore, and Ledyard, John (1977), "Optimal Allocation of Public
Goods: A Solution to the 'Free-Rider' Problem," *Econometrica* 45: 783–810.

(b) Applications

The pigs experiment is reported by

Baldwin, B. A., and Meese, G. B. (1979), "Social Behaviour in Pigs Studied by
Means of Operant Conditioning," *Animal Behaviour* 27: 947–57.

Political competition as a location game is modeled by

Downs, Anthony (1957), *An Economic Theory of Democracy*, New York, Harper and
Row.

The NATO data come from

Oneal, John R. (1990), "The Theory of Collective Action and Burden Sharing
in NATO," *International Organization* 44: 397–402.

Chapter 3: Understanding Conflict and Cooperation

(a) Theory

The notion of gains from trade goes back a long way in economics, to

Ricardo, David (1975, first published 1817), *The Principles of Political Economy
and Taxation*. London: Dent.

That differences in beliefs are an unreliable basis of gains from trade in argued more rigorously by

*Milgrom, Paul, and Stokey, Nancy (1986), "Information, Trade, and Common Knowledge," *Journal of Economic Theory* 26: 17–27.

That games played without repetition usually have inefficient outcomes is shown by

*Dubey, Pradeep (1980), "Nash Equilibria of Market Games: Finiteness and Efficiency," *Journal of Economic Theory* 22: 363–376.

On cooperation in games played repeatedly, see

*Abreu, Dilip (1988), "On the Theory of Infinitely Repeated Games with Discounting," *Econometrica* 56: 283–96.

*Fudenberg, Drew, and Maskin, Eric (1986), "The Folk Theorem in Repeated Games with Discounting and with Incomplete Information" *Econometrica* 54: 533–54.

(b) Applications

Useful discussions of implicit versus explicit contracting in respectively U.S. and Japanese business are

Macauley, Stewart (1963), "Non-Contractual Relations in Business," *American Sociological Review* 28: 55–67.

Dore, Ronald (1983), "Goodwill and the spirit of Market Capitalism," *British Journal of Sociology* 34: 459–482.

Experiments with the repeated prisoners' dilemma are reported in

Axelrod, Robert (1984), *The Evolution of Cooperation*. New York: Basic Books.

Marwell, G., and Ames, R. (1981), "Economists Free Ride, Does Anyone Else?" *Journal of Public Economics* 15: 295–310.

Rapoport, Anatol, and Chammah, Albert M. (1965), *Prisoner's Dilemma*. Ann Arbor: University of Michigan Press.

Chapter 4: Weighing Risks

(a) Theory

For more on risk aversion and decision-making under uncertainty, see

*Diamond, Peter A. and Rothschild, Michael, eds. (1978), *Uncertainty in Economics*. New York: Academic Press.

Hey, John D. (1979), *Uncertainty in Microeconomics*. New York: New York University Press.

Kreps, David M. (1988), *Notes on the Theory of Choice*. Boulder: Westview Press.

Machina, Mark (1987), "Choice under Uncertainty: Problems Solved and Unsolved," *Journal of Economic Perspectives* 1: 121–154.

*Sinn, Hans-Werner (1983), *Economic Decisions under Uncertainty*. Amsterdam: North-Holland.

The classic account of moral hazard and insurance is

Arrow, Kenneth J. (1965), *Aspects of the Theory of Risk Bearing*. Helsinki: Yrjo Johnssonin Saaatio.

(b) Applications

The cited study of managers' risk attitudes (which also contains a useful survey of other empirical studies of risk attitudes) is

MacCrimmon, Kenneth R., and Wehrung, Donald A. (1986), *Taking Risks: The Management of Uncertainty*. New York: Free Press.

Chapter 5: Gaining Bargaining Power

(a) Theory

Modern game theory's account of bargaining is reviewed in:

Binmore, Ken, Osborne, Martin A., and Rubinstein, Ariel (1992), "Noncooperative Models of Bargaining," in *The Handbook of Game Theory with Economic Applications*, edited by R. Aumann and S. Hart. Amsterdam: North-Holland.

Osborne, Martin J., and Rubinstein, Ariel (1990), *Bargaining and Markets*. San Diego: Academic Press.

Sutton, John (1986), "Non-Cooperative Bargaining Theory: An Introduction," *Review of Economic Studies* 53: 709–724.

The outside-alternatives and cost-of-delay bargaining games follow

Binmore, Ken, Rubinstein, Ariel, and Wolinsky, Asher (1986), "The Nash Bargaining Solution in Economic Modeling," *RAND Journal of Economics* 17: 176–88.

*Rubinstein, Ariel (1982), "Perfect Equilibrium in a Bargaining Model," *Econometrica* 50: 97–110.

The acquiring of alternative bargaining partners as a way of improving one's bargaining position is explored by

*Wolinsky, Asher (1987), "Matching, Search, and Bargaining," *Journal of Economic Theory* 32: 311–33.

Many of the ideas in this chapter, including the role of focal points and the value of commitment, are due to

Schelling, Thomas C. (1960), *The Strategy of Conflict*. Cambridge: Harvard University Press.

For more on focal points, see

Kreps, David (1990), "Corporate Culture and Economic Theory," in *Perpectives in Positive Political Economy*, edited by J. E. Alt and K. A. Shepsle. Cambridge: Cambridge University Press.

Myerson, Roger B. (1986), "Negotiation in Games: A Theoretical Overview," in *Uncertainty, Information, and Communication*, edited by W. P. Heller, R. M. Starr, and D. A. Starrett. New York: Cambridge University Press.

The cited focal-point experiments are reported in

Roth, Alvin E. (1987), "Bargaining Phenomena and Bargaining Theory," in *Laboratory Experiments in Economics*. Cambridge: Cambridge University Press.

Commitment in bargaining is analyzed by

*Crawford, Vincent P. (1982), "A Theory of Disagreement in Bargaining," *Econometrica* 50: 607–38.

(b) Applications

A more down-to-earth account of bargaining, an account of the tricks of the negotiating trade by a consultant who bills himself as "the world's best negotiator" is

Cohen, Herb (1982), *You Can Negotiate Anything*. New York: Bantam.

The cited State Department seminar for foreign-service officials is described by

Winham, Gilbert R. (1979), "Practitioners' Views of International Negotiation," *World Politics* 32: 111–35.

The story of the baseball strike is told by

DeBrock, Lawrence M., and Roth, Alvin E. (1981), "Strike Two: Labor-Management Negotiations in Major-League Baseball," *Bell Journal of Economics* 12: 413–25.

The Chinese river-boat example of the use of commitment comes from

Cheung, Steven N. S. (1983), "The Contractual Nature of the Firm," *Journal of Law and Economics* 26: 1–22.

The example of the takeover raider's commitment strategy comes from

Lax, David A., and Sebenius, James K. (1986), *The Manager as Negotiator.* New York: Free Press.

Licensing as a form of commitment is analyzed by

Shepard, Andrea (1987), "Licensing to Enhance Demand for New Technologies," *RAND Journal of Economics* 18: 360–67.

Chapter 6: Using Information Strategically

(a) Theory

The analysis of screening originated with

*Rothschild, Michael, and Stiglitz, Joseph E. (1976), "Equilibrium in Competitive Insurance Markets: An Essay on the Economics of Imperfect Information," *Quarterly Journal of Economics* 90: 629–50.

The extension of the first game in this chapter to less trivial situations of bargaining with asymmetric information is done in

*Myerson, Roger B. (1979), "Incentive Compatibility and the Bargaining Problem," *Econometrica* 47: 61–73.

*Myerson, Roger B., and Satterthwaite, Mark A. (1983), "Efficient Mechanisms for Bilateral Trading," *Journal of Economic Theory* 29: 265–81.

For more general versions of the bargaining-with-delay game, see

*Fudenberg, Drew, and Tirole, Jean (1983), "Sequential Bargaining with Incomplete Information," *Review of Economic Studies* 50: 221–48.

*Sobel, Joel, and Takahashi, Ichiro (1983), "A Multistage Model of Bargaining," *Review of Economic Studies* 50: 411–26.

*Cramton, Peter C. (1985), "Sequential Bargaining Mechanisms," in *Game-Theoretic Models of Bargaining*, edited by A. Roth. Cambridge: Cambridge University Press.

*Grossman, Sanford, and Perry, Motty (1986), "Sequential Bargaining under Asymmetric Information," *Journal of Economic Theory* 39: 120–54.

*Gul, Faruk, Sonnenschein, Hugo, and Wilson, Robert (1988), "Foundations of Dynamic Monopoly and the Coase Conjecture," *Journal of Economic Theory* 39: 155–190.

For more on extracting profit when the other party's willingness to pay is not known, see

*Baron, David P., and Myerson, Roger B. (1982), "Regulating a Monopolist with Unknown Costs," *Econometrica* 50: 911–30.

*Maskin, Eric, and Riley, John G. (1984), "Monopoly with Incomplete Information," *RAND Journal of Economics* 15: 171–96.

The disruptive effects of quality uncertainty on the workings of markets are analyzed by

Akerlof, George A. (1970), "The Market for 'Lemons': Quality Uncertainty and the Market Mechanism," *Quarterly Journal of Economics* 84: 488–500.

Research on bargaining under uncertainty is surveyed by

Kennan, John, and Wilson, Robert (1990), "Bargaining with Private Information," Technical Report No. 5, Stanford Institute for Theoretical Economics.

Signaling games were invented by

Spence, A. Michael (1974), *Market Signalling: Informational Transfer in Hiring and Related Screening Processes*. Cambridge: Harvard University Press.

Surveys of the subsequent work, much of which asks how to correct the unsatisfyingly inconclusive nature of signaling models that results from their plethora of equilibria, include

Kreps, David, and Sobel, Joel (1991), "Signaling," in *Handbook of Game Theory with Economic Applications*, edited by R. Aumann and S. Hart. Amsterdam: North-Holland.

Mailath, George (1991), "Signaling Games," in *Recent Developments in Game Theory*, edited by J. Borland, J. Creedy, and J. Eichberger. London: Edward Elgar.

Game-theoretic analysis of reputation-building is reviewed in

Camerer, Colin, and Weigelt, Keith (1988), "Experimental Tests of a Sequential Equilibrium Reputation Model," *Econometrica* 56: 1–36.

Wilson, Robert (1985), "Reputations in Games and Markets," in *Game-Theoretic Models of Bargaining*, edited by A. E. Roth. Cambridge: Cambridge University Press.

An omitted topic: the models examined in this book do not explain why information is asymmetrically distributed; the theory of individuals' decisions about how much information to acquire is surveyed by

Rothschild, Michael (1973), "Models of Market Organization with Imperfect Information: A Survey," *Journal of Political Economy* 81: 1283–1308.

McMillan, John, and Rothschild, Michael (1992), "Search," in *Handbook of Game Theory with Economic Applications*, edited by R. Aumann and S. Hart. Amsterdam: North-Holland.

(b) Applications

The role of deception and strategic misrepresentation in everyday buying and selling is entertainingly recounted by

Leff, Arthur Allen (1976), *Swindling and Selling*. New York: Free Press.

The facts on the oil-field negotiations come from

Wiggans, Steven N., and Libecap, Gary D. (1985), "Oil Field Unitization: Contractual Failure in the Presence of Imperfect Information," *American Economic Review* 75: 368–85.

For an analysis of strikes from the point of view of game theory (and as well a useful survey of models of bargaining under uncertainty), see

Kennan, John, and Wilson, Robert (1990), "Strategic Bargaining Models and the Interpretation of Strike Data," *Journal of Applied Econometrics* 5.

and on the tactics and tricks used in labor negotiations, see

Walton, Richard E., and McKersie, Robert B. (1965), *A Behavioral Theory of Labor Negotiations*. New York: McGraw-Hill, Ch. III.

A case study of bargaining as a way of revealing information about valuations is

Cassady, Ralph (1968), "Negotiated Price-Making in Mexican Traditional Markets: A Conceptual Analysis," *America Indigena* 28: 52–79.

Do actual used-vehicle markets have any of the character of the stylized lemons market? A testable implication of this example is that, holding age of vehicle constant, vehicles bought new will require fewer repairs than vehicles bought used, as the owners of good vehicles will tend to withhold them from the second-hand market. This proposition is statistically examined, and rejected, by

Bond, Eric (1982), "A Direct Test of the 'Lemons' Model: The Market for Used Pickup Trucks," *American Economic Review* 72: 836–40.

The concept of signaling has been applied to advertising expenditures by

*Milgrom, Paul, and Roberts, John (1986), "Price and Advertising Signals of Product Quality," *Journal of Political Economy* 94: 796–821.

to negotiations between borrowers and lenders by

*Leland, H., and Pyle, D. (1977), "Information Asymmetries, Financial Structure, and Financial Intermediaries," *Journal of Finance* 32: 371–87.

and to interpersonal relationships by

Camerer, Colin (1988), "Gifts as Economic Signals and Social Symbols," *American Journal of Sociology* 94, Supplement, S180-S214.

Chapter 7: International Economic Negotiations

This chapter draws on material in

McMillan, John (1989), "A Game Theoretic View of International Negotiations: Implications for the Developing Countries," in *Developing Countries and the International Trading System*, edited by John Whalley. London: Macmillan.

McMillan, John (1990), "The Economics of Section 301: A Game-Theoretic Guide," *Economics and Politics* 2: 45–58.

For more the game-theoretic modeling of international economic negotiations, see

Abbott, Kenneth W. (1985), "The Trading Nation's Dilemma: The Functions of the Law of International Trade," *Harvard International Law Journal* 26: 501–532.

Crawford, Vincent P. (1985), *Dynamic Contract Theory, with Application to Country Foreighn Borrowing Strategies*. Princeton Studies in International Finance No. 59, Princeton University.

Feenstra, Robert C., Lewis, Tracy R., and McMillan, John (1991), "Designing Policies to Open Trade," *Economics and Politics* 3: 223–40.

Johnson, Harry G. (1954), "Optimum Tariffs and Retaliation," *Review of Economic Studies* 21: 142–53.

Ludema, Rodney D. (1991), "International Trade Bargaining and the Most-Favored-Nation Clause," *Economics and Politics* 3: 1–20.

GATT's enforcement mechanism and reciprocity rule are described by:

Dam, Kenneth W. (1970), *The GATT: Law and International Economic Organization*. Chicago: University of Chicago Press.

Negotiators' objectives are empirically examined by:

Cheh, John H. (1974), "United States Concessions in the Kennedy Round and Short-Run Labor Adjustment Costs," *Journal of International Economics* 4: 323–40.

Usefully detailed accounts of how some international negotiations proceeded can be found in:

Hamilton, Colleen, and Whalley, John (1989), "Coalitions in the Uruguay Round," *Weltwirtschaftliches Archiv* 125: 547–61.

Sathirathi, Surakiart, and Siamwalla, Ammar (1987), "GATT Law, Agricultural Trade and Developing Countries: Lessons from Two Case Studies," *World Bank Economic Review* 1: 595–618.

Winham, Gilbert R. (1986), *International Trade and the Tokyo Round Negotiations*. Princeton: Princeton University Press.

Useful teaching cases on international economic negotiations are published in the Pew Program in Case Teaching and Writing in International Affairs, from the Graduate School of Public and International Affairs, University of Pittsburgh; for instance:

Krauss, Ellis S. (1989), "Under Construction: U.S.-Japan Negotiations to Open Japan's Construction Markets to American Firms, 1985–1988," Case No. 145.

Odell, John S., and Dibble, Ann (1988), "Brazilian Informatics and the United States: Defending Infant Industry versus Opening Foreign Markets."

Chapter 8: Creating Incentives

(a) Theory

A useful introduction to the analysis of incentive questions, by the originator of many of the ideas in this book, is

Arrow, Kenneth J. (1985), "The Economics of Agency," in *Principals and Agents: The Structure of Business*, edited by J. Pratt and R. Zeckhauser. Boston: Harvard Business School Press.

The provision of incentives for the agent produce both large output and high quality is modeled by

*Laffont, Jean-Jacques, and Tirole, Jean (1989), "Provision of Quality and Power of Incentive Schemes in Regulated Industries," Working Paper No. 528, Department of Economics, M.I.T.

(b) Applications

The Adam Smith quotations in this and subsequent chapters come from

Smith, Adam (1976, first published 1776), *An Enquiry into the Nature and Causes of the Wealth of Nations*. Chicago: University of Chicago Press.

Smith, Adam (1976, first published 1759), *The Theory of Moral Sentiments*. Oxford: Clarendon Press.

On the importance of the topic omitted here, nonmonetary rewards, see

Leavitt, Harold J. (1978), *Managerial Psychology*, Chicago: University of Chicago Press, 4th ed.

Simon, Herbert A. (1957), *Administrative Behavior*, New York: Free Press, 2nd ed.

The analysis of Chinese agriculture comes from

McMillan, John, Whalley, John, and Zhu Li Jing (1989), "The Impact of China's Economic Reforms on Agricultural Productivity Growth," *Journal of Political Economy* 97: 781–807.

Tang, Anthony M. (1980), "Food and Agriculture in China: Trends and Projections 1952–77 and 2000," in *Food Production in the People's Republic of China*, edited by A. M. Tang and B. Stone. Washington: Food Policy Research Institute.

The facts on baseball players' earnings come from

Hadley, Lawrence, and Gustafson, Elizabeth (1989), "Earnings in a Three-Tier Market: The Case of Major League Baseball," unpublished, University of Dayton.

Empirical studies of the effectiveness of piece-rate payment systems are:

Seiler, Eric (1984), "Piece Rate vs Time Rate: The Effect of Incentives on Earnings," *Review of Economics and Statistics* 66: 363–76.

Ehrenberg, Ronald G., editor (1990), "Do Compensation Policies Matter?", Special Issue of *Industrial and Labor Relations Review* 43: 3-S-273-S.

The estimates of the relationship between academics' publications and salaries come from

Tuckman, Howard P., Gapinski, James H., and Hagemann, Robert P. (1977), "Faculty Skills and the Salary Structure in Academe: A Market Perspective," *American Economic Review* 67: 692–702.

Chapter 9: Designing Contracts

(a) Theory

Further results in the theory of contracts are surveyed by

Borland, Jeffrey (1991), "Multiple Agent Models: A Survey," in *Recent Developments in Game Theory*, edited by J. Borland, J. Creedy, and J. Eichberger. London: Edward Elgar.

Hart, Oliver, and Holmström, Bengt (1987), "The Theory of Contracts," in *Advances in Economic Theory*, edited by T. Bewley. Cambridge: Cambridge University Press.

MacDonald, Glenn M. (1984), "New Directions in the Economic Theory of Agency," *Canadian Journal of Economics* 17: 415–40.

Sappington, David (1991), "Incentives in Principal-Agent Relationships," *Journal of Economic Perspectives* 5: 45–66.

The analysis of contracting under asymmetric information follows

*Laffont, Jean-Jacques, and Tirole, Jean (1986), "Using Cost Observation to Regulate Firms," *Journal of Political Economy* 94: 614–41.

*McAfee, R. Preston, and McMillan, John (1987), "Competition for Agency Contracts," *Rand Journal of Economics* 18: 296–307.

The results on the nature of the contract that are stated in this chapter presume the contract is linear: conditions under which it is optimal for the principal to offer a linear contract are presented by

*Holmström, Bengt, and Milgrom, Paul R. (1987), "Aggregation and Linearity in the Provision of Intertemporal Incentives," *Econometrica* 55: 303–28.

(For the benefit of the theoretically inclined reader, the results about the nature of the contract used in this chapter rely on the assumptions made by Holmström and Milgrom. The assumptions include: the random disturbance follows a normal distribution, the end-of-period accumulation of costs follow a Brownian motion; the cost of effort to the agent is quadratically related to his level of effort;

the agent has constant absolute risk aversion; and the principal is risk neutral. Under these assumptions, as Holmström and Milgrom showed, the optimal contract is linear.)

On the relative performance evaluation, see

*Holmström, Bengt (1982), "Moral Hazard in Teams," *Bell Journal of Economics* 13: 324–40.

(b) Applications

The use of salespeople's reports in setting their compensation is described in

Gonik, Jacob (1978), "Tie Salesmen's Bonuses to their Forecasts," *Harvard Business Review* 56: 116–23.

Wotruba, Thomas, and Thurlow, Michael L. (1976), "Sales Force Participation in Quota Setting and Sales Forecasting," *Journal of Marketing* 40: 11–16.

The interpretation of Japanese general trading companies follows

Sheard, Paul (1989), "The Japanese General Trading Company as an Aspect of Interfirm Risk-Sharing," *Journal of the Japanese and International Economies* 11: 399–422.

The data on profit rates for military contracts come from

Fox, J. Ronald (1974), *Arming America: How the U.S. Buys Weapons.* Cambridge: Harvard University Press.

Chapter 10: Setting Executives' Incentives

Game-theoretic models of the internal organization of firms are surveyed by

Holmström, Bengt, and Tirole, Jean (1988), "The Theory of the Firm," in *Handbook of Industrial Organization,* edited by R. Schmalensee and R. Willig. Amsterdam: North-Holland.

Milgrom, Paul, and Roberts, John (1988), "Economic Theories of the Firm: Past, Present, and Future," *Canadian Journal of Economics* 21: 444–58.

Stories of American managers pursuing their own interests at the expense of their shareholders' interests are given in

Segal, Harvey H. (1989), *Corporate Makeover: The Reshaping of the American Economy.* New York: Viking.

The cited estimates of executive remuneration come from

Jensen, Michael C., and Murphy, Kevin J. (1990), "Performance Pay and Top-Management Incentives," *Journal of Political Economy* 98: 225–64.

A leading theorist's view of how to design executive-compensation plans is given in

Holmström, Bengt (1987), "Incentive Compensation: Practical Design from a Theory Point of View," in *Incentives, Cooperation, and Risk Sharing,* edited by H. R. Nalbantian. Totowa, NJ: Rowman and Littlefield.

On practical aspects of the design of compensation schemes, see

Rock, Milton A., and Berger, Lance A. (1990), *The Compensation Handbook.* New York: McGraw-Hill.

On the incentive effects of Japanese stockholding practices, see

Hoshi, Takeo, Kashyap, Anil, and Scharfstein, David (1991), "Corporate Structure, Liquidity, and Investment: Evidence from Japanese Industrial Groups," *Quarterly Journal of Economics* 106: 33–60.

The evidence on the role of the board of directors and on takeover threats as a source of discipline on managers is assembled by

Shleifer, Andrei, and Vishny, Robert W. (1988), "Value Maximization and the Acquisition Process," *Journal of Economic Perspectives* 2: 7–20.

Some evidence on product-market competition as a source of managerial discipline is assembled by

Scherer, F. M., and Ross, David (1990), *Industrial Market Structure and Economic Performance*, 3rd ed. New York: Rand McNally, pp. 668–72.

Games played within organizations are modeled by

Milgrom, Paul, and Roberts, John (1988), "An Economic Approach to Influence Activities in Organizations," *American Journal of Sociology* 94: S154–S179.

The historical development of the corporate form of organization is surveyed by

Rosenberg, Nathan, and Birdzell, L. E. (1986), *How the West Grew Rich: The Economic Transformation of the Industrial World*. New York: Basic Books.

Useful teaching cases on inter-firm relationships include:

"The Lincoln Electric Company," Harvard Business School Case No. 376–028.

"The Washington Post, A & B," Harvard Business School Case Nos. 667–076, 667–077.

"Case of Big Mac's Pay Plans," *Harvard Business Review* July-August 1974.

Chapter 11: Bidding in Competition

(a) Theory

The key references on bidding are:

*Milgrom, Paul R., and Weber, Robert J. (1982), "A Theory of Auctions and Competitive Bidding," *Econometrica* 50: 1089–1122.

Myerson, Roger B. (1981), Optimal Auction Design," *Mathematics of Operations Research* 6: 58–73.

*Riley, John G., and Samuelson, William F. (1981), "Optimal Auctions," *American Economic Review* 71: 381–92.

*Wilson, Robert (1977), "A Bidding Model of Perfect Competition," *Review of Economic Studies* 44: 511–18.

Overviews of the literature are given by

McAfee, R. Preston, and McMillan, John (1987), "Auctions and Bidding," *Journal of Economic Literature* 25: 699–738.

Milgrom, Paul R. (1987), "Auctions and Bidding: A Primer," *Journal of Economic Perspectives* 3: 3–22.

Wilson, Robert (1992), "Strategic Analysis of Auctions," in *Handbook of Game Theory with Economic Applications*, edited by Robert J. Aumann and Sergiu Hart. Amsterdam: North-Holland.

(b) Applications

Facts from around the world about the many varieties of auction procedures that are in use are gathered in

Cassady, Ralph (1976), *Auctions and Auctioneering*. Berkeley: University of California Press.

Some experiments on the winner's curse are reported in

Kagel, John H., and Levin, Dan (1986), "The Winner's Curse and Public Information in Common Value Auctions," *American Economic Review* 76: 894–920.

On the winner's curse in oil-rights bidding, see

Capen, E. C., Clapp, R. V., and Campbell, W. M. (1971), "Competitive Bidding in High-Risk Situations," *Journal of Petroleum Technology* 23: 641–53.

Hendricks, Kenneth, Porter, Robert H., and Boudreau, Bryan (1987), "Information, Returns, and Bidding Behavior in OCS Auctions: 1954–1969," *Journal of Industrial Economics* 35: 517–42.

The connection between the winner's curse and corporate takeovers is made by

Roll, Richard (1986), "The Hubris Hypothesis of Corporate Takeovers," *Journal of Business* 59: 197–216.

The winner's curse in cost estimation is analyzed by

Quirk, James, and Terasawa, Katsuaki (1984), "The Winner's Curse and Cost Estimation Bias in Pioneer Projects," Working Paper No. 512, California Institute of Technology.

The facts on art and wine auctions come from

Ashenfelter, Orley (1989), "How Auctions Work for Wine and Art," *Journal of Economic Perspectives* 3: 23–36.

The cited study of FDIC auctions of failed banks is

Sternberg, Theodore (1990), "Measuring the Winner's Surplus in First Price Sealed Bid Auctions: with an Application to the Market for Failed Banks," unpublished, Vanderbilt University.

The use of auctions by computer-bidders is described by

Waldspurger, Carl A., Hogg, Tad, Huberman, Bernardo A., Kephart, Jeffrey O., and Stornetta, Scott (1989), "Spawn: A Distributed Computational Economy," unpublished, Dynamics of Computation Group, Xerox Palo Alto Research Center.

On government-contract bidding, see

McAfee, R. Preston, and McMillan, John (1988), *Incentives in Government Contracting*. Toronto: University of Toronto Press.

Chapter 12: Bidding in Olympic Competition

This chapter is based on

McMillan, John (1991), "Olympic Bidding Games," *Negotiation Journal* 7:255–263.

A related analysis is

Lawrence, Robert Z., and Pellegrom, Jeffery D. (1989), "Fool's Gold: How America Pays to Lose at the Olympics," *The Brookings Review* 7, pp. 5–10.

Chapter 13: Organizing a Network of Subcontractors

For detailed references to the empirical studies that this chapter draws on, see

McMillan, John (1990), "Managing Suppliers: Incentive Systems in Japanese and United States Industry," *California Management Review* 32: 38–55.

On specific capital as a determinant of the make-or-buy decision, see

Klein, B., Crawford, R., and Alchian, A. (1978), "Vertical Integration, Appropriable Rents, and the Competitive Contracting Process," *Journal of Law and Economics* 21: 297–326.

Williamson, Oliver (1975), *Markets and Hierarchies: Analysis and Antitrust Implications.* (New York: Free Press).

For additional information on inter-firm relationships, see

Asanuma, Banri (1985), "The Contractual Framework for Parts Supply in the Japanese Automotive Industry," *Japanese Economic Studies* 15: 54–78.

Asanuma, Banri (1989), "Manufacturer-Supplier Relationships in Japan and the Concept of Relation-Specific Capital," *Journal of the Japanese and International Economies* 3: 1–30.

Joskow, Paul L. (1988), "Asset Specificity and the Structure of Vertical Relationships: Empirical Evidence," *Journal of Law, Economics, and Organization* 4: 95–117.

Kawasaki, Seiichi, and McMillan John (1987), "The Design of Contracts: Evidence from Japanese Subcontracting," *Journal of the Japanese and International Economies* 1: 327–49.

March, Artemis (1989), "The U.S. Commercial Aircraft Industry and its Foreign Competitors," in *The Working Papers of the MIT Commission on Industrial Productivity.* Cambridge: MIT Press.

Monteverde, Kirk, and Teece, David (1982), "Supplier Switching Costs and Vertical Integration in the Automobile Industry," *Bell Journal of Economics* 13: 206–13.

Walker, Gordon, and Weber, David (1984), "A Transaction Cost Approach to Make-or-Buy Decisions," *Administrative Science Quarterly* 29: 373–91.

Useful teaching cases on inter-firm relations include:

"G.E. vs. Westinghouse in large Turbine Generators, A, B, & C," Harvard Business School Nos. 9–380–128, 9–380–129, 9–380–130.

"International Business Machines (E): Negotiating with Electronics Component Suppliers," Harvard Business School No. 9–577–158

Index

Abbott, Kenneth W., 231
ABC (American Broadcasting
    Corporation), 152–58
Abreu, Dilip, 227
Aerospace industry, 169
Agent: *See also* Principal–agent
    relationship
    commitment from, 55
    effort level of, 98–100, 102–4, 109–10,
        198–99
    fixed–price vs. cost–plus contract for,
        115–16
    insurance, 40
    risk averse, 106–7
Agricultural trade policy, 76–77
Aircraft, submarines vs., 5
Airlines, scheduling of, 16, 144
Airport gates and landing slots, 144
Akerlof, George A., 230
Alaska pipeline, 141
Alchian, A., 236
Allen, Thomas B., 226
Alliances, international, 14–15
Alt, J. E., 228
Alternative opportunities, 57, 187–89
    analysis of, 187–89
    bargaining breakdown and, 188–89
    bargaining power and, 48–49, 83, 108,
        164, 187–89, 202
    in defining game, 180
American Broadcasting Corporation
    (ABC), 152–58
American Economic Review, 144
American Telephone and Telegraph, 215
Ames, R., 227
Angels, California, 146
Anticipation
    bargaining power and, 47–48
    in game situations, 9

Antique industry, 145–47
Archetypical bargaining game, 45–47
Arledge, Roone, 152
Arms-for-hostages deal, 55
Arms-length contracting, 106
Arrow, Kenneth J., 38, 227, 232
Art of War, The (Sun Tzu), 56
Asanuma, Banri, 237
Ashenfelter, Orley, 144, 236
AT&T, 215
Auction houses, 143
Auctions, 146–47. *See also* Open
    auctions; Sealed-bid auctions
Aumann, Robert J., 12–13, 225, 226,
    230
Australia, education in, 72
Auto industry
    production method in, 169
    risk-sharing vs. incentives in, 170–71
    signaling in, 73–74
    subcontracting hierarchy in, 176–77
    subcontracting patterns in, 163, 166–
        69, 174
Aversion to risk, *See* Risk aversion
Axelrod, Robert, 227

Bacon, Francis, 61
Baldwin, B. A., 226
Banking, 36, 68
Barcelona Olympics (1992), 153
Bargainers, chess players vs., 17
Bargaining, 52–57
    aggressive, costs of, 84–86
    costs of delay and, 49–50
    fairness in, 52–53
    informational handicap and, 60–61
Bargaining breakdown, 65–67
    alternative opportunities and, 188–89
    commitment and, 85

239

Bargaining power
alternative opportunities and, 48–49,
83, 108, 164, 187–89, 202
archetypical bargaining game and, 45–
47
buyer-seller strategic situations in, 46–
48
commitment and, 60, 176, 191–92
competition and, 48–49
distribution of, in subcontracting, 164
focal points and, 50–53
forming beliefs and, 47–50
in international trade agreements, 76–
88
knowledge and, 60–61
mathematical symmetry and, 52–53
private information and, 106–10
reputation and, 67
Section 301 and, 83
summarized, 57–58
technique and, 53–57
Baron, David P., 229
Baseball
collusion in, 146
earnings in, 94
repeated-game theory and, 146
Behavior. *See also specific strategies and
strategic situations*
irrational, 6
opportunistic, 30–31
rational, 6–7, 85
Beiber, Owen F., 122
Belgium, 15
Beliefs, differences in, 24–25
Berger, Lance A., 234
Bertrand Ltd. (Cournot-Bertrand game),
25–27, 30–31, 183–84
Best response, defined, 19
Best-response function, 183–84
Bethe, Hans, 4
Bewley, T., 233
Bidding, 131–159. *See also* Auctions;
Open auctions; Sealed-bid auctions
in competition, 133–49, 208–9
conspiracies in, 145–47
elements of, 133–35
experiments in, 141
for government procurement, 147–48
money-on-the-table problem in, 137–
38, 155
for oil rights, 141
in Olympic competition, 150–59
profit from, competition and, 138,
145–47
pros and cons of competition in, 173–
75
seller's strategies in, 142–43
summarized, 148–49
uncertainty in, 134–35
value and competition in, 143–45
winner's curse and, 139–41, 154–55

"Bidding on New Ship Construction"
(DeMayo), 116
Binmore, Ken, 228
Biotechnology industry, 107
Birdzell, L. E., 235
Bluffing, 46–47, 56, 66–67
Board of directors, 125–26
Boeing, 164
Boesky, Ivan, 93
Bond, Eric, 231
Book knowledge, experience vs., at
games, 8
Borland, Jeffrey, 225, 230, 233
Borrowing, 68
Boudreau, Bryan, 236
Boulware, Lemuel R., 56
Boulwarism, 56
Brazil, 84, 86
Britain. *See* United Kingdom
Bruyere, Jean de la, 102
*Bulletin of the American Mathematical
Society,* 5
Buyer–seller strategic situation
bargaining in, 46–48
commitment in, 53–54
differences in beliefs and, 24
discerning valuations in, 63–64
gains from trade in, 21–22
informational handicaps in, 60–61
information analysis in, 192–93
nature of product and, 56
reputation in, 54–55

Calgary Olympics (1988), 154–55
California
housing market in, 36
sales practices in, 110
California Angels, 146
Camerer, Colin, 230, 231
Campbell, Richmond, 226
Campbell, W. M., 236
Canada, 15–16
political parties in, 16
risk aversion in, 36–37
in Tokyo Round (GATT), 81
Capen, E. C., 236
Carpenter's Union Benefit Fund (New
York), 56
Cartels, 27–28
Cassady, Ralph, 231, 235
CBS (Columbia Broadcasting System),
152–58
Chammah, Albert M., 227
Chateau Margaux (1953), 144
Cheh, John H., 231
Chemical industry, 93–94
Chess, 48
Chess players, 17
Cheung, Steven N. S., 229
Chief executives, incentives of, 123–24
Chile, trade policy of, 82

248 *Index*

Profit motive, 93
Progressive Conservative Party (Canada), 16
Promotion, as incentive, 101, 118–19, 129
Psychologists
  on irrational behavior, 6
  measurement of risk aversion by, 36–37
Psychology, risk premium and, 35–36
Public utilities, 4
Pudd'nhead Wilson (Mark Twain), 39
Pyle, D., 231

Quality
  incentives for, 101–2
  in subcontracting decisions, 168–69
Quantity discounts, 64
Questionnaires, 36
Quirk, James, 236

Racing, odds at, 34
Raiffa, Howard, 225, 226
Rand Corporation, 5
Range of agreement, 48
Rapoport, Anatol, 227
Rare book auctions, 146
Rasmusen, Eric, 224
Rational behavior, 6–7
  bargaining breakdown and, 85
Rational decision, uncertainty in, 34
Rational pigs game, 13–15
  best response in, 13–14
  international relations and, 14–15
  real experiments and, 14
Rational responses, 17. *See also* Anticipation
  best, 19, 183–84
Rationalization, trial and error vs., 14
Reagan, Ronald, 8
Reasoning, forward-looking, 57
Reciprocity
  summarized, 87
  in trade negotiations, 80–81
Reebok, 123
Reed, John S., 123
Regis, Ed, 225
Regulatory agencies
  inheritance game and, 19
  in strategic situation, 4
  telephone companies and, 19
Relative performance evaluation, 118–19
Repeated games, 28–30
  analysis of, 184–85
  in antique industry, 145–47
  cooperation in, 8, 165–66, 184–85
  enforcement of international agreements and, 78–79
  equilibrium in, 29–30, 185
  prisoner's dilemma and, 165
  ratings in, 165

retaliation in, 145–47. *See also* Retaliation
trustworthiness and, 30–31. *See also* Reputation
Reporting, honest, 200–201
Reputation, 31. *See also* Repeated games
  bargaining power and, 67
  buyer-seller strategic situation and, 54–55
  in defining game, 180
  informational asymmetries and, 70
  value of, 67–68, 167
Retaliation, 31–32. *See also* Repeated games
  analysis of, in repeated games, 184–85
  and bidding conspiracies, 145–47
  deviations and, 29
  inefficient outcomes and, 28–29
  perpetual, 86
  in trade policy, 82
Return, expected, 34–35
Revelation principle, 5–6
Revenue sharing, 156–58
Ricardo, David, 226
Rich, risk attitude of, 36–37
Riley, John G., 229, 235
Risk, 33–41
  attitudes toward, 36–37
  diversification of, 37–39, 116, 170–71
  expected return and, 34–35
  gains from trade and, 39–40, 111
  inevitability of, 33
  insurance against. *See* Insurance
  probability and, 33–34
  risk premium and, 35–36
  size of, 111
  in sports, 29, 38
  in stock market, 33, 38
  trade in, 111
  U.S. and Canadian attitudes toward, 36–37
  utility function and, 185–87
Risk aversion, 35–37, 41, 111
  analysis of, 185–87
  commission rate and, 205
  contracts and, 106–7
  royalty schemes and, 157
  subcontracting and, 170–71
  summarized, 41
Risk neutrality, 38, 40, 116
  analysis of, 185–87
  risk-sharing contracts and, 206–7
  setting commission rate and, 205
  subcontracting and, 170–71
Risk premium, 35–36
  insurance and, 36
  marginal payment and, 113–14
  risk-sharing contracts and, 207
  of salespersons, 112–14
  setting commission rate and, 205